VINTAGE
THE SAFFRON STORM

Saba Naqvi is a journalist and the author of four books. She lives in New Delhi and has a ringside view of landmark events in contemporary India.

T0043170

PRAISE FOR THE BOOK

'Saba Naqvi lays before us the chronology of how we got here. From a party whose leaders were embarrassed on the day of its arch vandalism to one where rousing and stoking the mob has become the norm in New India'—Aakar Patel, author, *Our Hindu Rashtra*

'We have in Ms Naqvi's book an enjoyable, informative and pacey retelling of a crucial period in our history. Saba Naqvi covered the BJP for decades and was extremely familiar with the inner workings of the party and writes well, in a breezy anecdotal style. The book also tells us something about the differences between the workings of Messrs Vajpayee and Modi. Though he rarely gave interviews and was famously monosyllabic, Vajpayee ran an open prime ministership. He could get petulant about negative coverage (and Ms Naqvi narrates how she became a victim of prime ministerial pique) but his anger rarely lingered. And when there were failures, Mr Vajpayee and his senior aides were willing to discuss them'—Vir Sanghvi in *Business Standard*

'In this age of intense acrimony between the establishment and media, Naqvi remains very fair in her narrative. The characters in her book may be polarising figures, but she always draws them out objectively. The book is written in the conversational style that is the signature of a veteran journalist'—Sunetra Choudhary in *Elle* magazine

'A ringside view of the evolution of the BJP. That the author had direct access to all those who mattered in the Vajpayee years is self-evident . . . a very stimulating read'—*Times of India*

THE SAFFRON STORM

From Vajpayee to Modi

Saba Naqvi

VINTAGE

An imprint of Penguin Random House

VINTAGE

USA | Canada | UK | Ireland | Australia
New Zealand | India | South Africa | China | Singapore

Vintage is part of the Penguin Random House group of companies
whose addresses can be found at global.penguinrandomhouse.com

Published by Penguin Random House India Pvt. Ltd
4th Floor, Capital Tower 1, MG Road,
Gurugram 122 002, Haryana, India

First published as *Shades of Saffron: From Vajpayee to Modi* by Westland in 2018
This revised edition published in Vintage by Penguin Random House India 2024

ISBN 9780143458548

Typeset in Sabon by Manipal Technologies Limited, Manipal

www.penguin.co.in

For my friends and colleagues who have been part of this journey and those who continue to stand up for all our freedoms. They know who they are.

And for

Aruna and Saeed, who know who I am.

Contents

AUTHOR'S NOTE

The opening lines of the Author's Note would have to change between the years 2017, when the original book was written, and 2023, when I was updating the manuscript and adding chapters. The original lines of the Author's Note read as follows: 'Let me straight up address a question that I've been asked very often: how do you, as a Muslim, cover the BJP [Bharatiya Janata Party]? Perhaps my identity has been in the back of the minds of some BJP members, but honestly, I have never perceived it as a problem. And given the access I have got over the years, I give many members of the party credit for not judging me on the basis of my name but on my professional ability. My so-called "Muslim" identity therefore is not an issue in my mind as far as political coverage goes . . .'

Those lines are seriously outdated now as the BJP is currently driving the age I would describe as one of hard-line majoritarianism. The shades of saffron described in the first book have come together in a saffron storm. Individuals who happen to be from Muslim backgrounds, including this author, have all too often been either the target, or the collateral damage, of the politics of the ongoing era and vicious campaigns on social media. For all such troubles I don't see myself as a victim. I consider myself privileged to be a journalist through a turbulent age, as mine is a profession that gives a ringside view of history. Nothing deters me from the task and this book is, after all, not my story but that of the BJP that is recasting India.

The earlier version of this book had concluded with the coming to power at the Centre of Prime Minister Narendra Modi. Now, as I update the book, the BJP led by Modi will, in 2024, be seeking a third five-year term. The second most powerful individual in India after the PM is Home Minister Amit Shah, the deputy par excellence, the individual who oversees statecraft down to every detail as the BJP has gone from strength to strength. A new leader has also emerged in the form of Uttar Pradesh Chief Minister Yogi Adityanath, the head priest of a religious order who won a second term in office in India's most populous state in 2022. This is the triangle now at the top of the BJP's leadership.

In comparison, the national opposition lacks cohesion although moves have begun to forge unity. In terms of the vote share, there is an impressive bloc of parties attempting to take on the BJP, yet it's not just a question of winning votes. Since the second term of PM Modi began in 2019, the Opposition at times appears to face a merciless onslaught that works at multiple levels from media narratives to state agencies. But many do continue to fight on bravely.

As I wrote with data at the conclusion of the first version of the book, the BJP by 2014 had become India's richest political party ever. One needs to emphasize this in the updated book as the BJP's wealth has increased in proportion to its expanding power. Opposition parties are in comparison short of funds and face constant investigations by income tax and enforcement agencies. More so than in 2014, the BJP has a monopoly on political funding, while the financial clout of rivals is being systematically broken.

The BJP's saffron storm is, therefore, not just about ideological orientation; it is also about the ruthless application of power to deny critics and opponents an equal fighting ground. The storm is built on money power and implemented through police power, while the reshaping of the national consciousness is aided by a highly communalized broadcast media.

INTRODUCTION

IN THE SAFFRON MIX:
IDEOLOGY, MONEY, THE ED AND MEDIA

It would be after winning the second term in 2019 under the leadership of PM Modi that the BJP really set about implementing its ideological agenda in a systematic way. We would now witness significant changes in the very foundations on which independent India was birthed. It is therefore necessary to briefly go over the timeline of events of 2019 to understand the fundamental transformation of India.

On 23 May 2019, the results of the national election came and the BJP won 303 seats in Parliament, its highest tally ever, giving it a simple majority in a Parliament that has 545 seats. The Modi-led BJP had by now expanded its popular vote to 37.4 per cent in 2019, way above the 23.75 per cent vote and 182 Lok Sabha seats won by the BJP under its first PM, Atal Bihari Vajpayee, in 1999. As the book examines and describes later, the BJP has also fundamentally changed from a party that ran a successful coalition, to one that has lost almost all significant alliance partners.

The party has set its own rules and does not explain itself to any ally, even as it has transformed India. It is necessary to briefly go over the legal and structural changes that the BJP led by Modi has already brought about in India. On 5 August 2019, just a few months into Modi's second term, the disputed and troubled state of Jammu and Kashmir was stripped of its special constitutional status and downgraded to union territory. Its elected leaders were placed under house arrest, and the valley of Kashmir put under curfew amid a news blackout and internet shutdowns for over a year.

The BJP had kept its ideological commitment to remove the special status of the Muslim-majority state. This was Strike One. The second half of the year delivered another ideological bonanza when on 9 November 2019, the Supreme Court, in a unanimous verdict of the five-judge bench, ruled in favour of handing over the disputed land to the Hindu party, paving the way for the construction of a Ram temple at Ayodhya. The verdict stunned the nation's large Muslim minority that had always understood the 1992 demolition of a medieval mosque to be the most public crime in India's contemporary history. The court did describe the demolition of the Babri mosque as illegal but gave the land for the construction of those who supported this anyway. This ideological gift came through the court, but this was Strike Two of what the BJP has always called its core commitments in all party documents and manifestos.

Very swiftly, therefore, in 2019, the BJP passed laws with reference to Kashmir and could bask in the glory of a judgment on the Ayodhya Ram temple issue. Both these events dramatically gave new twists to old festering disputes and revealed the contours of the emerging Indian nation state. It should not surprise us then that in 2022, campaigns began questioning the existence of mosques at two other sites within the boundaries of Uttar Pradesh (UP): the Krishna Janmabhoomi at Mathura, where Lord Krishna is said to have been born (a mosque stands on part of the land), and the Gyanvapi mosque adjacent to the Kashi Vishwanath temple in Varanasi. Both are live issues, being fought in courts even as people are periodically mobilized to raise the issues at the sites.

Towards the end of 2019, on 12 December, the BJP would also pass the Citizenship Amendment Act (CAA) in Parliament that would fast-track citizenship requests from select neighbouring countries as long as applicants were not Muslims. This would lead to protests in many parts of the country, starting from the area of Shaheen Bagh in Delhi. It would be a moving display of citizens asserting their right to protest and hold up the Indian Constitution. However, an unfortunate spin-off was the protests becoming the trigger for riots in north-east Delhi in March 2020. The moot point about the CAA is that it uses religion as a basis for granting citizenship, which many believe is against the Constitution of India. It is being challenged in the Supreme Court but can be seen as Strike Three in the transformation of the constitutional fundamentals on which independent India was founded.

The first term of the Modi government beginning in 2014 had witnessed, among other things, the ghastly phenomenon of lynching (of mostly Muslims) by so-called cow vigilantes, that peaked in 2018 according to the data that is available.[1] India was most visibly showing its shift to majoritarianism in that one community was being privileged over others, and minorities, most often Muslims but also Christians, were becoming targets of hate crimes. But the key point to note is that it would be in 2019, the year when the Modi-driven BJP won a second term, that the Indian republic would see real politico-legal transformations that sought to untether the nation from the constitutional framework that was created after Independence.

* * *

THE CADRE

On 23 May 2019, the day Modi won a second term in office as PM, I was seated in a television studio located in Noida, on the outskirts of Delhi, having been contracted as an election analyst to a television network since 2012. Towards early evening, when the mandate was fully settled, I would receive a call on my mobile telephone from a veteran BJP/Rashtriya Swayamsevak Sangh (RSS) functionary. He was calling to say I told you so, seat by seat. I digress into elaborating on this anecdote as it is instructive about how thoroughly the cadres of the BJP/RSS had mapped constituencies and how accurate their assessments were.

I usually travel to the field during elections and had done so for the 2019 campaign as well when I went to parts of Uttar Pradesh, India's most populous state that sends the largest contingent of eighty Members of Parliament (MPs) to Parliament. In 2019, the state voted in seven phases, which means that voting for different regions was spread out across seven different dates by the Election Commission of India. I am familiar with the state and my family's ancestral village is located in what is called the Awadh region, a three-hour drive from the state capital, Lucknow. Having covered the first phase of polling, I had travelled to the town of Moradabad in western UP, which was voting in the third phase, and visited the office of the local BJP representative. There, I would run into an RSS functionary named Bhupendra Singh Chaudhary, who began a detailed analysis based on specific polling booths in the seats and expanded on the margins of victory or defeat that the BJP would have in those parts of western UP that had already voted. He had been in charge of handling the seats that had voted in the first phase in an electoral process spread over a month. He was now ready to give break-ups of the results that would come by his estimates, such as winning a seat by 5000 votes and losing another narrowly. His forecasting was very precise. We exchanged phone numbers and he had promised to call on result day. So he did, and said, 'Sister, I had told you so.' He had, indeed.

But the question is, how had he managed to calculate correct estimates on precise seats when other parties and the media were not reading the ground realities accurately? This is because first, the BJP has feedback from its formidable cadre machinery in each polling booth. The party claims to be the largest political party in the world even as the RSS, the Hindu nationalist, right-wing organization, is estimated to be the largest volunteer-based cadre organization in the world. Since the BJP was born out of the RSS,[2] this cadre works for the party in a very organized manner.

Second, when the BJP comes to power in a particular state such as UP, it maps neighbourhoods and electoral rolls in a very systematic way, which no other party does. I would call Bhupendra Singh again before the 2022 UP state polls, when the party was said to be facing a challenge and again, I was given a mostly accurate break-up of results in western UP that were different from the narratives in the media.

Bhupendra Singh was first made the cabinet minister for Panchayati Raj in the second term of the Yogi Adityanath government. And then on 25 August 2022, he was made the BJP's state unit chief in UP. My 2019 source, made after a chance meeting, would therefore turn out to be a very important and capable RSS functionary who had also had a short stint in the Vishva Hindu Parishad (VHP).[3] He certainly knew the ground realities of the state, seat to seat, with the mapping of neighbourhoods where polling booths are located. I have no doubt he will be serving the BJP well in the state that gives the party the largest chunk of its parliamentary majority.

The Home Minister of India, the PM's most trusted aide, Amit Shah, too, works with rigorous data sets and ground feedback from figures such as Bhupendra Singh. That is what makes the second most powerful man in the Modi establishment such a formidable executor of electoral strategies. Projections have been wrong about states such as West Bengal and Delhi, but since Modi stepped out of Gujarat and moved his seat to Varanasi in UP, where Shah and his team put the electoral template into place, the party's internal estimates about this crucial state have been mostly accurate. They have created structures that represent all sections of society, and these have been used to build the cult of personality around first, Modi, and later for the 2021 state campaign, around the incumbent CM Yogi Adityanath.

The huge cadre presence has also mastered the manner of using technical aspects of the electoral process, as I would discover during my extensive ground report journeys. I would learn that the Opposition forces mostly function on generating a wave and a sentiment, but today, in parts of India such as UP, that cannot breach the barriers of a formidable machinery. Besides the electoral task of motivating voters to travel to polling stations, often miles away, in the first-past-the-post system, the route to victory is often through creating divisions in the voter blocs of the opposing parties, or putting up dummy candidates that would shave off a small number of votes of social groups that would be unlikely to vote for the BJP. The Modi–Shah BJP does this well and multiple candidates stand from seats in order to get a few hundred votes.

The RSS–BJP cadre also scrutinizes electoral rolls in a very systematic way—hence an individual such as Bhupendra Singh would understand which caste and community live near which polling station and how are they most likely to vote. After election, the results are examined to see where the support and losses came from. Travelling through parts of UP during both the national election of 2019 and the state election of 2022, I would also come across Indian citizens with voter ID cards who had failed to find their names in electoral lists.

I first met Bhupendra Singh in Moradabad in 2019. Four days before voting in Moradabad in the 2022 state poll, I would meet Sher Mohammad, who has voted in every recent election and was, on the day of our meeting, deeply upset.[4] In his advanced years, he had been compelled to negotiate the internet as he was desperate to find his name in the lists, vote and assert his right as a citizen. But his name had vanished from the electoral rolls and even political workers of the leading Opposition party in the state, the Samajwadi Party (SP), were unable to help him. Almost in tears was Wasim Akram, who had found only one name from his family of ten in the voter list. The story went on and on till I walked down to a street where an SP worker was distributing slips to potential voters. People were angry and upset and the man handing out the slips said in a recorded video that only 20 per cent of those coming to take the slips found their names. This was a Muslim-dominated block of Moradabad and 80 per cent of the names had not yet been found.

The implications of the anecdotal evidence that I found on the ground are worrying. In 2019, a report in *Frontline* magazine stated that a 'No Voter Left Behind'[5] campaign found that the names of twelve crore Indians were missing from electoral rolls; of these, four crore were Dalits and three crore Muslims. This suggests that some of the weakest sections of society are being systematically excluded from the democratic process. The same year, an app called 'Missing Voters' was created by one Khalid Saifullah of RayLabs Technologies to help disenfranchised voters.[6] These are good initiatives, but the larger question is: how do people who have voted in the past find themselves missing from electoral lists? One innocent reason can be that they are migrant workers and when the electoral rolls are revised, the booth-level officers (BLOs) tasked with the job did not find them at the given address and hence they got left out. Here, one of the critiques of the system is that electoral rolls are revised not by full-time employees dedicated to the job but by government schoolteachers who can be careless or overburdened. In 2019, the 'No Voter Left Behind' campaign had found the most troubling levels of exclusions in India's most populous states, UP and Maharashtra.

Opposition parties in UP such as the SP have frequently accused the BJP regime of deliberately seeking to exclude minority voters, suggesting that the party seeks to change the electoral demography from the real demography.[7]

The process that culminates in name deletions on electoral rolls involves submitting applications saying that certain individuals or families are no longer voters of a particular locality. At this point, the BLOs are supposed to verify the facts, but again because they are not full-time employees, they frequently do not follow up and the names are just removed. The possibility also arises that the BLOs could be loyal to the ideology promoted by the state or would just be obeying instructions in removing names. Following a Public Interest Litigation (PIL) in the Supreme Court that challenged the constitutional validity of Rule 18 of the

Registration of Electors Rules, 1960, the Election Commission of India stated before the apex court that names of voters would not be deleted without giving them prior notice. This happened on 8 August 2023. What is also noteworthy is that the petition was filed by former bureaucrats who know how the system works.[8]

Across India, names of Dalits are also known to vanish from electoral rolls. We can only surmise that this could have possibly happened due to a certain prejudice that does not care about the choices voters from the traditionally marginalized sections of society would be making. Yet, I believe this could change for Dalits or the scheduled castes. The most significant trend of 2022, which makes the BJP's march formidable in UP, is the inroads it has begun making among Dalits. This only adds to its electoral heft as there has been an earlier acceptance among sections of the other backward classes (OBCs). On top of that, the BJP has the overwhelming support of the upper castes. The Dalit outreach happened in an overwhelmingly poor state through free rations in the years following the Covid-19-related lockdown that began in March 2020. The party has also given greater representation to all castes. Dalits make up 21 per cent of the population in UP and have traditionally been seen as the voter bloc of the Bahujan Samaj Party (BSP) led by Mayawati that is now withering away to the advantage of the BJP. Because of financial investigations, the BSP, once a radical force for change, appears to have deliberately chosen to become dysfunctional. The 2024 national election will be the next big opportunity for the BSP to either go with a strategy that helps the BJP but also results in the shrinking of its bases, or to again take the leap of working with the Opposition.

But to return to the issue of electoral rolls, since the groundwork of the BJP is the most formidable in India, this gives it a clear advantage in closely fought elections in states that it rules. What is also disappointing is the lack of preparedness of many Opposition candidates when it comes to these technical, bureaucratic aspects of the election process. For instance, when I confronted the SP candidate for Moradabad city with the question about missing voters, he said he had asked people to help out with laptops and technical assistance. But a query with a former election commissioner revealed that if a complaint is made, verification takes at least seven to ten days. Therefore, by the time many voters headed out to get their slips, it was too late for them to vote anyway. The Moradabad candidate I spoke to would lose two elections on the trot by a few thousand votes.

The last-minute distribution of tickets in many cases also limits the time an Opposition candidate has to ensure that voters are registered on revised electoral rolls. Conversely, the BJP, with its blueprints and cadre force, would have a keen understanding of the voters and electoral rolls, which would aid it in states where it is in power regardless of whether it changes the candidate or not.

THE MONEY

The earlier edition of this book had concluded with a chapter titled 'BJP Inc.', which gave details of how the national campaign of 2014 that saw Gujarat CM Modi become PM, was the most expensive in India's history. Since then, the party has become richer and the rest of the political parties of India, be they national parties such as the Congress, or regional players, have become comparatively poorer. This trend has been reinforced each year since 2014.

In 2018, the Electoral Bond scheme of the Modi government became active, and critics point out that instead of transparency, which the government promised, it adds to the lack of information about political funding. Electoral bonds can be purchased through the State Bank of India (SBI), and donors who contribute less than Rs 20,000 remain anonymous and do not have to furnish identity details. According to a written reply in the Rajya Sabha in April 2022, Minister of State for Finance Pankaj Chaudhary provided the break-up of the yearly sale of electoral bonds: Rs 1056.73 crore in 2018; Rs 5071.99 crore in 2019; Rs 363.96 crore in 2020; Rs 1502.29 crore in 2021; and Rs 1213.26 crore in 2022.[9]

In other words, since 2018 when they were effectively available, bonds worth Rs 9208.23 crore have been sold according to the data up to 2022. According to various estimates, more than 75 per cent of all electoral bonds have gone to the BJP.[10] An explainer in the *Indian Express* notes that the central criticism of the scheme is that since a government-run bank sells the bonds, it makes it possible for the government to know exactly who is funding the opponents. This also makes it hypothetically possible for the government to victimize big companies and/or extort them.[11]

The electoral bond scheme is currently being challenged in the Supreme Court. One of the petitioners in the case is the Association for Democratic Reforms (ADR), which does detailed analysis of political funding and criminal antecedents of elected representatives. Every year, it prepares a report that analyses the donations received by political parties, as detailed in their submissions to the Election Commission of India.

The report made public in June 2022 is revealing of the huge disparity between the BJP and other political parties.[12] The report focuses on donations of above Rs 20,000 received by national political parties during the financial year 2020–21. The total of such donations declared by national parties was Rs 593.748 crore, of which Rs 477.545 crore went to the BJP. By comparison, the Congress got Rs 74.524 crore.

What is also noteworthy is that there are specific states that donate larger amounts to national parties. First, a total of Rs 246 crore was donated to national parties from Delhi, followed by Rs 71 crore from Maharashtra and Rs 47 crore from Gujarat. Delhi is the national capital, while now Maharashtra and Gujarat both have the BJP in power. The donations analysed by the ADR would be money that is 'white' or given with receipts as opposed to 'black' money, which is hard to measure but is undoubtedly part of political financing.

Also instructive is the breakdown offered by the ADR of how much of the money the BJP received came from corporate donors. Corporates/business sectors donated Rs 480.655 crore to political parties, of which Rs 416.794 went to the BJP in the financial year 2020–21. In the same period,Rs 60.37 crore came to the party from individual donors, so clearly big business is the moving force behind the BJP's extraordinary riches.

In contrast, the Congress received just Rs 35.89 crore from corporate/business sectors and actually got more from individual donors who contributed Rs 38.634 crore. This is interesting when the data shows that only 18.804 per cent of total donations to political parties came from individuals, while the bulk of 80.804 per cent came from corporates. To conclude, the BJP received more than six times the total amount of corporate donations declared by all other national parties for the financial year 2020–21.

That would be the year when the Indian gross domestic product (GDP) would contract by 7.7 per cent. It was not just the BJP that remained rich. In the year of the Covid-19 lockdown, according to the *Forbes* 2021 list, the number of Indian dollar billionaires went from 102 to 140 in twelve months. This is also a measure of the glaring inequality of India and how it has been increasing in the Modi era. The year 2020 was one of terrible hardship, reverse migration and job losses across most sectors, but at the end of it, 140 individuals had wealth that was equal to 22.7 per cent of the gross domestic product of that year.[13] The BJP, therefore, not only gets most of its wealth from the corporate sector, but during its reign, it has also been possible for a few individuals and industries in some sectors to get phenomenally rich and richer.

The starkest example of this is the phenomenal growth of the Adani Group, led by Gautam Adani, who has been accused of getting preferential treatment in infrastructure and energy projects, besides loans and financing from the SBI and Life Insurance Corporation of India (LIC), because of his proximity to PM Modi.[14] Till the end of 2022, Adani was listed as the third-richest man in the world. But his fortune and credibility are believed to have been impacted following the publication of a report by American short-selling firm Hindenburg Research[15] in January 2023, which makes charges of stock manipulation and fraud. The Adani issue has been one of the big public debates of 2023, with most of the Opposition demanding that a joint parliamentary committee be set up to look into this. The government has not yet agreed.

Meanwhile, whether we attribute the BJP's success to the image of the leader, the cadre, the social engineering or the Hindutva ideology, the data clearly shows us that the entire project is underwritten by unprecedented amounts of money from the corporate sector, sections of which could have developed a client–patron relationship with the regime. Even as they are giving in one direction, there is pressure to withdraw funds from being given to political parties inimical to the BJP. Quite clearly, therefore, it is corporate-funded Hindutva that has succeeded in India.

But I would also add that it has been possible for the BJP to achieve this because unaccountable political funding had in any case been hollowing out Indian politics for several decades, particularly since the opening up of the Indian economy in the 1980s and 1990s. The Congress, in power for much of independent India's history, always blocked extending public scrutiny to political funding. It brought in the Right to Information (RTI) laws during the term of United Progressive Alliance (UPA)-I between 2004 and 2009, but it never agreed to extend it to cover political funding. It is therefore now a victim of its own strategies. Many regional parties, too, operated in this endemically corrupt system of political funding that we have allowed in India, with regimes built around families/dynasties that also kept a tight grip on political funds.

Till the Modi-led BJP arrived in New Delhi, all political parties functioned without transparency about the source of their political funds. The Congress avoided scrutiny for itself but also extended this principle to other political players. The Modi–Shah BJP would operate very differently, ensuring huge funds came their way even as funds sent to rivals were scrutinized and, all too frequently, subjected to income tax raids and Enforcement Directorate (ED) investigations.[16]

ENFORCEMENT REIGN

The ED is a multidisciplinary agency mandated with investigating economic crimes, notably those of money laundering through the Prevention of Money Laundering Act (PMLA) and violations of foreign exchange laws. It works under the Department of Revenue,

Ministry of Finance, Government of India. Although most of the political funding today heads to the BJP, as we have noted, almost all the inquiries, seizures and arrests involve Opposition figures.

We cannot raise questions about the due process of law and must also note that the entire world of political finance has been deliberately kept fuzzy and opaque by the political class, across parties. Yet, simultaneously, it does appear that in this era of BJP rule, the ED's scrutiny has selectively been of Opposition parties and their leadership. This so-called 'ED reign' is arguably the most lethal weapon the BJP has against the Opposition that has resulted in defections to the BJP and the consequent collapse of state governments.[17]

It is effective because the system we have nurtured has involved a huge infusion of unaccountable money into political parties. Therefore, there is financial rot in all political parties. Also, at the outset, it must be stated that much of the money the BJP raises does go back into their politics, cadre building and election campaign expense. The party infrastructure across the country has seen a huge upgrade in the Modi–Shah era. There is no shortage of funds to create structures and infrastructure, both physical and ideological. Opponents charge that huge amounts are also spent in bringing down Opposition regimes and accommodating defectors.[18]

Meanwhile, as Opposition leaders face inquisitions for their alleged corruption, the PM's Office (PMO) has also taken to declaring Modi's assets on their website. There is an attempt at the highest level to present the image of an upright leadership (regardless of the party's spiralling wealth). According to the details updated up to 31 March 2022, Modi's assets increased only modestly between 2021 and 2022 and he no longer owns any immovable property after donating his share in a residential plot in Gujarat.[19] Meanwhile, his movable assets increased by Rs 26.13 lakh between 2021 and 2022, totalling Rs 2,23,82,504 which includes a fixed deposit, his bank balance, national savings certificates, insurance policies, all jewellery and cash. The assets of eight cabinet ministers (of thirty) and two ministers of state (of forty-five) were also uploaded as on 8 August 2022, and showed modest increases.

The BJP is not the first party under whose rule agencies have acted against opponents. In 2009, the UPA did away with the requirement that another agency should file a first information report (FIR) under the PMLA before the ED could take up the case. This allows the agency to make arrests without a warrant in some conditions. Let us not forget the money laundering cases filed during the Congress-led UPA era, between 2009 and 2012, against opponents such as Madhu Koda in Jharkhand, Y.S. Jaganmohan Reddy in Andhra Pradesh and some members of the Karunanidhi family in Tamil Nadu.[20]

In the current era, this has gone up by many notches. Currently, the leadership of most Opposition parties is under the ED scanner. Take the Congress: In June–July 2022, Sonia Gandhi faced repeated grilling while Rahul Gandhi was grilled for fifty hours over five days. In 2019, former finance minister P. Chidambaram was arrested in what is referred to as the INX Media case and is out on bail; his son Karti Chidambaram faces several ED cases and many of his assets have been seized. (Chidambaram as finance minister had advocated greater powers for the ED, so there is a cruel irony here.)

There are cases against state Congress leaders as well. In Karnataka, for instance, there are several cases against Deputy CM D.K. Shivakumar. He was arrested in 2019 in a money-laundering case and is out on bail but frequently interrogated by the agencies.[21] On 25 October 2023, just a month before Rajasthan would vote in state elections, the son of CM Ashok Gehlot was summoned by the ED even as the premises of the state Congress chief were raided. It is now par for the course for opposition parties to face raids before elections.[22]

Earlier, the Central Bureau of Investigation (CBI) was accused by some of acting on behalf of the ruling regimes, but there are certain restrictions on its operations as it is governed by an Act that needs what is called a 'general consent' of state governments to investigate a case. Since 2015, ten states, eight of which were ruled by the Opposition, have withdrawn that consent. The ED currently has policing powers without the restrictions that the CBI had to face. For instance, arrests can be made, and the case built up later with the necessary paper records required for conviction.

On 27 July 2022, a three-judge Supreme Court bench upheld amendments made to the PMLA which gives the government and the ED virtually unbridled powers of summons, arrest and raids and makes bail nearly impossible. It also shifts the burden of proof of innocence to the accused rather than the prosecution, which many legal experts say goes against the idea of natural justice. An editorial in *The Hindu* would conclude that: 'At a time when the ED is selectively targeting regime opponents, the verdict is bound to be remembered for its failure to protect personal liberty from executive excess.'[23]

Laws against money laundering were always stringent and as we have noted, both the UPA and the National Democratic Alliance (NDA) made amendments that expanded their scope. A 2019 amendment, passed as a money bill, which meant that it avoided scrutiny in the Rajya Sabha, made it possible to apply the law retrospectively. This gave the agency a lot of latitude in digging into the past to create a current case against particular individuals. A recent but controversial decision by the Supreme Court (that is likely to be reviewed) has also allowed the burden of proof to be placed on the accused, who have to prove their innocence instead of the ED proving their guilt.

Data submitted by the finance ministry in the Lok Sabha in the first quarter of 2022 tells the story of how since 2014, the ED has been weaponized:

- Between 2004 and 2014, the ED carried out 112 searches in the course of investigating money-laundering cases. In the next eight years, this number shot up twenty-six times to 2974 searches. That's a phenomenal growth.
- The value of the assets attached by the ED also went up from Rs 5346 crore between 2004 and 2014 to Rs 95,432 crore between 2014 and 2022. (The cases and seizures are overwhelmingly against members of opposition parties.)[24]
- The cases registered under the Foreign Exchange Management Act (FEMA) and PMLA have jumped three times in the first three years of the second term of the Modi government as compared to the corresponding period in the first term.
- According to data shared by the Minister of State for Finance Pankaj Chaudhary in the Lok Sabha, ED registered 14,143 cases under FEMA and PMLA between 2019 and 2022 as compared to 4913 cases in 2014 to 2017. That's an increase of 187 per cent and reinforces this author's submission that it is in the second term that the regime and the agencies at its disposal have really rolled up their sleeves and got down to business.[25]
- On 21 September 2022, the *Indian Express* published a lead story that examined data and cases carefully and concluded that since 2014, there has been a fourfold jump

in ED cases against politicians and 95 per cent are from Opposition parties.[26]

* * *

The year 2022 saw the BJP consolidate its power when it won the UP state election for a second term. Uttar Pradesh sends eighty MPs to Parliament. The state with the second-largest contingent of MPs, forty-eight, is Maharashtra. That is why besides the UP mandate, the other significant political development of 2022 was the collapse of the three-party alliance government that ruled Maharashtra. This happened due to large-scale defections in the Shiv Sena when a chunk of legislators created their own group and would migrate and come to power in the state in alliance with the BJP. Later, in 2023, we would see a split in the Nationalist Congress Party (NCP), founded by veteran politician and former CM of Maharashtra, Sharad Pawar. Two significant state parties in Maharashtra are currently split with a faction moving to the BJP while the other remains with the original party.

I believe we can see the 'enforcement effect' in the two most important political events of 2022 involving these two most populous states of India. First, in the face of a fightback by the SP in UP, that upped its vote share to 32 per cent, the BJP still won the state poll comfortably with a 10 per cent lead in vote share. Yet, we must note that simultaneously, there was a party whose vote share crashed from 22 per cent in the last election in 2017 to just 12 per cent in 2022 and much of that vote went to the BJP. The party in question is the BSP. As mentioned earlier, the Mayawati-led party has been rendered dysfunctional and it is said that the leadership is afraid of corruption cases being activated and the leader landing up in jail.

On the result day itself, again seated in a TV studio as the mandate of the UP election was announced on 10 March 2022, I would write a quick analysis noting the shrinking of the BSP and how it benefitted the BJP.[27] The BSP got one seat in the state assembly of 403. In a more detailed column some weeks later, I would analyse the decline of Mayawati and the BSP. She had created a template of a transferable vote bank but barely campaigned in the state poll. 'No groundwork, no mobilisation through rallies, just some tweeting followed by ticket distribution. Even her signalling indicated greater comfort with the BJP than with an expanding SP. There is speculation about whether she did so deliberately: She understands transactional politics, right from ticket distribution to government formation. Currently, many of her voters are simply striking a better bargain with the BJP.'[28]

Of course, there were other factors at work in the BJP's win in the state poll, such as the huge ration delivery, social and caste outreach across all sections of society and the popularity of both the PM and the CM. But the diversion of traditional BSP votes to the BJP was a significant element in what unfolded.

The Maharashtra 2022–23 endgame is arguably as significant as UP because Mumbai is the financial capital of India, and money, as we have seen, is directly linked to politics. All circumstantial evidence and statements of leaders around Shiv Sena chief Uddhav Thackeray and NCP founder Pawar suggest that the ED played a starring role in the collapse of the coalition government. Although the BJP first gave the CM's post to the breakaway leader of the Shiv Sena, Eknath Shinde, the national party is in the driver's seat in the state, not because of the spread of its own vote share but due to its capacity to split other parties.

There was actually a stunning sequence of events that preceded the collapse of the Maharashtra government led by the former CM

Uddhav Thackeray that had been supported by the NCP and the Congress in the state. Sanjay Raut, Shiv Sena MP close to the now ousted Uddhav Thackeray, had on 8 February 2022, released a letter he had written to the Rajya Sabha chairman saying lawmakers of the party including him were being threatened with ED action if they did not topple the Maharashtra state government.[29]

By June 2022, the government had indeed been toppled, properties owned by Sanjay Raut and his wife were seized and they were facing an ED inquiry while Raut himself was arrested on 31 July. He would spend 100 days in jail before securing bail. One does not know the scale of the evidence against Sanjay Raut, but according to data[30] submitted by the government itself, in the seventeen years of the existence of the PMLA, the ED has secured twenty-three convictions of the 54,422 cases, which is 0.004 per cent.

Meanwhile, some of the Shiv Sena members that shifted across to the breakaway faction led by Eknath Shinde—made CM of Maharashtra on 7 July 2022 in alliance with the BJP—did indeed have ED inquiries. It would be interesting to see how such investigations will be pursued in comparison to those against opposing parties still ruling other states. In Maharashtra, more such splits and defections would follow a year later when in early July 2023, the nephew of Sharad Pawar and a politician in his own right, Ajit Pawar, joined the state government with a large chunk of Members of the Legislative Assembly (MLAs). Again, many of the individuals who left the NCP faced income tax and ED inquiries and the pincer of their properties being seized. Ajit Pawar is currently the deputy CM of Maharashtra. When he had not joined the front created by the BJP, the party would fiercely campaign against him for what is referred to as the 'irrigation scam'. There are currently multiple legal cases that challenge the splits in both the Shiv Sena and the NCP, and more twists could emerge from court rulings.

Besides the Shiv Sena and the NCP, two parties that have been put through the ED wringer are the Trinamool Congress (TMC), which is in power in West Bengal and defeated the BJP in a pitched election in 2021, and the Aam Aadmi Party (AAP), which is in power in Delhi and had on two occasions, in 2015 and 2020, trounced the BJP very thoroughly in the city state in elections into which the national party threw its all.

From 2015 onwards, various intimidation tactics were used against the AAP after the party won a historic mandate of sixty-seven of Delhi's seventy seats just six months after Modi won the national mandate. As the BJP had won all of the seven parliamentary seats in the national capital, there was a clear division of choice made explicitly by many Delhi voters between the AAP for the city state and the BJP for the national vote. The first term of the AAP was known for a constant stand-off between it and central government appointees. AAP founder-leader and Delhi CM Arvind Kejriwal faced multiple defamation cases and by mid-2016, eleven of AAP's sixty-seven MLAs were in custody. However, the cases against them would eventually not hold up in court.[31]

The AAP would win a second term in Delhi, getting sixty-two of the seventy seats, a marginal decline. The 2020 battle was pitched and communalized and took place in the midst of the protests at various sites in the national capital against the CAA. While the BJP tried to frame it as a Hindu–Muslim election, the AAP kept the focus on its governance record. That the city was on edge, however, became clear just weeks after the election result was declared on 8 February 2020. On 23 February, Hindu–Muslim riots broke out in the north-eastern part of the city, claiming fifty-three lives and large-scale destruction of property in the most densely populated part of the metropolis. The trigger for the riots was the seething resentment by some BJP members and supporters against the anti-CAA protests.[32]

After winning a second term in Delhi, the AAP also became more focused on its national ambitions, and in 2022, came into power in Punjab. Just months after that verdict, one of the most high-profile ministers of the Kejriwal-led regime, Satyendar Jain, was put under the ED scanner and arrested on 31 May. After a year spent in jail, he got interim bail, which has currently been extended on medical grounds. There have, however, been some revealing twists in his case.

On 21 July 2022, the media reported that his bail hearing was opposed by the ED on the grounds that it did not trust Delhi government hospitals to give a fair report as they 'can be managed by the accused'. Additional solicitor general S.V. Raju made this submission before a special judge.[33] It is a fascinating argument by one wing of the state, suggesting that institutions under a particular regime cannot be trusted as they would in all likelihood be biased. What is equally noteworthy is that a high court would accept the argument that Jain must not be given a health report by doctors working in Delhi government hospitals.

One wonders if the same argument would not extend to the ED itself, considering that it comes under the finance ministry, although it is expected to work without political bias—just as doctors should be trusted for their diagnosis. As for the Kejriwal-led party, worse was to come. On 9 March 2023, his right hand and the Deputy CM of Delhi, Manish Sisodia, was arrested in what is referred to as the liquor policy scam and at the time of writing, bail has been repeatedly denied to him. On 17 April that year, Kejriwal was questioned for nine hours by the CBI in the same matter. On 4 October, the most high-profile and active MP of the party, Sanjay Singh, was arrested by the ED in the same liquor policy case. Then, after Manish Sisodia was denied bail by the Supreme Court, Kejriwal would be summoned to appear before the agency on 2 November 2023. But he has at the time of writing, failed to appear and challenged the grounds for his summons. What is however clear is that the law is such that Kejriwal could be arrested at any time. Moreover, the ED lawyer has stated in court that the agency is considering making the party an accused in the case under the PMLA. If that happens, it would be the first time that a political party would face this. As stated, everything is pitched and relentless when it comes to investigating and attempting to pulverize Opposition leaders.

Another party in the firing line from the first term of the Modi regime is the TMC, which has been in power in West Bengal since 2011. There have been cases and inquiries against TMC members for some years now, but the state became a special focus after the 2019 Lok Sabha election, when the BJP surprised everyone by winning as many as eighteen seats of the forty-two. After that, serious moves began to break members of the TMC away and put the Opposition party on the mat.

As many as thirty-four TMC legislators would join the BJP, including some heavyweights such as Mukul Roy and Suvendu Adhikari, both key figures in the party.[34] Yet, in spite of all efforts by the national party, in the assembly election held in March 2021, the TMC won comfortably—although the BJP did emerge as the leading opposition party in the state. Some of the inductees into the BJP would return with folded hands to the TMC in a state known for violent reprisals along political lines. But let it also be stated emphatically that in 2017, both these high-profile inductees who joined the BJP were questioned in an alleged scam.

Roy was questioned by the CBI and Adhikari by the ED for alleged involvement in what is known as the Narada tapes scam that involved a sting operation.[35]

In 2022, a year after the TMC won a third successive term in West Bengal, it is the individual who has emerged as a potential successor to TMC chief Mamata Banerjee, who began to be routinely summoned for interrogation by the ED. The reference is to Abhishek Banerjee, the nephew of the CM and now the effective number two in the party. The pressure on the West Bengal party is intense and every other day, a new report of ED action makes news.

The ED action can at times also serve to reveal the terrible rot in the political finance system. Take the case of Partha Chatterjee, who held multiple portfolios in the West Bengal government. He would be suspended by the party five days after his arrest by the ED on 23 July 2022 and the alleged recovery of Rs 48 crore from his associate.[36] If we go by the version of events shared by the agency with the press, the case is as murky as they come and is known as the recruitment scam—allegedly, bribes were given to recruit teachers who had not cleared the basic tests. The fact that Mamata Banerjee would suspend Partha Chatterjee, who was believed to be close to her, shows that she is sensitive to the repercussions of the endless levelling of corruption charges.

But it must also be stated that so far, like the AAP, the TMC, too, has prevailed electorally in spite of the cases that are designed to damage its image, intimidate legislators and cut financial supply lines.

There has also been the targeting of Mahua Moitra, the high-profile TMC MP. She is a former banker who has been known for her very articulate arguments about businessman Gautam Adani and she has openly accused PM Modi of 'favouritism and cronyism'. There is currently an orchestrated campaign to get her disqualified as an MP and the TMC has appointed her district president of the party in Krishnanagar (Nadia West) that falls within her parliamentary constituency.

Members of parties in the Opposition spectrum can therefore meet any fate—from seizure of properties and time in jail to cancellation of their membership of Parliament. As things stand now, Sonia and Rahul Gandhi can be put behind bars, as can the leadership of the AAP, TMC, NCP and the faction of the Shiv Sena run by the founder's family. A constant target is the Rashtriya Janata Dal (RJD), whose founder, former CM Lalu Prasad Yadav, has already served a jail term and is currently out on bail. The party has the largest chunk of seats in Bihar and is in power in the state in an alliance with Nitish Kumar, the CM and leader of the JD(U) that walked out of the ruling alliance arrangement with the BJP in August 2022. Lalu Yadav's son Tejashwi Yadav is the deputy CM of the state and is now also facing ED cases.[37]

The Jharkhand Mukti Morcha (JMM), which is in power in Jharkhand in alliance with the Congress, is also in the firing line of police action and corruption cases. Chief Minister Hemant Soren reportedly faces a potential disqualification and did take the MLAs of the ruling alliance to Congress-ruled Chhattisgarh, presumably to avert defections.[38] But he would return to his state to call for a trust vote that was passed comfortably in September 2022, which means that a no-confidence motion against his government can only be moved after six months. But this is another instance of Opposition parties corralling their legislators for fear of defections brought about by the mix of threats and financial inducements.

Indeed, under this sort of merciless pressure, the back-room stories of Indian politics, impossible to substantiate, are about Opposition parties reportedly coming to some sort of understanding with the BJP in order to buy a modicum of mercy. We can never elaborate on such stories but can say with some certainty that some Opposition parties are atrophying since there is the very basic human fear of incarceration and seizure of assets.

Media reports suggest that the enforcement style of politics can be used as a pressure tactic to sort out internal matters within the BJP itself. From the names in the public domain, former Karnataka CM (four terms, each of which would not be completed) and BJP veteran B.S. Yediyurappa and some of his close aides have faced income tax (IT) raids and cases can always be activated as a way of taming the relatively independent figure and making him fall in line with the party diktat.[39, 40] Yet, as Yediyurappa is a caste strongman, with some influence over the Lingayat community of Karnataka, there are limits as to how far such tactics would be taken to sort out power tussles within the BJP. Besides, the corruption charges against him go back several decades. The BJP uses both carrot and stick on Yediyurappa. He was compelled to quit the chief ministership in July 2021,[41, 42] but then, as an act of appeasement, included in the party's most influential national forum, the Parliamentary Board, in August 2022. Eventually, in May 2023, the BJP would lose the state government that was put together with defections from the Congress and JD(S) and the Congress would come to power in the state, in an election that gave a fillip to the entire national Opposition. In November 2023, the BJP would again turn to the Yediyurappa family, when his son Vijayendra Yediyurappa was given charge of the state unit.

The truth is that the finances of all political parties are questionable.[43] But it is possible that constant raids and seizures reinforce the image of all the other political parties as being corrupt even as the BJP is never questioned on becoming the richest party in India's history. Yet, the pervasive ED pressure is also the trigger for the disparate opposition parties seeking to unite to save themselves. The Indian National Developmental Inclusive Alliance (I.N.D.I.A.) has been formed in 2023 with the singular purpose of taking on the BJP in 2024. But what is needed for the alliance to work is not just a national revival of the Congress but in some states, the capacity of the party to come to an understanding with precisely those forces that defeated them in recent decades.

Meanwhile, there can be little doubt that big money has corroded politics and that there is also no big leader in sight who can carry the moral halo required to really cleanse the system. There was a time when even leaders of small parties or movements were intellectual giants and committed to the people as opposed to trying to hang on to power and assets. Congress MP Rahul Gandhi who walked the length of India in his Bharat Jodo Yatra, from 22 September 2022 to 23 January 2023, has been trying to foreground public morality, ethics and values. But he is not a creator of a mass movement or the founder of a party; he is a dynast trying to reinvent his own party and find the right tone, tenor and courage to take on the BJP in an age that they dominate.

In conclusion, we can say that politics often does not appear to be a level playing field in India.

Meanwhile, the Supreme Court's July 2022 ED judgment mentioned earlier will have far-reaching consequences even on the manner in which corporates and business houses engage with political parties, particularly those in the Indian Opposition. There is another complex legal matter before the Supreme Court. A seven-judge bench is to decide if amendments making the PMLA more stringent, which bypassed Rajya Sabha scrutiny, should have been made through the money bill route (money bills need to be passed only by the Lok Sabha).[44] Till then, however, we have a politico-legal framework that disadvantages any political party that is not in power on the side of the BJP.

MEDIA AND SOCIAL MEDIA

Many reasons have been offered by analysts for the BJP's huge win in the 2019 national elections. Among them was the Pulwama-Balakot cycle of events generating a muscular nationalist sentiment, Modi's popularity, no Opposition candidate with much credibility plus money and cadre working for the BJP.

Some commentators said 2019 was a post-caste and post-identity mandate and noted the breach in class segments that voted for the BJP. I would agree that India had changed and shifted its axis dramatically. But I believe that the change has also been driven by technology in general, and the telecom revolution ushered in by Jio, the mobile and data service launched by Reliance Industries in 2016. The 2019 poll was therefore a post-Jio election as, in Modi's first term, India became the nation with some of the cheapest data tariffs in the world, and thus one of the world's largest consumer of wireless data. On a lighter note, it is now frequently said that data is cheaper than atta (wheat)!

A September 2018 story in the *Wall Street Journal* began with the sentence that India's richest man is catapulting hundreds of millions of poor people straight into the mobile internet age.[45] It noted that Mukesh Ambani, head of Reliance Industries, 'one of India's largest conglomerates, had shelled out $35 billion of the company's money to blanket the South Asian nation with its first all-4G network'.

The plunge in prices led to a surge in data traffic to 1.5 billion gigabytes a month, according to Amitabh Kant, the then chief executive officer of the NITI Aayog. In December 2017, Kant posted on his Twitter account (now renamed X): 'Mobile data consumption is higher than USA & China put together.'[46] To clarify, China has more data consumers than India in absolute terms, but in terms of percentage of the population, India is ahead. In 2012, India contributed to only 2 per cent of the world's mobile data traffic and China held a 10 per cent share, while the Western market accounted for 75 per cent. By 2022, India held a 21 per cent share of the global mobile data traffic and China 27 per cent, while the Western markets of North America and Europe account for only a quarter of the global traffic for mobile data services.[47]

Jio's subscription base, meanwhile, would grow even after the company began charging for data services as the company's entry had crashed the rates for data in India. The Telecom Authority of India (TRAI) releases data on both wireless and wired telephone connectivity and in the last few years, the growth is significant in both rural and urban segments. Jio is the market leader with Airtel closely following it. The 'Jio effect' therefore is there for all of us to see as today, in a matter of a few years, it is par for the course to see farmers, labourers, drivers and domestic help watch content on their mobile phone when they get a moment away from their hard day's work.

That, I believe, is the big transformation in India—and initially, only the BJP understood it. With millions of Indians now owning smartphones and data becoming dirt cheap, the BJP's messaging is now spread through content designed for WhatsApp forwards and social media platforms. In any election-bound state, the BJP conscripts an entire team that creates content and distributes it with local nuances. District and constituency-specific content is churned out by motivated cadre. And yes, anyone who has been on a WhatsApp group of the *bhakts* (the BJP-faithful) would know that the content can be blatantly communal, incendiary and full of false facts.[48]

Simultaneously, another level of this pyramid is the TV channels that churn out debates and 'reports' favourable to the national ruling party. They build the image of the PM, never question the nationally dominant party and, all too frequently, organize polarizing debates about Indian Muslims, from which bites are then shared at the ground level through WhatsApp by the social media army of the BJP. The website Newslaundry that monitors TV debates has produced a lot of content on this theme, calling it 'Bloodlust TV' and more.[49] The website Alt News explicitly calls out a lot of the fake news and communal propaganda distributed by the BJP's social media ecosystem and is therefore quite fiercely targeted by the state.

Ideological content against minorities is today actually manufactured and produced by television channels (often run by traditional media groups) and they have certainly played a role in altering the national consciousness, particularly in the Hindi-speaking parts of the country. Broadly, many TV anchors routinely suggest various conspiracies involving Muslims many times over. This ranges from the idea of Muslims creating an exodus of Hindus, of hatching a master plan to reproduce and overtake the Hindu population, and of seducing Hindu girls as a form of love jihad. The minority community is presented as anti-national, intolerant, prone to rioting and deserving of everything that they get because they, well, asked for it. Historical grievances and stereotypes about the Muslim male are part of this messaging that is both overt and subliminal in that it touches ancient prejudices and complexes even as it creates contemporary discourse. Medieval Mughal emperors are often pulled into this discourse, and this cannot be dismissed as being just ridiculous because it is so toxic.

It can therefore be said that public discourse has been re-engineered in India and this rides on the new technology. The figures for social media applications in India are mind-boggling: Twitter may generate the greatest controversy but actually has a smaller number of users in India in comparison to other social media platforms. Facebook has the largest audience size from India in comparison to other nations and the numbers for YouTube and WhatsApp are also phenomenal and growing. Indians consume a lot of political content on these platforms. Indeed, there is a trend now of political parties also reaching out to individuals considered to be social media influencers as opposed to traditional print media.

Beyond the so-called engineering of 'news', there is also a concerted attempt to recast popular culture altogether with organized trolling and filing of frivolous criminal cases against certain shows created for OTT platforms, which have now become very cautious in their commissioning. There was also in 2022 a boycott demanded of big Bollywood movies made by traditional production houses that included actors who happen to be Muslim or are perceived as being liberals. Simultaneously, films such as *The Kashmir Files*, *The Tashkent Files* and *The Accidental Prime Minister*, which promote the right-wing narrative, are fiercely backed by this ecosystem. In the case of the controversial *The Kashmir Files*, the film was made tax free by most BJP-ruled states, which means the ticket price was low. In 2023, the film *The Kerala Story*, about Indian women being fooled and entrapped into fighting for ISIS, was used as a propaganda tool by the BJP/RSS ecosystem when state elections in Karnataka took place in mid-2023. The BJP would lose that election, yet they do have an understanding of attention spans being very short in the age of social media. Messaging has to be short but reinforced repeatedly.

For instance, these past eight years, there has been one repeated message: Modi! Modi! Modi! No choice, no choice, no choice! That is how the cookie crumbles these days.

When I had begun the journey of covering the BJP in the late 1990s, the world was very different. It was gentler, kinder and I could still have a swagger about being an Indian in a secular, federal republic. The BJP was also a colourful party where I would make many friends and develop multiple sources. It was the beginning of an era. In the years since, as I have tracked and covered the party, the institutional sub-culture of the BJP would change, as would that of the country. The BJP has already pulled off quite a feat. Let us now go to the beginning of the party's journey in power.

1

THE VAJPAYEE MORNING

My engagement with the Bharatiya Janata Party (BJP) began in an age of relative innocence. Journalism does at times take us to places where we end up witnessing history. It was a morning assignment to cover the swearing-in ceremony of Atal Bihari Vajpayee on 19 March 1998. I had been on the BJP beat for a year and dutifully turned up very early at the modest ceremony held in the open-air forecourt of Rashtrapati Bhavan. The chairs were empty at first, and then they filled up and suddenly the moment came without much fanfare: the amiable Atalji (as he was popularly known), with friends across the political spectrum, took the oath of office in Hindi. Next to be sworn in was the more austere, Lal Krishna Advani, very much the architect of the BJP's ascent to power.

It was a significant moment in contemporary politics. The BJP had ended what was called its 'untouchability', a phrase which was used freely those days to describe the party's presumed inability to get allies. After emerging as the single largest party in 1998, but short of a majority, it had shown great pragmatism in hammering out a Common Minimum Programme with regional parties (this meant excluding three commitments in its election manifesto: construction of a Ram temple at Ayodhya, repeal of Article 370 of the Indian Constitution that gives special status to Jammu and Kashmir, and the enactment of a Uniform Civil Code).

Even in retrospect, it would be a mistake to view this coming-together of disparate parties only as a gathering of anti-Congress party forces. For its pivot was a party that had a very distinct ideological mooring that challenged the concept of secularism on which post-Partition India had been built, mostly by the Indian National Congress, with brief interruptions by messy coalitions that collapsed quickly, never surviving full terms.

The Vajpayee moment was both about the centrality of the BJP, and equally about sensible coalition formation. Those who scripted the first rule of the BJP included some spectacular figures besides Vajpayee and Advani. The one-time trade union activist and socialist, George Fernandes, was a central character in the National Democratic Alliance, or NDA, as the coalition came to be known; sworn in on that day was also the late Ramakrishna Hegde, former chief minister of Karnataka; and Surjit Singh Barnala, former chief minister of Punjab.

If there were regional satraps who had left an indelible mark on Indian politics, the future too was present, taking oath of office: Nitish Kumar, who would later become chief minister of Bihar, and Naveen Patnaik, who would go on to become the chief minister of Orissa.

The ceremony that I witnessed in 1998 was therefore a marker of the changing political landscape. It was just the beginning.

* * *

But the story behind the Big Moment that day was that Atalji was sulking and annoyed. He had been advised against making Jaswant Singh, his friend and close associate, the finance minister, because the Rashtriya Swayamsevak Sangh (RSS) had vetoed it. There were credible sources who later revealed that the then chief of the RSS, K.S. Sudarshan, had personally told Vajpayee not to appoint Jaswant as the finance minister. (L.K. Advani would later say in private conversations that he believed Vajpayee should have ignored the RSS chief at that point).[1]

What unfolded was very typical of the internecine RSS–BJP pressure play that would characterize the Vajpayee era. In 1996, while heading a government that had lasted just for thirteen days, Vajpayee had picked Jaswant as his finance minister. But 1998 was different in the sense that unlike the thirteen-day rule of 1996, that was never expected to last, this time the BJP was looking at running a 'real government' for the first time in its history.

That is why other opinions also weighed in. The RSS felt that Jaswant Singh was too strong a votary of the free market, a maverick, a liberal, and somehow didn't conform to the image that the sangathan (organization; yet another term to describe the RSS) endorsed. The fact of the matter was that at the time, the RSS wanted a finance minister who would vigorously promote their brand of swadeshi (homespun) economics that advocated protectionist policies. In the last-minute wrangling over portfolios, the RSS had pitched heavily for the ideological purist, Murli Manohar Joshi (who was later allocated the ministry of Human Resource Development or HRD).

This is when Atal Bihari Vajpayee put his foot down. Although he'd acquiesced to not making Jaswant Singh the finance minister, he made his opinion clear that he would not agree to the RSS running the Finance ministry through their nominee. Eventually, a compromise was struck and Yashwant Sinha, the bureaucrat-turned-politician, was pitchforked to the Finance portfolio. In a sense, Vajpayee had his revenge, as Yashwant was not from the RSS, but a former IAS officer who became a career politician, first as a Socialist by joining the Janata Dal (JD), and then the BJP in 1996. What also went in his favour was past experience as he had served as finance minister from November 1990–June 1991 during the brief prime ministership of Chandra Shekhar.

Eventually, the same Yashwant Sinha, a pivot of the Vajpayee era, would indeed abandon the BJP of the Modi era, and become a vocal critic. In the year 2022, he would be propped up as a presidential candidate by opposition parties against the BJP's nominee, Draupadi Murmu, and be defeated. Tragically for him, by this time, even some opposition parties were beginning to support the BJP candidate, because she was an adivasi woman nominee and some were under various pressures. The idea of joint opposition action certainly collapsed during the 2022 presidential election.

(Ironically, Jaswant Singh, the man who was Vajpayee's first choice for finance minister, but blocked by the RSS, would also not survive the party in the latter years and be expelled for a book he wrote on Mohammad Ali Jinnah. He was, however, the main fire-fighter on many fronts during the Vajpayee era and a chapter about this colourful figure who has now passed away, is there later in the book.)

* * *

There were two other dramatis personae from the south of India who played crucial roles in the Atal Bihari Vajpayee government in 1998. They couldn't be ignored, although they were hardly seen in Delhi, preferring instead to pull strings like master puppeteers from their respective state capitals of Hyderabad and Chennai. This was a classic coalition regime. Chandrababu Naidu was then the chief minister of Andhra Pradesh and leader of the Telugu Desam Party or TDP. In 1998, he was still negotiating the 'secularism' question and hence chose to give outside support to the BJP, which meant that the TDP would not participate in the government but wouldn't pull it down either. This also meant that he and other regional satraps had the advantage of extracting many lucrative deals for their respective states, even as they pretended to be one-foot-in-one-foot-out on the secularism front. But the troubles with Naidu would mostly happen behind the scenes.

Not so with the All India Anna Dravida Munnetra Kazhagam or AIADMK, led by the late J. Jayalalithaa, that was out of power in Tamil Nadu, but had eighteen MPs in Parliament.

Although the actress-turned-politician would eventually join the government, she made life difficult for Vajpayee over the mandatory letter of support.

One of my most vivid memories leading up to 19 March 1998 is about spending several hours outside Atal Bihari Vajpayee's residence at 7, Safdarjung Road, even as senior BJP leaders, along with alliance partners such as George Fernandes sat inside, with tension writ large on their faces. They had spent hours in a huddle waiting for Jayalalithaa's letter of support, which was to be sent to the then President K.R. Narayanan. The endless waiting game was exacting as all the alliance partners had already sent in their letters to the President by 12 March, save Jayalalithaa who had kept them waiting for forty-eight hours. The man of the moment was obviously Atal Bihari Vajpayee, whose annoyance at the delay was overtly visible to all of us waiting for Jayalalithaa's decision.

Finally, the letter arrived, but Jayalalithaa would make an intemperate ally and eventually play her part in bringing down the BJP government, leading to another election in 1999. Her severing of ties actually proved to be a blessing in disguise for the NDA, which went on to win a comfortable majority in the next elections. Subsequently, the Dravida Munnetra Kazhagam (DMK) would replace the AIADMK as NDA's partner from Tamil Nadu, but not before the lady had stirred up several little storms. Surviving Jayalalithaa was in fact one of the first challenges faced by the NDA.

* * *

I witnessed this remarkable scene standing in the portico of Vajpayee's residence. The NDA regime was barely two months old and there was already a crisis brewing. I recall the moment when the lady arrived looking furious, and what followed is imprinted vividly in my memory.

It was a hot day. An air-conditioned Tata Sierra drove into the portico. First a retainer stepped out and rushed to place a stool below the car door. Then the folds of the cloak the lady wore those days, billowed in the wind. One regal foot appeared, then the other, and then Jayalalithaa appeared, smiling sweetly at the media. The cloak swirled yet again as she turned around and marched off into Vajpayee's living room.

The meeting over, Jayalalithaa marched out with her cloak swirling back again and decided on an impromptu press conference. At this point in the ensuing drama, Jaswant Singh played major-domo and escorted her to the marquee on the patio. There, deliberately or otherwise, oblivious of the prime minister's assurance to Parliament about not misusing Article 356 (that restricted the Centre's hand in dismissing state governments), she announced that she expected the BJP to keep up the pressure on the DMK government in Tamil Nadu. 'They know what to do,' she declared perfunctorily, and then got into the car and drove off leaving the fine men of the BJP quaking in her wake.

* * *

In the run-up to the 1998 elections, the BJP had made a commitment of not misusing Article 356, in the manner the Congress party had done several times over in the past. It was apparent that Atal Bihari Vajpayee wanted to position the BJP as a party that respected and promoted federalism and he was really committed to this constitutional ideal. But the irrepressible Jayalalithaa (although she had extracted six berths for the AIADMK) exhorted the Vajpayee government to destabilize the DMK government in Tamil Nadu and help her tide over several corruption cases that she was facing. At one point of the tug of war with her, the late Pramod Mahajan told me that an exasperated BJP had informed Jayalalithaa that they were ready to change position on Article 356 but, 'she should convince us that we can constitutionally get away with it.'

The scene I had witnessed in the portico of Vajpayee's home was triggered by the then Union Special Secretary (Home) Ashok Kumar giving a clean chit to the DMK-led Tamil Nadu government on the law and order front after a visit to the state. That drove her into a rage that we witnessed and the hapless bureaucrat was transferred as an act of appeasement.

But the debilitating fallout was tension between the Home ministry and the Prime Minister's Office (PMO), fuelling speculation that all wasn't well between Advani and Vajpayee.

There were many theories floating around and if there was one question which came up repeatedly, it was whether the Home ministry had *deliberately* put its hand into a hornet's nest by sending a team to Tamil Nadu. That sort of conjecture about competing power centres led by Vajpayee and Advani would henceforth remain a constant feature in the Atal-led NDA years.

In a matter of a few hours, Jayalalithaa made the new government look shaky. She also began a war of words with Commerce Minister Ramakrishna Hegde, and Urban Development Minister Ram Jethmalani over other matters not worth recounting today, although the personalities involved were iconic. In the first two months, it seemed as if the obsessive preoccupation with Jayalalithaa and her battles would end up paralysing the government and destroy its credibility. While some felt that Vajpayee was being too mild in handling her, on her part, she had been jailed in December 1996 and was fighting a slew of corruption cases with her back to the wall. Eventually she would bring down the government, only to witness it being resurrected. She would remain a force to reckon with in Tamil Nadu politics till her passing in 2016.

The starkest difference between the Vajpayee and Modi eras is that from a multiplicity of power centres in the old BJP and rivalries at the very top, we now have a singular leadership that faces no challenges from within the party. The ideological movement of the cadre organization, the RSS, has ironically been best served by a personality cult built around one individual.

2

THE JOURNEY

The Jana Sangh was founded in 1951 by Shyama Prasad Mukherjee with the clear intent of it being the political arm of the RSS. Almost two and a half decades later, in 1977, the Jana Sangh merged with several other parties that were ideologically Left, Right and centrist; but they were all opposed to the Congress party in the post-Emergency era. That is how the Janata Party was born; but within a short span of three years, it split in 1980 over the 'dual membership' issue of former Jana Sangh members who still swore allegiance to the RSS. That is when former members of Jana Sangh decided to form a separate party that allowed them the freedom to pursue their brand of politics which had its genesis in the RSS ideology and on 6 April 1980, the BJP came into being with Atal Bihari Vajpayee as its first president.

I suspect it may have come as a bit of a surprise for many members of the newly-formed Bharatiya Janata Party, but in his first presidential address, Vajpayee played down the RSS–Jana Sangh connection and instead focused on the legacy of Jayaprakash Narayan (popularly known as JP), the Socialist leader, whose Sampoorna Kranti or Total Revolution against the Congress and

Indira Gandhi had led to the imposition of the Emergency and creation of the Janata Party. In his autobiography, *My Country My Life*, L.K. Advani writes,

> There was considerable speculation in political circles about whether the new party would mark the revival of the Jana Sangh. Atalji dispelled these speculations with a categorical assertion in his presidential speech. 'No', he said. 'We will not go back. We do not want to project that we want to revive the Jana Sangh in any way. We will make use of our experience in the Janata Party. We are proud to have been associated with it. And although we are out of it now, we do not want in any way to disown this past . . .'[1]

Through most of his tenure as prime minister too, Atal Bihari Vajpayee wanted the BJP to maintain a distance from the RSS and hard-line elements within his party, as well as the ideological family.

* * *

I began covering the BJP in 1997, and as one of my first assignments, I travelled to Chitrakoot (on the Uttar Pradesh–Madhya Pradesh border) to meet one of the great Jana Sangh ideologues, who had scripted his party's entry into the Janata Party and thereby orchestrated the dissolution of the Jana Sangh.

The late Nanaji Deshmukh was a giant in the iconography of the Hindu Right. After the failure of the Janata Party experiment, he decided to renounce public life and chose social work in some of the most backward regions of Uttar Pradesh. It was perhaps appropriate that he should have shifted to Chitrakoot, where

Lord Ram, according to legend, was supposed to have spent part of his fourteen-year-long *vanvas* (exile). The context being the appropriation of Ram as the icon for the revival of Hindu Right in Indian politics.

In the Nineties, Chitrakoot was one of the most unspoilt of Indian pilgrimage sites. There were no pesky *pandas* (or pandits) playing mediators between man and God, nor hordes of pilgrims seeking salvation. But what I remember clearly was an army of monkeys on every rooftop, every street corner—the sort who are used to being venerated and pampered, not the kind you shoo away out of fear.

This tiny, dusty little town had great mythological significance. Situated on the Bundelkhand plateau on the Uttar Pradesh–Madhya Pradesh border, Chitrakoot reverberated with the legend and lore of the Ramayana. The Kamadgiri mountain is where Ram is believed to have lived with Sita and Lakshman; the Gupt Godavari caves, where all the rivers converged to pay homage to Ram; and the idyllic Janaki (another name for Sita) Kund on the banks of the river Mandakini, where, legend has it, that Sita would sit down to rest after her daily bath.

That said, Chitrakoot was hellish in the summer with temperatures hitting 50 degrees Celsius. I remember reaching the place, getting over my fear of monkeys and making my way to a bright pink building which Nanaji had named after his late friend and founder of the Indian Express group, Ram Nath Goenka. He told me how the newspaper baron was instrumental in coaxing Indira Gandhi to release him from jail after a seventeen-month-long imprisonment during the Emergency. He would also tell me that it was RNG (as Goenka was known popularly) who had persuaded him to stand for elections in 1977.

On his release, as mentioned earlier, Nanaji became one of the architects of the Jana Sangh's merger into the Janata Party, although he'd refused to join Prime Minister Morarji Desai's cabinet. He would tell me, 'The Janata experiment failed not because of the Jana Sangh members' dual membership of the RSS but because three men, Desai, Charan Singh and Jagjivan Ram, all wanted to be prime minister.'

Once the Janata project failed, Nanaji Deshmukh abruptly quit public life for what the RSS projects as the noblest of tasks in its lexicon, described as 'nation-building'. And so Nanaji began working in Gonda in Uttar Pradesh, the district from which he'd entered Parliament. He set up a project, which yielded impressive results: 2000 tube wells in two years, and improved methods of cultivation in 2800 villages, he claimed. The headquarters for the project was located in a building called Jayaprabhagram, named after his close friend, Jayaprakash Narayan or JP, with whom Nanaji had formed a strong relationship during the Bihar movement in 1974 that had led Indira Gandhi to impose the Emergency in the first place.

His address at Chitrakoot was an outhouse attached to the Goenka memorial called Siya-Ram Kutiya. I recall drawing Nanaji's attention to pictures of Mahatma Gandhi alongside portraits of the RSS founder, K.B. Hedgewar, as also M.S. Golwalkar or 'Gururji'. Is the RSS trying to appropriate Gandhiji? I asked him, in the context of M.K. Gandhi having been killed by an individual committed to the Hindu Right-wing ideology.

'I don't see a contradiction . . . like Gandhi, the RSS also believes that India lives in her villages . . . If it had not been for the RSS, I wouldn't have thought of devoting my life to the country. Whatever Nanaji Deshmukh is today is because of the RSS.'

After his retirement from mainstream politics, Nanaji took it upon himself to promote the RSS's vision for India. He promoted schools for adivasis or tribals who were made aware of their Hindu identity; set up Ayurveda research centres; a rural university that educated village folk about ancient Indian shastras. His mission also included transposing the 'ancient Indian idyll' to the modern age, and one of its most important symbols was the *gaumata* or the holy cow. Nanaji was particularly proud of his *gaushala* or cowshed, in which he bred ten different varieties of cows and offered to take me on a guided tour of the place.

In retrospect, I must thank Nanaji for having revealed an entirely new world to me—for the first time, I saw several men sincerely, and with a great deal of reverence, collecting samples of cow urine. Even before I could express my utter astonishment at what I had witnessed, Nanaji said, 'Did you know that scientists are now discovering that desi ghee made from the milk of Indian cows does not contain cholesterol?' I murmured something in response, reeling as I was under the influence of large quantities of cow urine!

But the most important lesson I learnt from my meeting with Nanaji was that the Indian Right had strong ties with captains of Indian industry. For instance, amongst the most prominent of his followers was the then Bombay Dyeing Chairman, Nusli Wadia.

'I knew his mother, Jinnah's daughter, Dina very well,' said Nanaji to me. He pointed to a school in the vicinity which followed the gurukul system, that the RSS believes prevailed in the idyll of ancient India. It was named after Surendra Paul, the younger brother of NRI industrialist, Swraj Paul. We later went into Ramnath ashram, which was a hostel for 200 adivasi students, whose day began with yoga. But it was the brochure which got my attention. It said, 'Lord Ram, with his compassionate behaviour, had won the hearts of the *vanvasis* . . . the forest dwellers were the strength of Lord Ram.'

Nanaji was in a chatty mood that day and proceeded to speak about his most ambitious project which involved 'hand-picked' couples who were to be given instructions in 'moral, cultural, and economic development' in about a 100 village clusters. He said, '*Mera kaam saat peediyon tak chalega*' [My work will continue for seven generations after me]. I asked him if the aim was general social upliftment or creating a 'Hindu' rashtra or nation?

'There is no Hindu–Muslim problem in our country. Politicians create it. And as for Hindu rashtra, that was just word play,'[2] he said.

All the themes that were dear to this Jana Sangh ideologue would get full play seventeen years later, when Narendra Modi led the BJP to a fabulous victory in 2014. However, the metamorphoses would begin a few months after my visit to Chitrakoot, because the following year, in 1998, the BJP for the first time in its history would taste real political power at the Centre, as the head of a coalition government.

In hindsight, now that India has its first adivasi or tribal President in Draupadi Murmu, elected in July 2022, the significance of RSS outreach must be noted. It has for years worked in tribal pockets trying to define and keep adivasis in the Hindu fold and avert the possibility of conversion to Christianity due to the consistent work done by the church in some of the poorest parts of India. Individuals such as Nanaji Deshmukh (he passed away in 2010) were the backbone of the framework that the RSS quietly created in India, even in the years when the BJP was not in power.

* * *

Atal Bihari Vajpayee was a moderate in the party as he established on the foundation day of the BJP in 1980. His faith in the federal nature of India too was established in this speech and in many others made during his long and impressive parliamentary career. But if winning elections is a marker of a political party's success in a democracy, then what Vajpayee said during his foundation day speech carried little weight.

Four years after its founding, in 1984, the BJP was reduced to just two MPs in Parliament with Vajpayee himself facing a humiliating defeat from his seat in Gwalior in Madhya Pradesh (he lost by a margin of over two lakh votes to the late Madhavrao Scindia of the Congress). This was the general election which took place after the assassination of Indira Gandhi in which the sympathy factor helped the Congress get its largest ever election tally—still unmatched by any party.

For the BJP, this created an existential crisis. The Eighties also saw the emergence of caste-based identity politics in the Gangetic belt that threw up a challenge first to the Congress, but also to the central ideological tenet of the BJP–RSS that aimed (in principle at least) to unite all Hindus across divisions of caste. As a reaction possibly to both caste power and dynastic rule, the BJP at some time began to experiment with what can be called its core ideology. This culminated in the Ram temple movement that would transform politics as it signalled the arrival of the BJP as a national force.

The Ram janmabhoomi movement was actually initiated by the Vishwa Hindu Parishad (VHP) which had begun a campaign that was centred on three sites: Ayodhya, Kashi and Mathura. L.K. Advani later stepped in and began a vigorous campaign and rath yatra (journey in a chariot) that focused on Ayodhya, believed to be the birthplace of Lord Ram. The VHP/BJP claim was that the Babri mosque stood on a temple to Lord Ram that had been demolished by Muslim rulers. Several seminal books have been written on the Ayodhya issue and this is not the place to revisit it, as it involves a contested history, mythology, religion and politics.

The rath yatra, which was led by L.K. Advani from Somnath to Ayodhya in 1990, may have lit a divisive trail of riots and disturbances across north India, but it did signal a new consciousness as the 'political Hindu' had finally arrived. Yet, after the demolition of the Babri mosque on 6 December 1992, the same L.K. Advani would go on record to say that India couldn't be conquered by stridency alone and post 1993, the search for allies and the incremental vote share began. Advani, the architect of the revival, completely reversed his earlier stand and recommended that the BJP needed to project a more moderate image than ever before. We can say that the BJP leadership concluded that a sort of forced moderation was a more prudent strategy for India at that time.

Meanwhile, Atal Bihari Vajpayee who kept a distance from the Ram temple movement and in private conversations objected to its agitational stance, became more acceptable as the leader who practised moderation within a party such as the BJP. It was therefore decided that the party would build a personality-oriented campaign around him in 1998—his long record as a parliamentarian stood him in good stead, besides friendships and respect that he had earned across the political spectrum.

Was Vajpayee really opposed to the Ram temple movement? I believe at some level there was a genuine revulsion, perhaps even aesthetic, in the way things were panning out around the mandir-masjid. I remember following him to Surat in Gujarat during the campaign trail. One day, even as he stepped out of his car, a volunteer who appeared to be in a state of frenzy, began shouting,

'Jai Shri Ram' (Hail, Shri Ram). I vividly recall Vajpayee turning around and snapping rather poetically, '*Bolte raho Jai Shri Ram; aur karo mat koi kaam!*' [Keep shouting Jai Shri Ram; do little else!] It was one of those Vajpayee moments I shall always remember.

Around the same time, Atal Bihari Vajpayee granted me an interview, which was published in *India Today* magazine where I then worked, as part of one of the first cover stories I wrote on the BJP. We spoke about many things, but the major thrust of the interview was that he wished to separate the BJP from RSS. 'It is ridiculous to say that the BJP would be remote controlled by the RSS. The RSS has views of its own. The BJP has views of its own. And the BJP is adjusting to a more real situation.'[3]

Another memory from the 1998 campaign is of the time when a reporter asked the BJP's prime minister-designate point-blank (which seems impossible to do these days) what if his party lost the elections. Unfazed, and with a twinkle in his eyes, Vajpayee had retorted, 'Then it will be *agli bari*, Atal Bihari' (The next time over, Atal Bihari.) The campaign slogan in 1998 was, *Abki bari Atal Bihari* [This time around, it's Atal Bihari]. It was this self-deprecating humour in Hindi that made the man liked even by political adversaries.

On 4 December 1997, the then President of India, K.R. Narayanan dissolved the eleventh Lok Sabha. There was a certain irony in the fact that it coincided with the BJP holding its first all-India Muslim Youth Conference at a stadium in Delhi. Vajpayee couldn't resist cracking a joke even on that day—'People may suggest that we have an understanding with the President to dissolve the Lok Sabha on the day we have our first Muslim conference.'

I remember being told by party cadre how they had instructions not to raise the 'Jai Shri Ram' slogan. Naturally, I attended the event and was quite amused to see silence on Ram, but leader after leader going up on stage and reciting Urdu couplets, showering praises on Muslim heroes, many I hadn't even ever heard of. L.K. Advani proceeded to give examples of India's composite culture: he spoke of Hindus visiting Sufi shrines, and Meo Muslims.* K.R. Malkani, veteran Jana Sangh leader, who at that time headed the Deendayal Research Institute, came up with two gems which I dutifully noted in my reporter's notebook—'*Ram–Rahim ek hain, Krishna–Kaaba ek hain*' [Ram and Rahim, as Krishna and Kaaba, are one and the same], he said in the spirit of oneness. But the very next line had prompted Atalji to stare at Malkani, who said, 'No Muslim will oppose Atalji even if he stands from Islamabad.'

However, the news point for me that day was a significant statement by L.K. Advani who appealed to Muslims to give up their claim on the Babri Masjid in Ayodhya, while assuring them that he would personally negotiate with the VHP to find a settlement to the Kashi and Mathura disputes.†

* * *

But some years had passed since the demolition of the Babri mosque on 6 December 1992. The hero of 1998 was Atal Bihari Vajpayee. On the day he filed his nomination for the Lok Sabha elections from Lucknow, he conducted himself like a typical

---

* An ethnic sub-group found in Mewat region spread across Rajasthan and Haryana—some of whom keep alive their rich oral tradition that also involves telling in ballad form, *Pandun ki Kada*, the Mewati version of the Mahabharata.

† By this time the fallen Babri mosque haunted several senior leaders within the BJP as protracted legal battles, both criminal and civil, had begun. The original VHP campaign was not only limited to Ayodhya, but had involved demands linked to three sites in Kashi, Mathura and Ayodhya (all in UP), where they claimed temples were demolished to build mosques.

'pseudo secularist', a phrase that was put into regular usage by his close ally, L.K. Advani. Vajpayee tried, in a manner of speaking, to keep all the gods happy. He held a havan in the morning; then visited a Christian college where he released a version of the New Testament in the Awadhi dialect; and ended his day at an Iftar, that was attended by several of the city's notables.

What could one make of this, except conclude that the party that had spearheaded the Ram temple agitation was, in 1998, consciously trying to blunt the counter-polarisation. This was not about attracting new voter blocs that were traditionally hostile to them, but about getting new alliance partners and making it easier for regional parties to tie up with the BJP led by Vajpayee. The party was reaching out to an audience that had till now shunned saffron. It would be a mistake to imagine that the BJP was trying to change itself as some commentators of that age did; it was always about positioning itself in ways that had favourable outcomes in coalition formation.

At that time, its ideology was not as acceptable as it clearly is today, and the BJP had to soften the sharp edges. The Vajpayee-led BJP was telling small regional players that it could be the alternative choice for those who had traditionally never trusted it. It was simultaneously saying that it needed to be at the centre of any anti-Congress arrangement that could bring stability in the age of fractious coalitions. All of this was pegged on one man, Atal Bihari Vajpayee, a leader who had kept his moderate image intact, despite his life-long association with the RSS.

From the very outset, the calibration of ideology was a significant feature of the BJP's rise in national politics. Since the Vajpayee era was fundamentally about coalitions, this 'moderation' bit was carefully nuanced. In hindsight, only a man as sophisticated as Vajpayee could have pulled off the trapeze act.

Every now and then he played along with the hardliners, but would manage it in a manner which kept his non-radical image intact. It shouldn't however be forgotten that he was after all an astute politician and therefore, whenever he didn't agree with his party's Hindutva agenda, he used the ready alibi of managing the pulls and pressures of a coalition government. The BJP had posited its most acceptable face for 1998. The problem was that a section of the party began to suggest that the face was just 'a mask'. And therein lies another sub-plot to the story of the BJP in the era of Atal Bihari Vajpayee.

3

THE MASK

In 1997, K.N. Govindacharya was considered to be the most influential general secretary in the BJP. In those days of expansion and recalibration, the Tamil Brahmin, who had spent years in Varanasi and worked in undivided Bihar, spoke excellent Hindi. He also stood out amongst other RSS full-timers, because of his impish humour and the intellectual ability to understand other ideological traditions.

It was Govind (as I called him) who'd actually worked on what he called 'social engineering' that involved spreading the BJP's mass base beyond the party's traditional bastion of two communities in north India—the traders or Banias, and Brahmins.

Simultaneously, he had also stressed on the importance of projecting leaders of the Other Backward Castes (OBCs) like Kalyan Singh and Uma Bharti in the post-Mandal era* even as the RSS kept up its traditional work amongst the Adivasis.

---

* The report of the Mandal Commission that recommended reservations for the OBCs had been accepted by Prime Minister V.P. Singh in 1990, thereby redefining the contours of Indian politics. Both Uma Bharti and Kalyan Singh were from the Lodh community that is included in the list of backward castes entitled to reservations, and

Govindacharya was known to exert greater influence over L.K. Advani than he had over Atal Bihari Vajpayee. For instance, at a BJP National Executive meeting in 1992, Vajpayee had lost his customary cool and said, 'I have one question for Govindacharya. If you want to honour one leader, is it necessary to denigrate the other?' Obviously, the reference was to Govind's open adulation of L.K. Advani.

On 18 September 1997, two British diplomats called on Govind at the party headquarters, accompanied by an Indian analyst who was hired by the British High Commission. Govind would later accept that he had a long interaction with the diplomats, but denied what was subsequently reported in the Indian press.

Here's what happened: almost a fortnight after this famous meeting, on 6 October 1997, several articles appeared in some Hindi dailies including the widely circulated *Punjab Kesri*. In these stories, Govind was quoted as saying: 'Vajpayee is not the internal strength of the BJP, merely a mask. A mask is useful only for theatre.' In another remark, Govind appeared to be almost bragging when he said, 'You are talking to the RSS representative in the BJP. I am the sole individual who now communicates between the RSS and BJP.'

The most devastating article was written by none other than Bhanu Pratap Shukla, former editor of *Panchajanya,* the official RSS mouthpiece. The story created an instant stir as Shukla was an insider and it was presumed that he had access to reliable sources about the internal goings-on in the party and RSS. Other newspapers and magazines quickly picked up the story

---

both would become for brief periods chief ministers of Uttar Pradesh and Madhya Pradesh. Their projection at the time was significant in the evolution of the BJP.

and reported that Govindacharya had indeed called Atal Bihari Vajpayee a *mukhauta,* a mask.

In the days when Facebook and Twitter did not exist, it took a while for the story to circulate, but it did with lethal consequences for Govind. When the story broke, Atal Bihari Vajpayee was away in Bulgaria. But after his return, he shot off two letters.

The first was a curt note to L.K. Advani, in Hindi. Translated, it read: 'On returning from my foreign trip, I read an interview given by Shri Govindacharya. You must have read it as well. Vijayadashami greetings to you.' The second letter was addressed to Govindacharya demanding an explanation for his remarks.

There was more. Both letters were leaked to the media. The next day, when Vajpayee went for a book release function that was attended by top BJP and RSS leaders, he commented, 'I wonder why I am being invited to speak here when I am only a mask.'

And then there was some more. Two days later, at a BJP youth convention, Vajpayee was even more assertive and said, 'It's not the party that makes a prime minister. It's the people who do so.' The message was not lost on the BJP and RSS leadership. At the time, several opinion polls suggested that Vajpayee's popularity exceeded the party's; no matter how brilliant or useful Govindacharya may have been, Atal Bihari Vajpayee was definitely more powerful.

K.N. Govindacharya's influence in the BJP would subsequently be curtailed and by early 2000, he was forced to leave the party of his own volition. When I spoke to him, he denied making the mukhauta remark and told me by way of an explanation, 'Atal and Advani are like Ram and Bharat for me, and Atalji is Ram, from the Ramayana.'

Be that as it may, that 'mukhauta' word had done its damage and would stick for years thereafter whenever opponents wished to attack Atal Bihari Vajpayee. What that word did really is expose the fundamental neurosis at the heart of what I would call 'Project Vajpayee': on the one hand, there was his undeniable acceptance across the political spectrum, his formidable parliamentary experience, and his dizzying mass appeal. On the other, there was always the doubt: was Vajpayee and the new-look, moderate, BJP for real? Or was it just an expedient cover for an agenda set by some high priests in the RSS's headquarters in Nagpur? Was the country being tricked by a master strategist to wrest power under false pretences? After all, Govindacharya had allegedly said that a mask was only useful in theatre.

The Govindacharya episode also reveals that the idea of 'engineering' society was nurtured by the RSS for several decades before the party actually became a force among all sections of society in the Modi era.[1]

* * *

In 1998, Atal Bihari Vajpayee traversed the country making meaningful speeches about *swasthya*, *shiksha* and *suraksha* (health, education and security). He openly admitted to being irritated by questions about the Ram temple in Ayodhya, the Uniform Civil Code, or the revival of the Hindu rashtra. Even occasional queries about Kashi and Mathura would irk him no end, and he would choose to keep silent.

However, it was also true that the building of a grand Ram temple in Ayodhya was a core issue that the BJP couldn't afford to ignore, as it had contributed to its great electoral leap in 1991. Vajpayee therefore made a subtle change in tack and said that it was no longer necessary for a BJP government to enact a legislation to build a temple at Ayodhya. 'We will resolve the issue through dialogue—the same way we resolved the Azadari dispute between the Shias and Sunnis of Lucknow. A law will not be needed.'

Ram mandir could never be jettisoned by the BJP. There were other voices like that of Kushabhau Thakre, who later became party president—'Can anyone think about India without Ram?' he once asked me, but added with utmost honesty that, 'We can only implement our ideology if we have the strength to do so. *Yeh sab hamara karyakram hai, lekin shakti nahin hai'* [All this is on our agenda but we lack the strength to pursue it].' That was a euphemism for saying that their ideology will not be jettisoned, but only deferred for some more time.

Vajpayee was different from the run-of-the-mill RSS worker because he perceived politics as an art of the possible. It wasn't as if he wasn't close to the Sangh Parivar; it was rather well known that he enjoyed a great rapport with the then RSS sarsanghchalak (supreme leader or chief), Rajju Bhaiya. That said, Vajpayee also had some contempt for those in public life who did not have the ability to win elections. He was always more comfortable in the company of former Rajasthan chief minister Bhairon Singh Shekhawat, Jaswant Singh and, later, Pramod Mahajan, all traditional politicians, and all figures who have passed away, including Vajpayee himself.

One of Vajpayee's famous retorts to the 'mukhauta' controversy hinted at his impatience towards back-room organizers such as Govind. 'I must be enjoying the full confidence of the party or else I would never have been bestowed with the highest honour of being the prime ministerial candidate.'

Yet, among the hardliners, Vajpayee did not come out tops. Sadhvi Rithambara, notorious for her venom-spewing remarks about Muslims during the Ram janmabhoomi movement, described him as, 'half a Congressman'; while the then chief of the Vishwa Hindu Parishad, the late Ashok Singhal, was barely on talking terms with him.

As far as the Advani–Vajpayee relationship was concerned, it had layers of complexities. On the one hand, there was mutual respect based on long-standing friendship and association. Advani, typically like several RSS functionaries, was adept at handling the nitty-gritty of organizational matters—something Vajpayee had no patience for. But once Vajpayee settled into the prime ministership, the question about who was more powerful remained unanswered. Advani because he had greater party and RSS backing? Or Vajpayee because he had greater mass appeal?

It was the clear-headed Advani who would describe what the BJP was going through as, 'The transformation of an ideological movement to a mass-based party. That is why there are hiccups at every stage. Take the recent agonizing over the party's manifesto. While a manifesto may be so much as paper for most political parties, every small nuance is pored over in the BJP.'

In sum, by the time of the swearing-in ceremony on 19 March 1998, the BJP had shown far greater flexibility than it was credited with having. The umbilical cord to the RSS had not been cut, yet the Vajpayee facade was instrumental in convincing several parties to go along with the BJP. Vajpayee himself said quite artfully, 'Sometimes circumstances may have forced us to take a hard line. But the BJP has always been a moderate party.'

There's no denying that putting the NDA together required deft work and it revealed the political intelligence of both Advani and Vajpayee. Ironically, it was during the 1998 campaign trail that Vajpayee would frequently attack the United Front (UF) coalition (that got outside support from the Congress party) for lack of ideological clarity with lines such as, '*Kahin ka eent, kahin ka roda, Bhanumati ne kunba joda*' [A brick from here, a brick from there, that's how Bhanumati got her flock together]. The BJP had done pretty much the same, but the difference was that they would make it work.

As for the Govindacharya issue, Vajpayee would eventually deal with it with a sense of humour. There was a point when he stopped referring to Govind by his name, and would privately tell members of his inner circle how 'Rajneeshacharya' (reference to a godman with a large following) did this or that. Apparently, once Vajpayee genuinely forgot his name and referred to him as 'Dronacharya'!

4

THE OPEN HOUSE

The first six weeks of Atal Bihari Vajpayee's prime ministership were rocky largely because of J. Jayalalithaa's shenanigans, but also because of significant changes that were confronting the BJP and the RSS.

First, the point that must be made about the early BJP that came to power during the Atal phase was that it was talkative. There was a view on everything, and often multiple views, and the beauty of it was that its leaders and workers were more than willing to express themselves openly (the next avatar of the BJP in 2014 would be entirely different). In hindsight, I would put it down to the fact that the BJP did not originally come from a high command culture such as that in the Congress party and the RSS preferred backseat driving. The other hallmark of the BJP of those days was that everybody could legitimately aspire to rise from the ranks, and hence there was hectic jostling for posts and perks of office. It appeared messy, but there was a certain health to the proceedings.

For a reporter it was a delight, as there were multiple sources of information. First, the PMO under Atal Bihari Vajpayee was remarkably open and within it, various officers would be willing to speak to journalists. There was also the Home ministry led by L.K. Advani and as he was a power centre, a daily visit became routine for several journalists. The party office was yet another favourite haunt and besides the appointed spokespersons who gave daily briefings, there were full-time RSS pracharaks like Govindacharya who lived there and were often ready for a chat or an informal briefing.

In the good old days, when daily TV news followed newspaper headlines, it was a ritual for many of us to first attend the party briefing at Ashoka Road and then walk around to the back of the office to meet leaders in their offices or living quarters. (It was during one such occasion that I met Narendra Modi for the first time in 1998–99.) Moving away from convention, press briefings also began to be held at the RSS office in Jhandewalan, a clear indicator that they were no longer coy about their stakes in the BJP.

This became evident when the time came to find a president for the party, as L.K. Advani had become part of the government as Union minister for Home Affairs. The choice fell on the seventy-six-year-old Kushabhau Thakre, a loyal pracharak of the RSS who had been specially deputed to work with the BJP. In the choice of Kushabhau Thakre, the RSS exerted a firm grip over the party even if the government intended to appear autonomous. In those days, it was amusing to see the political class outside the BJP ask: Kushabhau who? And then take a minute to distinguish the spelling of his name from that of the first family of the Shiv Sena, then an ally of NDA.

Kushabhau was no political genius, but an able backroom organizer, which was a mandatory skill for any long-time RSS worker. When I asked him to describe himself after he became

BJP president in April 1998, he said, 'I am the man with the towel. Someone who sits in the back with a big towel, wiping the tears of party workers, the defeated candidates, those who've got nothing . . .'[1]

It was clear that he wanted to be perceived as the behind-the-scenes man. It is important to stress that figures like Kushabhau lived simply in the party office, eating their meals in the common mess. On becoming president, he was given an extra room with a hand shower in the bathroom and I remember how he fussed about the little luxuries. 'I prefer to sleep in the open on a charpoy (cot). All my life I have lived in one room, what will I do with the second room?' When the issue of giving him security came up, there was again some fretting: 'Why? I am not a dangerous man. Why should I have security?'

However, Thakre had work to do and focus on what was a matter of some importance for the BJP those days—how does an ideological movement remain subordinate to the government? He took a cue from L.K. Advani when the outgoing president laid it bare in his opening speech at the National Executive meeting in April 1998, where Kushabhau was formally appointed. 'The interests of the coalition at the Centre must be paramount. The party's strategies in the states must be subordinate to its national strategies.' After that the newly elected BJP president repeated this ad nauseam, 'The national agenda is the BJP's agenda. There is no party agenda different from that of the coalition government.'

Yet, having been part of the Sangh Parivar long enough, Kushabhau was aware that the BJP as a political party would wither if it became dependent on the government. 'If we do not separate the party, we will end up just like the Congress. Fifty years ago the Congress was an ideal, even for an RSS man like me. Today, look at the mess it is in,' he often said to me.

Kushabhau Thakre was an interesting character, initially brushed off as an insignificant figure since no one in Delhi circles knew him. Men like him actually marked the difference between the Congress party that just seems to flounder after losing power, and the BJP that always tried reinventing itself to return to power. Kushabhau came with a long and impressive record of a grassroots worker who was said to have been instrumental in building the edifice for the RSS and BJP in Madhya Pradesh. Conversations with him therefore helped me understand the role of cadre-building in the BJP.

He said he had two main tasks—as mentioned earlier, he felt that overdependence on government saps the lifeline of a political party, hence he strove to maintain some autonomy. Simultaneously, he was tasked with keeping the party and Sangh cadres motivated enough so that they didn't overdo the trend of looking for power or other favours from those in the government. This, however, proved to be an impossible task, as it obviously went against very human nature. During the Vajpayee era, many did seek out-of-turn favours and were unconcerned with the morality of it all. In 2002, for instance, a scandal broke over the allocation of petrol pumps to cadre and their families by the BJP regime.

I recall asking Kushabhau Thakre if his role in the party was limited to back-seat driving for the RSS? 'Our critics who raise the RSS bogey don't understand us properly. They talk of remote control by the RSS, but the RSS gives small instructions, just one or two instructions. Otherwise the BJP handles its own affairs.'

I found his statement rather amusing and when I asked him if the RSS just gave 'one or two instructions', he not only repeated himself, but also added the reason why—it was because 'centralized control was un-Hindu'.

Even as Kushabhau Thakre immersed himself in his new role as party president, it was said that he had limited contact with Prime Minister Vajpayee who preferred to discuss party matters with L.K. Advani. Vajpayee's careful distance from pracharaks was a reality that the Sangh had to contend with, and find ways to handle. If one looks at pictures of those days, unless I had imagined it, in a few, Atalji looks bored when he was in the frame with those he perhaps viewed as dull non-entities.

Kushabhau Thakre would pass away in 2003, towards the end of the Vajpayee tenure, and never lived to see the age of Modi; that would have no doubt made him very happy.

5

THE HOUSEHOLDER

There was nothing dull about Atal Bihari Vajpayee. On the public stage, he had endured for four decades before he became prime minister. Parliamentarians across generations, including Jawaharlal Nehru, had taken note of his Hindi oratory. But he made a great subject for analysis because of the ideological contradictions that made up the persona.

Consider just two facts: he had the image of a moderate, despite a life-long link to the RSS. And he was called a bachelor, even though he had a full family life.

By the time a journalist like me engaged with the Vajpayee story, he was already in his seventies with an entire life behind him. It was only after he became prime minister that the 'private Vajpayee' came into focus. His living arrangements got attention not because mainstream media deliberately wanted to transgress his privacy, but because after he settled in, it was clear that the real gatekeepers to the prime minister's house were his adopted daughter, Namita, and her husband, Ranjan Bhattacharya. Their daughter, Niharika, was clearly adored by the prime minister, and their home was full of photographs of the child with her grandfather.

The centre of Vajpayee's home was however a lady called Mrs Kaul who kept a rather low profile, and was only seen, and heard little, even during official dinners and public events those days. Their relationship seemed to have endured better than several legal and conventional marriages. Here are the simple facts as recounted in several Vajpayee biographies. Atal Bihari Vajpayee met Rajkumari Haksar, a distant relative of the Nehru–Gandhi family, during his student days in Gwalior (Madhya Pradesh). They had a life-long association though she married another man, B.N. Kaul. Meanwhile, even as Atalji became busy with politics, he kept in touch with the couple and often visited them in Delhi, where Mr Kaul taught at Ramjas College in the university.

I have no special insight into the personal life of Vajpayee and what it took to maintain such a long and enduring bond between two individuals who were not tied by the social convention of marriage. But the reason and the fact that it never came up for discussion in the press was also because Vajpayee wasn't secretive about it in any way. He was devoted to Mrs Kaul as she was to him, and he treated Namita like his own daughter. He never hid anything from the world.

I once ran into Namita after Vajpayee's retirement and she, much like daughters who end up taking care of their parents, said how looking after Baapji (as she called Vajpayee) and her mother took up quite a bit of her time and energy. (Mrs Kaul would pass away in 2014 at the age of eighty-eight.)

Vajpayee, the 'bachelor' prime minister, therefore, had a demanding family life, and like a conventional householder, his surrogate daughter and others made their presence felt during his prime ministership. In 1996, Ranjan Bhattacharya was appointed Officer on Special Duty (OSD) in the Prime Minister's Office, but after Vajpayee's government fell prematurely within thirteen days, he reverted to his hotel marketing business. In 1998, Atal Bihari Vajpayee once again felt the need for a family member to accompany him through the gruelling campaign, and Ranjan obliged him by travelling with him.

While working on a profile of Atal Bihari Vajpayee, I had a long interaction with Ranjan and met him several times subsequently. In so far as travelling with him during electioneering was concerned, here's what he told me: 'Baapji is very reserved. He doesn't communicate with many people. That's why I was there to look after his personal needs, his health etc. Baapji has always insisted I am just a family member. Nothing more. But yes, I'll be involved when he is electioneering.'[1] Therefore, the 1998 campaign saw Ranjan constantly by Vajpayee's side, and amongst other things, screening uninvited callers and hangers-on. I remember Ranjan saying he was forced to change his phone number thrice in two months.

The surfeit of information that one could gather on Vajpayee was also proof how open the first BJP regime was. As mentioned earlier, the party spoke, his family spoke, and his friends also spoke. Ranjan was polite and diplomatic, while Namita was always forthright and blunt. She was a teacher in one of Delhi's leading private schools and would often bring her students home. As I was working on a feature on Vajpayee, one of the parents of her students told me, 'My kids have run across the lawns, clambered on to Vajpayee. He may be the prime minister today, but to kids he is just nanaji who liked having them around, and lived in a great big house with lots of men carrying guns.'[2]

I collected a lot of trivia for the piece, as for the first time an individual's image was being built up in a systematic way from within the BJP. It was the sort of personality-centric piece done on prime ministers and reads like a bit of a puff job today. So,

I would dwell on things such as the names of the dogs in the household, the books Vajpayee read and what he ate and so on!

It was such an open prime ministerial home that I even got to know the burly, moustachioed Shiv Kumar, who can be seen in many pictures of those days. Shiv Kumar had been Vajpayee's man Friday for nearly three decades, even before he became prime minister, and herein lies a story about the bonds that Vajpayee shared within the Sangh Parivar. In 1969, it was on the instructions of the Jana Sangh that Shiv Kumar gave up his law practice to work full-time for Vajpayee, the upcoming MP, and remained with him ever since. 'I've been Atalji's chaprasi (peon), cook, bodyguard, secretary and constituency manager, all in one,' he said while talking about his relationship with the prime minister. From Shiv Kumar I would pick up past anecdotes such as Vajpayee going to Disneyland and the Grand Canyon in 1993 after his official engagements in the US were over.

While working on the profile, I even located a 'Modi' who turned out to be the prime minister's close friend: his first name being Mukund, who was a New York City paediatrician with a practice in Brooklyn East and a home in Staten Island. At the time, he was the founder-president of the Overseas Friends of BJP, and he told me of Vajpayee visiting restaurants in New York (he apparently loved Mexican food) and going to catch Broadway shows such as *Fiddler on the Roof, Evita,* etc.

As for Vajpayee's fondness for food, I can add my own two bits here. I once sat next to him at a dinner on the lawns of the prime ministerial residence where he ate appam and chicken stew with great relish, and with such undivided focus that he was quiet all through and would just nod or smile in reply to direct questions. That was his manner: pleasant, indifferent, easy, charming, all in one go. I figured that at times he was genuinely bored with having to answer questions. He excelled in nuances though, a mere suggestion, a joke in answer to a question. He had, I believe, a natural inclination for obfuscation and a genuine distaste for stridency.

And then there was also another old friend in Vajpayee's life, the Supreme Court advocate and member of the then BJP National Executive, N.M. 'Appa' Ghatate. The two knew each other since 1957 when Ghatate would come to Parliament only to hear Vajpayee speak. Apparently, the then Speaker of Lok Sabha, Anantashayanam Ayyangar, once told Appa that in the House, Hiren Mukherjee, the Communist MP, was the best orator in English, while in Hindi it was the 'newcomer', Atal Bihari Vajpayee. When Ghatate repeated this to Vajpayee, the latter typically responded, '*Toh phir bolne kyon nahin deten hain?*' [Then why does he not let me speak?]

Appa Ghatate, from a Maharashtrian family with links to both the Hindu Mahasabha and the RSS, was utterly devoted to Vajpayee and by 1998 had put in three years of work editing a three-volume collection of Vajpayee's parliamentary speeches. He had also absorbed the Vajpayee brand of politics and was very critical of the Modi era in private and the post Vajpayee lack of openness in the party.

But in his advancing years he basically liked to remember the era of Vajpayee. 'He hardly spoke in private. We have travelled together for hours without exchanging a word. But the minute he went on to the public stage, he was a changed man.' There were other little interesting details that I gathered: that he never learnt to drive, and was neither religious nor superstitious. Apparently, he had had a hearty laugh when Lord Ganesha was said to have 'drunk' milk across Indian temples, in 1995.

Such was Ghatate's fascination with his old friend that long after Vajpayee lost power, and even after he passed away on 16

August 2018, Appa would call and stay in touch, searching out people who had memories of the Vajpayee days. When I wrote the lead opinion in the *Times of India* edit page after Vajpayee's passing, Appa called me almost in tears and said he agreed with my assessment and Vajpayee would have done so too. I was quite moved by Appa's sincerity given the rocky journey I would have with the Vajpayee establishment, detailed later in the book.[3]

Appa would call me a few weeks before his death in 2021 and try to fix another lunch meeting that alas I could not make. A few months earlier, he had insisted on my meeting him for lunch at a popular Chinese restaurant in Delhi's Ambassador hotel. He had ordered too much food. With Appa's passing, the last memory keeper of the Vajpayee age was gone, except for Advani.

Were Vajpayee and Advani ever friends? By the time I began covering the BJP, the two men came across as very different people. For one, unlike Vajpayee who loved his food, L.K. Advani was an austere eater. I've sat down for lunch at his Pandara Road residence where all he ate was one chappati, a bowl of dal, and two vegetables. That may have been the reason why he was in much better health than Vajpayee by the time the two veterans brought the BJP to the national centre stage. Although Vajpayee was far more eloquent, Advani was more forthcoming in his comments. He was direct in his responses and was never vague about the direction he intended to follow at any given time.

6

THE ATOMIC FALLOUT

On 11 May 1998, less than two months after the NDA came to power, India carried out three simultaneous nuclear tests in the desert of Pokhran, in Rajasthan. In effect, with Operation Shakti (meaning, strength) as it was code-named, India declared itself the sixth nuclear weapon State in the world; the US reacted swiftly and led in imposing sanctions, but two days later, two additional tests at home were conducted yet again.

L.K. Advani has an intriguing line in his book, *My Country My Life*,[1] about Pokhran II. He writes, 'The first and foremost task was to make India a nuclear weapons power—a vital commitment in every election manifesto of the BJP since 1967.' Since the BJP was only formed in 1980, I presumed this implied that Advani saw no difference between the Jana Sangh and his party!

A week later, Pakistan followed with a nuclear test, as a result of which tensions escalated between the two nations that had fought wars in the past. In 1974, Indira Gandhi had conducted nuclear tests in Pokhran, then code-named 'Smiling Buddha', and referred to as Pokhran I; Vajpayee had now moved ahead with Pokhran II. However, in the aftermath of the nuclear tests, there were varied opinions within the security establishment and civil society on whether Pokhran II was a strategically wise decision.

But it made for good politics in that it not only delighted the BJP, but empowered it and its core constituency. Atal Bihari Vajpayee's perceived political weakness temporarily vanished with five big bangs. Advani would write in his book, as follows:

> As I look back I find that the people of India noted many contributions of the Vajpayee government . . . but our government's greatest achievement was instilling a sense of pride, confidence and hope in Indians, both within and outside India.[2]

But the decision to carry out nuclear tests was Atal Bihari Vajpayee's alone and initially only he and his National Security Adviser (NSA), Brajesh Mishra, were aware of the plan, and outside of the government, Dr A.P.J. Abdul Kalam, the then head of Defence Research and Development Organisation (DRDO), who later became the President of India. It was only after the final plan was approved did the core team let Home Minister L.K. Advani know of this 'historical' moment. The others who were brought into the loop were Finance Minister Yashwant Sinha, Defence Minister George Fernandes, Jaswant Singh, then Deputy Chairman of the Planning Commission, and Pramod Mahajan, the young BJP leader from Mumbai who would be made political adviser in the PMO. This would henceforth remain the core group that ran things during the Vajpayee era.

After Pokhran II, Vajpayee began to add *Jai Vigyan*, hailing scientific temper, to former prime minister Lal Bahadur Shastri's famous slogan, *Jai Jawan, Jai Kisan,* which extolled the contribution of farmers and soldiers in nation-building. But

there was yet another slogan which did the rounds those days—
Jai Atom Bomb—which possibly captured the BJP's post-nuclear
test gung-ho mood perfectly.[3] For a brief spell, party leaders and
cadre exulted as if they had altered political equations with five
Big Bangs.

The reason I elaborate on that time is because the idea of being
'anti-national' also emerged at that point in the Vajpayee era.
It began to be suggested that anybody who voiced their protest
against the tests could be inclined to be what is today deemed as
'anti-national'. The then general secretary of the BJP (who would
also be Vice President of India), M. Venkaiah Naidu, openly
described all contrarian views as 'unpatriotic'.

The post-Pokhran II period can be described as the time
when the BJP began to effectively use the technique of 'hyper
nationalism' to put critics on the back-foot. This began in the age
of Vajpayee and was taken to new heights in the post-2014 era
defined by Narendra Modi.

It must also be pointed out that the BJP always admired
(grudgingly) Indira Gandhi's use of the nationalism card. In
1971, after India intervened to liberate East Pakistan (later called
Bangladesh), Atal Bihari Vajpayee, then known as the most
articulate Jana Sangh leader, had praised her. After Pokhran II,
Vajpayee made it a point to state in Parliament that he had spoken
in admiration of Indira Gandhi when she'd announced India's
nuclear programme in 1974.

The BJP viewed the Big Bangs as their chance to dominate the
'nationalist' space that was till then dominated by the Congress
party. In 1998, they were also helped along by the fact that the
Congress had dithered on taking a position on the issue. Amongst
other things, it had taken the then Congress President Sonia
Gandhi ten days and a lot of soul-searching to finally come out

against the nuclear tests. At the seventh death anniversary of her husband, Rajiv Gandhi, she had said rather sardonically, 'Real strength lies in restraint, not in the display of shakti.'

Sonia's long silence over the nuclear tests was the outcome of two distinct views within her own party. While the then Leader of Opposition, Sharad Pawar, was not shy of clambering on to the 'national pride' bandwagon, Congress spokesperson Salman Khurshid, AICC Secretary Mani Shankar Aiyar and Economic Affairs Secretary Jairam Ramesh, all considered to be close to Sonia, had advised outright condemnation. Initially, it was AICC Foreign Affairs Chairman K. Natwar Singh's view of cautious praise that prevailed.

In her consultations with party men, Sonia is believed to have conceded that 'the tide is in favour of the BJP'. Eventually, however, the sceptics had their way based on the strength of the argument that the Nehru–Gandhi foreign policy consensus had been destroyed by Vajpayee. While still shying away from attacking the tests upfront, the Congress decided to take on the government for generating a war hysteria. In the climate that prevailed post Pokhran II, Sonia's 'foreign' origin was being raked up yet again.

The Left parties were the most direct in accusing Prime Minister Vajpayee of 'trying to equate the bomb with patriotism and whip up a jingoistic fervour,' while the Samajwadi Party (SP) chief Mulayam Singh Yadav accused the BJP of communalising the issue.[4] The Opposition began to suggest that the 'bomb' was a sort of secret weapon that the imaginary Hindu rashtra had devised to silence its enemies!

There came a point when it became necessary for Home Minister Advani to intervene and rubbish any speculation of having built a so-called 'Hindu bomb' while countering Pakistan's suggestion that India's nuclear tests bore out the Two-Nation theory. His quote was carefully constructed, as follows:

> The fact that Farooq Abdullah and Dr. Abdul Kalam could be working for their country with the same patriotic dedication as any other Indian does not fit into the false framework of the Two-nation theory on which Pakistan is based.[5]

Yet, there were strong undercurrents of Hindu nationalism surging through the Sangh Parivar. I recall Govindacharya telling me that, 'Like the feeling attached to Ayodhya, the nuclear tests are an emotional nationalist assertion.' The BJP had indeed begun the process of 'owning' the nationalism space, something it would do much more overtly two decades later.

At that time, however, it was still tentatively feeling its way, post Pokhran. For instance, the BJP's state executive in Rajasthan had chalked out a plan for Prime Minister Vajpayee to hold a public meeting in Ramdevra (situated twelve kilometres from Pokhran; a place revered for a saint called Ramdev), following which rallyists were to scoop out sand from the area and use it as a symbol to galvanize the party in the state where elections were due later that year.

It finally took the intervention of the prime minister to scuttle this agitprop. Addressing BJP workers at his residence, Vajpayee had said, 'No party or individual can take the credit for the tests.'[6] He later cancelled a public meeting in Bangalore (now, Bengaluru) that was organized by the party to felicitate him on the 'Big Bomb'. Even Dr Farooq Abdullah, who was then part of the NDA, played an interesting cameo in Vajpayee's post-Pokhran script. He accompanied Vajpayee to Pokhran where he said, 'Lord Ram is not the God of the Hindus alone. He is the God of the entire world and so, is the lord of Farooq Abdullah.'

Meanwhile, leaders of the Vishwa Hindu Parishad, who, as mentioned earlier, believed that L.K. Advani had stolen the thunder of the Ram temple movement begun by them, had their own ideas of celebrating what they called 'Jai Shri Bomb'. They announced the construction of a shaktipeeth (a site consecrated to the Mother Goddess) at Pokhran. 'We are not concerned with the BJP,' thundered the then VHP General Secretary Giriraj Kishore as he announced the plan to build the shrine. The 'Shakti,' he said, would be 'depicted by a *tandav nritya* (dance) of Shiva and Durga.'

The tandav had indeed begun.

7

ALL THE KING'S MEN

1 May 1998 wasn't merely a watershed moment in India's nuclear policy. It was arguably also the moment when Prime Minister Atal Bihari Vajpayee acquired a certain presidential grandeur. The Vajpayee who'd announced the Pokhran tests to a bewildered world wasn't quite the genial parliamentarian. With the national flag fluttering in the background, two aides standing ramrod straight, the ceremony had appeared like the swadeshi version of press conferences in the White House.

As mentioned earlier, in the context of comparing his style with that of L.K. Advani, Vajpayee was a man who liked grand strategy, but lacked the patience for finer details. He would be in his element while addressing a public gathering of 50,000 people but could be reticent with five in a room. He was easily bored and averse to hangers-on or groupies. Those who imagined themselves to be part of his coterie, often found themselves out of favour when he heard of them acting in his name.

Yet, there was a small circle he relied on and trusted without question. The first to arrive in the PMO most mornings was his Personal Secretary, Shakti Sinha, an IAS officer, in his hallmark checked bush shirt. A low-key man with an affable disposition, Sinha had worked with Vajpayee since 1996 and had become such an integral part of the Vajpayee establishment that insiders often joked that the nuclear tests (named Operation Shakti) were actually named after Sinha! The other reason often cited for his closeness to the prime minister was that Shakti Sinha was related to Vajpayee's adopted family by marriage. (Years later, during Narendra Modi's prime ministership, Shakti Sinha would land the prestigious post of director of the Nehru Memorial Museum and Library or NMML at Teen Murti, the historic home of India's first prime minister.) There would therefore be ideological continuity in spite of the big differences between the Vajpayee and Modi eras.

But back then, Shakti Sinha appeared to work diligently as Atal Bihari Vajpayee's assistant. As a routine, every morning, the late Pramod Mahajan, trouble-shooter, spin doctor and spokesman in the Prime Minister's Office, would arrive to join over the morning pow-wow. Mahajan was a skilled practitioner of realpolitik with strong links to Mumbai's business community. He would prove to be a key figure during the Vajpayee era and in the early days, along with Shakti Sinha, was accused of orchestrating Vajpayee's appointments by excluding certain individuals.

There was a third man who had Vajpayee's ear, but one never heard complaints of him having agendas or trying to manipulate the prime minister—the imposing Major (retd) Jaswant Singh. He was Vajpayee's key adviser on more matters than his formal designation of deputy chairman, Planning Commission. Besides the important job of placating Jayalalithaa, he was put on every task force, from Defence to IT.

It was said that Vajpayee, the master of the Hindi flourish, was very impressed with Jaswant Singh's Queen's English. Hence,

Jaswant was also utilized for his drafting skills, as he could lift a dull statement with some grand prose. One could imagine Singh poring over a draft of the prime minister's speech and declaiming, 'No, no, no, my dear. We'd better put that sentence differently.'

By keeping Jaswant Singh by his side, Vajpayee was also in a way making a point to the RSS that had objected to him becoming Finance minister. But the war of attrition went on and the RSS ensured that Jaswant was also excluded from Kushabhau Thakre's BJP National Executive team. But Vajpayee then got his own back by ensuring that Jaswant be given a Rajya Sabha ticket.

So, one may ask: did Atal Bihari Vajpayee have a special fondness for English-educated policy-diplomats? Perhaps, if we include the great dependence on his principal secretary, who came to head the PMO. Brajesh Mishra was the son of former Madhya Pradesh chief minister D.P. Mishra, once considered to be Indira Gandhi's 'Chanakya' for his great strategic skills. After retiring from the foreign service, Brajesh Mishra joined the BJP in 1991 and became the head of its Foreign Affairs cell. By then, amongst other things, Mishra had already earned a reputation for being a hawk on China. Both Vajpayee and Brajesh were more interested in Foreign Affairs and Defence and less so in economic issues.

It would, however, be a low-key figure of the Vajpayee PMO who would become quite popular with the media. The PMO drafted a senior Press Trust of India (PTI) journalist, Ashok Tandon, as an OSD on the recommendation of BJP media cell. Initially described as a lightweight, he went on to become one of the most popular media advisers to a prime minister in recent decades. Ashok Tandon may have been inclined towards a particular ideology, but he was neutral in the matter of giving access to all journalists. Besides, he understood the requirements of the media. The Manmohan Singh PMO that followed was lower on the scale of access, and as for the current Narendra Modi PMO, there is virtually no access for most journalists and the ritual of dropping by to talk to an officer is long over.

* * *

A few months into Vajpayee's prime ministership, stories began to circulate about his poor health. The man described as brilliant, brave and charming in May 1998, post Operation Shakti, was by the end of June perceived as tired and listless. What was also worth noting was that stories about his ill-health were being spread by members of the RSS or those who pledged loyalty to alternative power centres in the BJP.

The campaign actually began in mid-June 1998 during the summer recess of Parliament, when the seventy-three-year-old Vajpayee took a five-day break at his summer home in Manali (Himachal Pradesh), near a hotel where Ranjan Bhattacharya had business interests. All of a sudden, stories about the prime minister's ill-health began appearing in obscure dailies, forcing the BJP to issue a formal denial. But just as suddenly, the rumours died away.

I was told to investigate and learnt that Atal Bihari Vajpayee had lost a kidney in 1985, and by the time he became prime minister, he was also wearing a hearing aid. That's probably one of the reasons he looked vaguely bored when others were speaking, but came into his own when he had to speak. But unlike his predecessor P.V. Narasimha Rao, who had had a bypass surgery before he became prime minister, Vajpayee had no cardiac trouble, his blood sugar levels were normal, and he had the average health condition of a seventy-plus Indian man. If rumours about his poor health got some traction, it was partly due to Vajpayee's style of functioning coming under intense scrutiny. Political observers suddenly realized he was a man of a few words, hadn't granted a single television interview, walked slowly and often struck a meditative pose with his eyes firmly shut at public functions. On top of it all, there was official confirmation[1] that he had also cancelled a few public functions at the last minute.

The situation was therefore ripe for the rumour mills to work overtime. The *Asian Age* newspaper led with stories attributed to the enonomist-turned-politician Dr Subramanian Swamy, who claimed that Vajpayee was being treated for prostate cancer at the Sitaram Bhartia Institute of Science and Research in Delhi and was scheduled to travel to New York's Sloan Kettering Institute of Cancer Research for advanced treatment.[2]

Dr Swamy also proclaimed, rather preposterously, that Home Minister L.K. Advani would stage a coup d'etat when Vajpayee goes for treatment to New York. 'I'll produce documentary evidence of Vajpayee's condition very soon,'[3] said Swamy who then ran a one-man show called the Janata Party and was not yet a member of the BJP. In those days he was actually very close to Jayalalithaa, although they would have a terrible falling out later.

In spite of repeated denials from both the government and party, Swamy succeeded in bringing Vajpayee's health into focus and provided enough grist for speculation. I met Vajpayee's foster son-in-law, Ranjan Bhattacharya, who told me that Vajpayee had undergone an annual check-up at the All India Institute of Medical Sciences (AIIMS) for the past decade, and more so after he became prime minister as it was mandatory for him to do so. 'He went for these routine tests over two days in mid-June and all the results were absolutely clear.'[4]

Inquiries revealed that Atal Bihari Vajpayee had indeed visited the Sitaram Bhartiya Institute on a Saturday morning in mid-June for a bone scan, one of the compulsory tests for the prime minister. The reason: his radiologist at AIIMS had shifted to the institute and his personal physician had recommended that the scan be done there. It was also confirmed that he would be headed to New York for a five-day trip starting 24 September 1998, to address the UN General Assembly. However, no visit to any hospital in the US had been scheduled in his itinerary.

The rumours about Vajpayee suffering from cancer were eventually put to rest. But Vajpayee's health remained a story throughout his prime ministership. Later in his tenure, I remember detailed stories about the problems in his knees and the replacement surgery he had to undergo.

8

SATYAMEV JAYATE

Thirteen was not a lucky number for Atal Bihari Vajpayee. In 1996, his government had lasted for a mere thirteen days after failing to muster the required majority. In 1999, his government lasted for thirteen months and fell by just one vote during a no confidence motion in Parliament, triggered by events that followed the withdrawal of support by J. Jayalalithaa.

I was in the House that day, 17 April 1999, and remember the sudden hush in the lobby of Parliament and then the thrill of big breaking news. In a fraction of a second, the government of the day had ceased to exist, but as events would turn out, it would soon be resurrected.

But a quick recap of the first phase of Vajpayee's prime ministership must highlight, besides Pokhran II, his famous bus journey across the Wagah border to Lahore on 20 February 1999 about which I will expand later. What had also happened during the first year in power was a certain breakdown of trust between Vajpayee and some members of the larger ideological family.

This was quite visible during the celebrations to mark the government's first anniversary. It could have been an occasion to put aside differences and present a united front. Instead the anniversary celebrations generated a lot of heartburn and highlighted the resentment of cadre who felt excluded. At the heart of the problem was something as amusing as a glitzy show titled 'Satyamev Jayate', which was held in the backdrop of a monument in Delhi's Hauz Khas.

It was the brainchild of Pramod Mahajan about whom it was said facetiously that he could have been an event manager in his last birth. He wanted a grand show eulogizing Prime Minister Vajpayee's first year in office. Quite late in the day, he roped in theatre director Amir Raza Hussain, the late actor Om Puri, a few pop bands (Silk Route from India and Junoon from Pakistan), and the show was ready to roll!

Except that it was a disaster, and at various levels. First, not all the RSS and BJP workers who thought they deserved to be there were invited, resulting in a lot of disappointment. Despite the big and talented names associated with the show, it was badly produced and was full of glitches. A bus that was meant to showcase Vajpayee's famous Lahore journey refused to move, with its front wheel stuck firmly to the ground! Apart from the fact that it was a shoddy show, it made little sense. While the *sutradhar* or narrator, the late Om Puri, spoke in Hindustani, the scenes from Indian history were explained in English. Even as the actor-turned-VJ Jaaved Jaffri thought on his feet and tried to make up for the bloopers, it just did not come together. In retrospect, the music bands were the only part of the show that worked.

But there was yet another public relations disaster happening outside the venue. More than 3000 people were issued passes for the grand show, although the site could only accommodate 1000. On top of it was the strict security drill as the prime minister was expected to arrive. In the commotion that followed, several RSS pracharaks who held valid passes, failed to make their way inside, and were seen arguing with security personnel, while members of the government sailed through. Then there were those with 'blue' and 'gold' invite cards, who entered with great ease, and they were mostly invitees of the first family. Naturally, more heartburn.

I recall a senior RSS functionary expressing his frustration openly to me. 'If our views are not important, why should we attend the show, even if we get an invite? Am I going to call up someone in the PMO for an invitation? If he doesn't remember to invite us, why should we even attend such a function?'

There was yet another modest event meant to commemorate Atal Bihari Vajpayee government's first year in office—a high tea at the BJP's national headquarters in central Delhi by the then BJP president, Kushabhau Thakre. Even this event created a minor controversy despite the fact that it had a quasi-governmental sanction. While L.K. Advani, Murli Manohar Joshi, Ram Naik, Som Pal and Uma Bharti attended the function, the most important man of the moment, Prime Minister Atal Bihari Vajpayee, failed to make time for it.

BJP apparatchiks tried to gloss over the prime minister's absence by saying it saved them the trouble of over-intrusive security! A dull speech, tea and chaat, and the BJP president's little event was over. The only noteworthy point made by Thakre that day was that the anniversary had fallen on the Hindu New Year, the fifty-second century of the Kalyug. I heard him out, but when I looked around, I noticed how this auspicious coincidence had failed to enthuse the parivar that appeared singularly apathetic about the entire jamboree.

But what stands out in my memory of that day was a comment made by a BJP general secretary, who took it upon himself to try and play down the subtle tension between party and government.

'Once a man gets married, he will naturally pay more attention to his wife than his mother,' he had said. 'The mother may feel hurt, but her importance isn't diminished,'[1] he told the few journalists who were at the BJP's national headquarters. That general secretary was Narendra Modi.[2]

9

THE COLLAPSE

If one were to describe the first year of Prime Minister Atal Bihari Vajpayee's tenure in office after the euphoria over the nuclear tests, it can be managed in one word: Tough. By the time J. Jayalalithaa withdrew support to the Vajpayee government in 1999, she had run down most of the principal players in the regime.

About L.K. Advani she'd said: 'He is a Home minister without any concern for the nation's security and he is working in tandem with extremist outfits. He is a man suffering from selective amnesia.' About Pramod Mahajan, she made many insinuations, 'I do not answer to every Tom, Dick and Harry. We, the AIADMK are a responsible party. People close to Vajpayee took hefty bribes to transfer the enforcement director.'[1] She didn't spare George Fernandes either, because he had created a controversy by sacking the then Naval Chief, Vishnu Bhagwat. 'What prompted him to sack Bhagwat and also describe China as enemy number one? He must be moved to a lesser ministry . . .'

In the midst of all this drama, what was most interesting was the cameo played by the irrepressible Dr Subramanian Swamy, then president of the Janata Party. On one famous occasion, Dr Swamy threw a tea party and invited both Sonia Gandhi and Jayalalithaa who was then threatening to 'weigh my options'; she had conveniently forgotten that in 1998, she had likened the possibility of Sonia becoming prime minister to a 'national tragedy'. Less than a year later, Jayalalithaa would be seen holding Sonia Gandhi's hand tightly, whom she now called 'my old friend', for the benefit of politics and the waiting media. Vajpayee and company squirmed. Dr Swamy still chuckles when you mention the tea party and his career as a 'one-man demolition squad'.

By now Prime Minister Atal Bihari Vajpayee appeared hemmed in from all sides—his first Independence Day speech from the ramparts of the Red Fort on 15 August 1998 was lacklustre; he looked extremely tired, disoriented, and had walked out after losing a shoe that had to be recovered.

* * *

But it is to his credit that in the interim, nine months after Operation Shakti, he did try valiantly to recover some grandeur by positioning himself as a man of peace—by taking the historic bus journey to Lahore across the Wagah border.

On 20 February 1999 at 4.10 p.m., Vajpayee, accompanied by twenty-two eminent citizens, arrived at the Wagah check post. As expected, there was a lot of hype and mega coverage of the two-day trip. The Indian press, hugely excited at the possibility of witnessing a historic peace deal event, followed in separate buses and wrote reams describing their brief foray into forbidden territory, Pakistan. Nine months after the two nations seemed to be on the verge of triggering a nuclear arms race, the prime ministers of India and Pakistan, Atal Bihari Vajpayee and Mian

Nawaz Sharif, were hugging each other like long-lost friends. It was South Asian *pappi-jhappi* (kisses and hugs) routine at its best. The Pakistan Rangers' and Indian Border Security Force's (BSF) bands strained to outdo each other. Punjabi bhangra dancers did their robust gigs in front of the bus as it drove into Pakistan. Some of the Indian visitors also got into the mood and did a bit of bhangra themselves.

Sharif arrived early to receive his Indian guest and, as a goodwill gesture, moved beyond the check post on his side into No Man's Land and then briefly on to Indian soil. Finally, from the border, Vajpayee and Sharif flew off to Lahore in a helicopter.

Among the Indians were well known personalities like dancer Mallika Sarabhai, poet-lyricist Javed Akhtar, painter Satish Gujral, journalist Kuldip Nayyar, cricketer Kapil Dev, actors Dev Anand and Shatrughan Sinha. The 'evergreen' Dev saab (as he was popularly known as) said famously, 'This was the greatest moment of history. Future generations will remember Vajpayee and Sharif.' Indeed, they did, but for entirely different reasons.

Little did people know that the 'bus of peace' carrying the Indian prime minister never drove into Lahore, because of security concerns. It was only the one carrying the entourage that zipped thirty-five kilometres into the city.

Meanwhile, Vajpayee's official delegation included, among others, Jaswant Singh, by then External Affairs minister. Some years later, after the NDA was out of power, Jaswant Singh wrote a delicious little anecdote in his book, *A Call to Honour*.[2] He recalled that just when the prime minister's team had boarded the plane in Delhi to leave for Amritsar, from where the short drive to Wagah would begin, Vajpayee's assistant remembered that he had left the prime minister's hearing aid behind. A car had to speed from Race Course Road (the prime minister's residence is still located on this road, which has now been renamed as Lok Kalyan Marg) to the airport with traffic police frantically clearing the route. Finally, the hearing aid was brought, enabling Vajpayee to hear out what his Pakistani counterpart had to say. Not that in the end it mattered very much at all.

10

THE CARETAKER PRIME MINISTER

On 17 April 1999, the Atal Bihari Vajpayee government collapsed by a single vote. If that in itself wasn't a historically ridiculous precedent, the prime minister would additionally set a record for heading a caretaker government for the longest period of nearly six months, longer than even the short-lived five-month tenure of Prime Minister Charan Singh in 1979–80. The reason why Atal Bihari was made to hold a position, despite having lost the confidence vote in Parliament by one vote, was because in the public eye, he was seen to have the moral right to continue in office till the next general elections.

However, legally speaking, a caretaker regime cannot exceed six months because that is the maximum interval under Article 85 of the Constitution between two sessions of Parliament. The Constitution is, however, not so clear on the powers of a government in this interregnum—it doesn't have any provisions for a caretaker government as such; therefore, this was interpreted as there being no legal constraints on the functioning of the Vajpayee government. However, propriety and convention decreed that a government that was voted out, refrains from taking measures involving policy changes.

There was however a past precedent to such a recommendation and that being in 1979 when the then President, N. Sanjiva Reddy, while dissolving the Lok Sabha had stated that, 'The Government of India will not take any decision during this (caretaker) period which sets new policy or involves new spending of a significant order or constitute major administrative executive decisions.'

Almost two decades later, while dealing with the I.K. Gujral government—which resigned in November 1997 before being actually voted out—President K.R. Narayanan's approach wasn't so negative. In a letter to the prime minister in December 1997, he sought to define the status of a caretaker government more generously: 'The present government is not a caretaker government under our Constitution. It has full authority to be used with discretion.' It needs mention here that K.R. Narayanan was still President during the early part of the Vajpayee era.

Still, the operative word in Narayanan's communique to the Gujral regime was 'discretion', a term so subjective that it didn't prevent Inder Kumar Gujral from issuing a Prasar Bharati ordinance that put the board, that oversaw Doordarshan and AIR, outside the purview of Parliament. (This was later reversed by the NDA.) In that context, the then Cabinet Secretary Prabhat Kumar's circular dated 1 May 1999 stating that the Vajpayee administration will continue to function like a normal government was hardly surprising and guided by the precedent.

Curiously, the caretaker period gave Vajpayee a breather, for he was freed from Jayalalithaa's routine threats to topple his government. The BJP lost no time and swiftly got into an election mode intending to take every advantage while still holding office. I recall a PMO official telling me in confidence that while the government doesn't intend to go overboard (by way of initiating any policy decision), it won't be hamstrung either. As it turned out later, the government had to take huge decisions regarding national security and that being the Kargil war.

Meanwhile, the Congress as the main Opposition party raised a pertinent point: how could there be a non-functioning government for six months? It was a logical question to ask, except for the fact that it was the Congress that had fiercely opposed early elections that were scheduled to be held in June 1998. But as politics often makes people resort to convenient amnesia, the Congress insisted that among other things, Vajpayee's lame-duck regime shouldn't effect bureaucratic transfers and was particularly livid over the transfer of the Home secretary.

It was during that period that I'd interviewed the former Prime Minister I.K. Gujral. He perceived things a little differently from the Congress and said, 'There may be many occasions when the Vajpayee government will have to take vital decisions. It would not just be the government's right but also its responsibility to elucidate India's stand on key issues.' At the same time, he believed that in the absence of Parliament, the government must explain to the public why it was taking specific steps.

'The government is well within its rights in transferring the Home secretary, but it should have given a reason for doing so. Prudence demands that whatever would have been discussed in Parliament should now be explained to the public.'

By then, the BJP had already pressed the fast forward button. The Finance Bill was passed by the Lok Sabha without any changes, launching populist schemes listed under Yashwant Sinha's budget, as any party faced with an election would do. These included a new national programme for rural industrialization, a scheme to provide ten kgs of free food grains to senior citizens, and an increase in the allocation for rural infrastructure.

While researching for this book, I discovered that as caretaker prime minister in 1979–80, Charan Singh had also taken populist steps—such as, reducing prices of diesel and kerosene, but when he proposed State funding of elections, the then President Neelam Sanjiva Reddy had said a firm no (in hindsight, it would have been a good thing) and stepped in to stop Charan Singh from issuing an ordinance. He informed the prime minister that he would overturn the decision as the move involved a major change in existing electoral laws.

Then there was yet another precedent in 1991 when President R. Venkataraman had stepped in during Chandra Shekhar's prime ministership and praised the prime minister for readily agreeing to his suggestions. This finds mention in *My Presidential Years,* in which Venkataraman recalls how he had to curtail the government from issuing new licences. The book also describes how the then Law Minister, the maverick and unstoppable Dr Subramanian Swamy, had apparently pestered President Venkataraman for permission to sign a contract with Hyundai Heavy Industries and another with Boeing. When the President refused to give his assent, Swamy had asked what would happen if the Cabinet refused to heed the President's advice. The President had then told him that he would study the Constitution and act accordingly. Eventually, the government did not press the point.

But if there was one big difference between Vajpayee and his predecessors as caretaker prime ministers, it was that he and his party were very much in the electoral reckoning, while Charan Singh, Inder Kumar Gujral and Chandra Shekhar were catapulted to the position and weren't ever seen as permanent fixtures. That is why, by and large, even the bureaucracy cooperated with Vajpayee and didn't ignore him as a flash in the pan.

11

THE KARGIL WAR

Then suddenly, a war was upon us and it would change the script for Prime Minister Atal Bihari Vajpayee. The highest Himalayan ranges became the arena for a short, but bloody conflict between India and Pakistan. The story is now well known. Even as the Indian and Pakistani prime ministers were hugging each other, first in Wagah, and then Lahore, operatives sent by the Pakistani army were encroaching into Indian territory in the Kargil district of Jammu & Kashmir's remote and high altitude Ladakh region. So secluded was the terrain that India discovered only four months later in May 1999, when local shepherds reported sighting men in Pathan suits, traditionally worn in Pakistan. Further investigations revealed that they were trained mujahideens on a covert mission to occupy Indian territory, apparently at the order of Pakistan's new army chief, General Pervez Musharraf.

The obvious conclusion was that a nuclear-armed Pakistan was yet again seeking to internationalize the Kashmir issue by violating disputed territory that both countries claimed, but where peace is held by respecting what is known as the Line of Control (LoC).

When Atal Bihari Vajpayee called Nawaz Sharif in May that year to speak about the 'betrayal', the Pakistan prime minister claimed to have no knowledge of what the army had done, which wasn't impossible given the way civilian rulers have been manipulated or summarily dismissed by Pakistan's army. Five years later, Nawaz would speak about Vajpayee's telephone call and say:

> I suppose I should have known all about it. But frankly I had not been briefed. I hold Mr. Musharraf responsible for this. I did not know I was being stabbed in the back by my own General.[1]

Yet, later there were accounts by a few in the Pakistani establishment suggesting that the prime minister possibly knew, but we can never know for sure.

But I am quite certain that Atal Bihari Vajpayee was genuinely dismayed at what had unfolded, despite his efforts to broker peace with Pakistan. After going through several accounts of the time, and my own gut sense from the day-to-day coverage of the entire Vajpayee era, I believe that after Pokhran II, he wanted to go down in history as a man who brought peace to neighbouring countries that had been engaged in a long drawn conflict since 1947. There were well-sourced stories at the time about Intelligence inputs being ignored, and critics suggesting the central government was inattentive when the Pakistanis had crept in. But the broader picture that remained with the public was that this was a war in which the Pakistanis had occupied vantage points on the high mountains and the Indian Army fought a tough battle for seventy-four days to reclaim the territory.

It is perhaps better to recall the Kargil war from the prism of those who were at the helm of affairs at the time. In his memoirs, *My Country My Life*, L.K. Advani writes:

In the second week of May 1999 the prime minister called me for an urgent meeting. The Army had informed him about some strange movement of unidentified people crossing the LoC (Line of Control) in Kargil district. It being a high altitude and rugged region with sparse population the first intrusions were detected quite accidentally by local shepherds on 3 May who were occasional informers of the Indian army. The army sent out patrols and found that the intrusions extended not only to the Batalik sector but also to Dras, Mushkok and Kaksar sectors. The infiltrators were heavily armed and had entrenched themselves at heights of 16,000 to 18,000 feet along a 150 kilometre stretch of the Indian side of LoC and threatened the strategic Srinagar-Leh highway that lay below. Consequently defence minister George Fernandes visited the area on 12-14 May. Upon his return he and senior officers gave the prime minister a detailed briefing on a situation whose gravity had certainly not been fully understood earlier.[2]

On 26 May 1999, the Indian Army launched a counter offensive code-named Operation Vijay. As mentioned earlier, Pakistan had made early advances into the Kargil sector, and the mandate was to beat them back without crossing the LoC. After an intense debate, the Indian Air Force was deployed with instructions not to cross the LoC. Even as the war progressed, there were many casualties on the Indian side, as soldiers on the ground had to go uphill where they proved easy targets for Pakistanis who had occupied vantage positions.

Pakistan's early defence was that these were insurgents from the Kashmir valley, acting autonomously in protest against the Indian State. Later, the argument was made that the LoC itself was disputed.

But what went well from the Indian perspective was the release of transcripts of a conversation between General Musharraf (while on a visit to China) and Lt Gen. Aziz Khan, the then chief of general staff. (The entire conversation is reproduced in Jaswant Singh's memoir, *A Call to Honour*.)

The telephone conversation was pretty damning stuff and it was just a matter of time before the Pakistanis dropped the pretence. There were no mujahideens; Pakistani soldiers dressed as civilians were given hand-held weapons and other ammunition as part of a deliberate plan. Years later, Shahid Aziz, who was the head of ISI during the Kargil conflict, admitted as much in a signed article in a Pakistani daily.

At the end of the war, the official death toll for India stood at 527 and 1363 wounded, including one Prisoner of War (PoW). The official figures for Pakistan stood at 357–453, although later many from their military establishment, including Nawaz Sharif, claimed that thousands were killed.

I did not cover the war, my focus being politics, but we were all involved and it was in a sense the first war in my adulthood. I shall never forget the eleven-hour battle fought by Indian soldiers to reclaim Tiger Hill on 4 July 1999. Finally, twenty-two days later, on 26 July 1999, the Indian Army concluded Operation Vijay after announcing a complete eviction of Pakistani troops.

By the time the guns fell silent, what went well in Vajpayee's favour was that there was enough credible evidence to show that the Kargil conflict was a consequence of aggression from Pakistan.

In his memoirs, Jaswant Singh quotes a letter by the then US Deputy Secretary of State, Strobe Talbott, dated 4 January 2000.

> During Kargil, India held fast to the moral high ground, in the face of enormous provocation, and resisted the temptation to take retaliatory steps which would at best have cost India its unprecedented international support.[3]

Jaswant Singh also mentions a meeting with the then US Secretary of State, Madeleine Albright, in July 2000, during which she said, 'Jaswant, it was a masterly handling of the Kargil crisis. You did not put a foot wrong.'

In the end, the Kargil war was not only viewed as a military victory, but a moral win for Prime Minister Vajpayee.

* * *

Even before the guns fell silent in Kargil, the BJP was quick off the mark to start campaigning for the elections that were scheduled in September–October that year. It was an eventful year for me. Besides following Vajpayee and other BJP leaders around, I vividly recall running into Narendra Modi at the BJP headquarters. In 1998, the current prime minister was one of the general secretaries of the BJP, in charge of the sangathan, which meant that he was the link between the party and RSS. He remained in Delhi till 2001, after which he was sent to Gujarat as chief minister.

But back then, Atal Bihari Vajpayee was at the centre of attention. The man who was India's thirteenth and sixteenth prime minister respectively, was on his way to becoming its seventeenth as well.

Contrary to the current view, the 1999 election was the first big presidential-style poll campaign mounted by the BJP. It was on a smaller scale than Narendra Modi's 2014 campaign, but it was nevertheless presidential. The 'branding' of Vajpayee became an oft-quoted term in BJP circles of those days. Two leaders who came to be known as 'Young Turks' (the term was first used in reference to Chandra Shekhar whose prime ministership had lasted for a mere seven months) plunged themselves into the campaign: Arun Jaitley and Pramod Mahajan. The latter played a more significant role owing to his proximity to the Vajpayee establishment and particularly the first family.

The first time I heard the word 'Teflon' being used to describe an Indian politician was when Arun Jaitley, always the master of phrases, told me, 'Like Ronald Reagan in the US, Vajpayee as the triumphant leader of a triumphant nation has become Teflon-coated.' Pramod Mahajan, who was then the Information and Broadcasting Minister, was not so good with glib phrases. But he had this to say about the prime minister: 'During the caretaker days, respect for Vajpayee has become reverence, admiration has become adulation. Everything has changed in a 100 days.'

On the sidelines, however, there was some discomfort in the party and parivar as Vajpayee was looming way above the others, especially L.K. Advani, whose performance as Home minister was not impressive. Pramod Mahajan, the most reliable insider those days, whose off-the-record political assessments were often accurate, once openly admitted to the dilemma faced by the party and ideological family. He felt that for a cadre-based party like the BJP, projecting an individual (Atal Bihari Vajpayee) as opposed to a collective, was going against the grain. Although Pramod Mahajan was still an important strategist for the impending elections, his disastrous anniversary jamboree wasn't forgotten either. The prime minister shot down his idea of celebrating 15 August as Vijay Diwas (Victory Day), as he'd felt that to solely focus on the Kargil war on Independence Day would be a bit crass.

Meanwhile, the 'Brand Vajpayee' team first toyed with the idea of hiring a professional advertising agency, much like what the Congress party had done in the past, and famously during Rajiv Gandhi's campaign, evoking the rather mushy but unforgettable slogan: 'My Heart Bleeds for India'. They zeroed in on Dhar & Hoon, who roped in the advertising guru, Tara Sinha, to handle the campaign. But the three-member team of Jaitley, Mahajan and Arun Shourie, tasked with overseeing the campaign, were not satisfied with the first cut. As a result, the deal with Dhar & Hoon was called off and there was talk of bringing in Trikaya Grey, another leading advertising agency those days.

In due course it was felt that while the agencies were producing commercially attractive copy, it lacked political heft. The job eventually went to an in-house group known as 'Taskforce BJP', with the creative input handled by Sushil Pandit, a man we frequently now see on Indian television news speaking aggressively about Kashmiri pandits and rubbishing any opposing views as being 'anti-national'.

The campaign was focused on Vajpayee and was unabashedly personality-centric. It would soon be splashed across national dailies: 'A leader you can trust. In war. In peace.'

The first time that I went searching for a quote from Narendra Modi at the BJP's national headquarters, was also during the 1999 elections. 'Vajpayee has become a leader. Sonia is a mere reader,' he had said then. It would be the beginning of his relentless attack on Sonia Gandhi.

12

THE SONIA FACTOR

Campaign 1999 was the first big contest between a BJP leader and Sonia Gandhi who had finally come into her own and taken control of the Congress party. By 1999, as Congress president, she was not only deeply involved in the running of the party but also in the entire electoral process that she had once been reluctant to be part of (her son, Rahul Gandhi, took over as president on 16 December 2017 for two years when again Sonia became president till Mallikarjun Kharge took over in 2022).

Even as the BJP was celebrating the success of Pokhran II that they were linking to 'national pride', Sonia Gandhi had retaliated by saying that, 'Real strength lies in restraint, not in the display of shakti.' As part of the entire 'nationalistic narrative' they were trying to own, the BJP launched a strong attack on Sonia Gandhi's 'foreign origins'.

This was actually a card handed over to them by a group of ex-Congressmen, led by former Maharashtra chief minister and strongman Sharad Pawar, who had unsuccessfully challenged Sonia's leadership within the Congress. On failing to do so, Pawar exited the party and formed the Nationalist Congress Party

(NCP). In his memoirs titled *On My Terms: From the Grassroots to the Corridors of Power,* which was released in 2015, Pawar claimed that it was Sonia herself who had highlighted her foreign origins:

> On 15 May 1999, the Congress president called a meeting of the CWC. For no apparent reason, she suddenly pulled out a sheet of paper and read aloud: 'I was born outside India. If this becomes an issue in the campaign, how would it impact our party's performance in the election.'[1]

As any robust Opposition party in a democracy, the BJP made most of what was obviously an inner-party feud within the Congress party. The unrelenting attack on Sonia Gandhi's Italian roots, despite the fact that she had made India her home, was perhaps one of the reasons that made her so tentative about the seat to make her debut into the Indian Parliament. She eventually chose Bellary, a seat in Karnataka, that had always been won by the Congress (it's about 250 kilometres from Chikmagalur from where Indira Gandhi had stood for a by-election in 1978 after the ignominy of the Emergency, and the subsequent Janata Party rule).

The battle for Bellary was fought in a dry, rocky region and the most outstanding feature was the magnificent ruins of the Vijayanagar empire in Hampi. Despite its long distance from New Delhi, Bellary was remarkable for never having broken its record of returning the Congress party; by the time Sonia went there in 1999, Indira Gandhi had been dead for fifteen years, but was still worshipped like a goddess in and around the town.

From then to now, of course, something big has changed: it is now known for the Bellary brothers who ran a huge and illegal mining empire. But back then, Indira 'amma' was the Earth Mother, and therefore her daughter-in-law, Sonia, was safe.

Given the background, the Congress's cat-and-mouse game to mislead the Opposition about Sonia's choice of Bellary as her constituency was astonishing. In hindsight, one can safely say that the Congress's paranoia was rooted in an exaggerated idea of the BJP's game plan. In this instance, the team of Sonia's advisers certainly gave some bad advice.

Apparently, right from the time she had decided to enter electoral politics, Sonia Gandhi was keen to contest only from Amethi in Uttar Pradesh, the seat of her late husband, Rajiv Gandhi. Yet she ended up in Bellary because sundry arguments were trotted out by the Congress: the BJP would go to any lengths to make sure that she didn't enter Parliament, even to the extent of putting up an ailing, dummy candidate whose death would lead to the election being countermanded; the sitting BJP MP from Amethi, Sanjay Singh, would resort to large-scale violence to get the polls countermanded; and finally, if she stood from just one constituency, the BJP would try to pin her down to that seat.

Sonia obviously bought into these arguments and gave the go-ahead to a hare-brained plan to throw the Opposition off its track. The evening before the last date for filing nominations, Sonia took off for Hyderabad in a commercial flight, accompanied by her secretary, Vincent George, party General Secretary Ghulam Nabi Azad, and her security personnel.

Azad made it a point to deliberately mislead the media into believing that Sonia was headed for Kadapa in Andhra Pradesh. When asked about Sonia's eventual destination, he retorted: 'If we were going to Bellary, why would we be in Andhra Pradesh?'[2]

As part of this elaborate charade, a small seven-seater aircraft and a helicopter were parked at Hyderabad airport. The flight plan given to the crew was that Sonia would take the chopper to Kadapa, and Azad would fly to Bellary. Finally, the lady, accompanied by her entourage, drove to the airport and took off for Bellary, presumably smug in the belief that the BJP had been fooled.

Not quite. The BJP came up with a stunning counter and I would eventually ferret out the interesting details of what followed. Several workers of the Congress party were well aware of the smokescreen that the high command was creating in its attempt to mislead the Opposition about Sonia's eventual destination. Besides Bellary and Kadapa, the Congress was also putting out rumours that Madam Gandhi may eventually contest from Medak in Andhra Pradesh, which was held by her mother-in-law at the time of her assassination in October 1984. The BJP was first tipped off about this so-called 'grand plan' on the morning of 17 August 1999, just a day before the final date for filing nominations. The civil aviation authorities had informed the ruling party that Sonia was booked for Hyderabad from where she could proceed either to Kadapa or to Bellary, in Karnataka.

By noon, the BJP had learnt that the then Andhra Pradesh Congress chief, the late Y.S. Rajasekhara Reddy, had proceeded to his constituency, Kadapa, instead of waiting on Sonia, as was the protocol. By evening, the BJP was alerted that the Special Protection Group (SPG) was making security arrangements in Bellary.

Meanwhile, BJP General Secretary Venkaiah Naidu (later Vice President of India) was in Bengaluru working out details of seat distribution, even as news of Sonia Gandhi's movements began to filter in.

He immediately got into action and choreographed a game plan to counter the Congress president.

He first telephoned the chief minister of Andhra Pradesh, N. Chandrababu Naidu, in Hyderabad. The two discussed the possibility of propping up a candidate who could give a fight to Sonia in Kadapa. Should it be a strong local leader or an outsider? Why not a film star, suggested Chandrababu, who had piggybacked to political prominence as the son-in-law of the charismatic cinema idol, N.T. Rama Rao.

Over the next few hours, there were four telephone conversations between the two Naidus. The chief minister suggested the names of two popular actresses—Jayapradha, then a TDP Rajya Sabha member, and Vijayashanti, described as the 'female Amitabh Bachchan' of Telugu cinema, who had joined the BJP the year before. Eventually both felt that Vijayashanti, who had great mass appeal, would be a perfect choice for a backward rural constituency like Kadapa.

The question now was to get the lady's consent. It was well past midnight and Vijayashanti was in Chennai. Venkaiah Naidu then got in touch with his contacts in the film industry. At the unearthly hour of 1.30 a.m., Vijayashanti had two visitors—film director Chitty Babu, who was a member of the BJP, and Devi Vara Prasad, the well-known producer of several films starring the late NTR, and superstar Chiranjeevi.

Even as both men were trying to persuade Vijayashanti into agreeing to the plan, Venkaiah Naidu reached out to Home Minister L.K. Advani, who was then campaigning in Karaikudi in Tamil Nadu. Finally it took a woman to convince another—Vijayashanti consented after Advani's daughter, Pratibha, spoke to her at 2 a.m.

That done, the next step was to ensure that Vijayashanti reached Kadapa before the 3 p.m. deadline for filing nominations. One chopper was kept ready for her at Tirupati, while the then Civil Aviation Minister (later Minister for Parliamentary Affairs who passed away in 2018), Ananth Kumar, made sure that another helicopter was on standby at Chennai.

Meanwhile, a parallel operation was also being put in place. The same night, the BJP leadership received an Intelligence tip-off that security in Bellary was being tightened. Things began to suddenly hot up in Bengaluru where Commerce Minister Ramakrishna Hegde was hammering out last minute details of the seat adjustments with Venkaiah Naidu. When asked about a possible candidate to prop up against Sonia Gandhi in Bellary, Hegde suggested Sushma Swaraj's name. But there was a problem—Sushma had publicly announced that she wouldn't be contesting the forthcoming polls. Who now would persuade her to change her mind?

Ramakrishna Hegde took the lead in this endeavour and rang Sushma Swaraj around midnight; Venkaiah also followed it up by calling her immediately thereafter. After some debate over the issue, Sushma Swaraj agreed to pick up the gauntlet if the BJP leadership decreed. Venkaiah Naidu now moved with great alacrity. At 1.30 a.m., he called BJP President Kushabhau Thakre. A sleepy Thakre liked the idea in principle but advised Venkaiah to get it ratified from both L.K. Advani and Atal Bihari Vajpayee. Naidu contacted Advani yet again in Tamil Nadu.

Excellent idea, said the Home minister, but clear it with the Prime Minister as well? Reluctant to wake up Vajpayee at that hour, Venkaiah Naidu meanwhile utilized the time to tie up every loose end. He worked through the night to make all the travel arrangements and got the paper work in order for Swaraj to file her nomination.

Finally, Sushma Swaraj was booked on an early morning commercial flight from Delhi to Bengaluru. A helicopter was procured and parked discreetly at the Jakkur airfield in north Bengaluru. At 6.30 a.m., Venkaiah Naidu finally mustered up the courage to call the prime minister who gave his consent after ascertaining that Sushma was ready to meet the challenge.

Soon thereafter, Sushma Swaraj, dressed traditionally as a married Hindu woman, complete with a bright red bindi, sindoor in the parting of her hair, colourful bangles adorning her wrists and a mangalsutra around her neck, embarked on one of the most high-profile electoral battles of her political life. She landed in Bellary wearing BJP colours (a green blouse, and a bright orange sari), and in one of her first statements proclaimed that she represented the swadeshi brand against the 'videshi' Sonia.

It became the battle royale of 1999: the BJP's 'behenji' versus the Gandhi 'bahuji'. 'It is a battle for Indian self-respect,' Sushma declared. Quick with words, she picked up a few Kannada phrases and used them to full effect. The BJP believed they wouldn't lose even if Sonia technically won the election. The BJP had won this round, and the Congress president was in a sense, ambushed in Bellary.

As a counter, the Congress hurriedly announced the next day that Sonia would also contest from Amethi. The early announcement this time around was aimed at pre-empting the suggestion that she would stand from Amethi (where nominations closed on 14 September) only if the trend in Bellary was unfavourable.

In the end, despite the constant manoeuvering and war room-like strategies, it was Sonia Gandhi who won the Bellary seat by a margin of 56,000 votes, although it was clearly a low margin given the seat's electoral history. There was also no doubt in anyone's mind that Sushma Swaraj had made her mark as a great campaigner and smart politician. She passed away in 2019 and must go down in BJP history as one of the best women parliamentarians of the party who served as leader of the Opposition in Lok Sabha, between 2009 and 2014, during the second term of Manmohan Singh's UPA.

When Hegde and Venkaiah Naidu had first suggested the idea of fighting Sonia Gandhi, by her own account shared with this reporter, she had come up with a clever response: 'It would be like fighting the Kargil war. I'll either be a glorious martyr or a triumphant victor.'[3]

13

CAMPAIGN 1999

In 1998, Atal Bihari Vajpayee used to be greeted at rallies with cries of, *'Raj tilak ki karo tayyari, aa rahen hain Atal Bihari'* [Get ready for the coronation, for here comes, Atal Bihari]. In response, he would say jocularly, *'Jab Bhagwan Ram ke rajtilak ki tayyari ho rahi thi, tab unko chaudhah saal ke vanvaas me jana padah'* [When preparations were underway to anoint Lord Ram, he was forced into fourteen years' of exile].

But a year later, in 1999, he struck a sombre tone, almost sounding like a victim:

> They (the Opposition) united to pull us down but could not unite to form an alternative government. We lost the confidence motion by just one vote. So come out and cast your vote. It could make a difference.[1]

At the same time, he also showcased himself as the 'victor' following the Kargil war. This was a different Vajpayee who, at the advice of his strategists, was selling himself over the NDA, or the one-year record in office.

He was also very restrained, something he had always practised. So when Sonia Gandhi accused him of *gaddari* (treachery) at a rally in Ujjain, and when the Congress made the charge that he had collaborated with the British during the Quit India movement in 1942, he was injured innocence itself. 'I can't speak the language Sonia is using. Let there be criticism but there should not be baseless allegation. *'Meri zindagi khuli kitab hai* [My life is an open book],' he had said in his defence.

Sonia Gandhi was making the same mistake with Vajpayee that she would make years later with Narendra Modi. A personalized attack proved to be counterproductive as both men were, in different ways, bigger than the parties they represented. But in 1999, Sonia persisted with the gaddari theme as she was also forced to respond from a disadvantaged position: her foreign origin. She had once said, 'The government betrayed the nation by not acting in time in Kargil. So many of our young men were martyred.'[2]

As it turned out, 1999 was a vicious election in terms of the rhetoric. There were very offensive comments against Sonia from those campaigning for the NDA. For instance, Pramod Mahajan reportedly compared Sonia to Monica Lewinsky, and then denied he had done so. Then a Congress spokesman, the legendary lawyer Kapil Sibal described Prime Minister Vajpayee as a 'habitual liar' who was 'not only sleeping when the enemy came but also actively connived and consorted with the enemy.'[3]

At a meeting in Bellary, Defence Minister George Fernandes piped up to ask, 'What is Sonia Gandhi's contribution to the nation? Yes, there is one contribution—the two children she gave birth to. She contributed two people to the 100-crore population. Is there anything else?' I wonder if such a statement in today's times, when social media watches every word carefully, would have passed muster? Not only was it disparaging, but also grossly patronising towards a woman. But as mentioned earlier, no one was innocent in the dialogue of the deaf.

On behalf of the Congress party, senior leader Ghulam Nabi Azad (who quit the party in 2022) seemed to transgress accepted boundaries when he asked: 'How does Vajpayee have a son-in-law? Who is married to whom?'[4] The AICC office also distributed extracts from *The Morarji Papers* that had created controversy, as it was basically drawn from documents during Morarji Desai's rule, and traced the collapse of the Janata government. In the extract, the former prime minister had referred to a rumour that his External Affairs Minister Vajpayee, 'spent more time imbibing alcohol and flirting with women than in the administration of his ministry.'[5] Possibly because he was a high Brahmin, the mainstream press never questioned Vajpayee about his adopted family, but the politicians were making up for what my fraternity had decided not to do.

It just went on and on. In the course of the campaign, Pramod Mahajan likened the NCP leader Sharad Pawar to the Hollywood actress, Elizabeth Taylor. 'He marries, divorces, remarries and again divorces.'[6] Although Pawar had left the Congress, he was still fighting against the BJP.

The process of front organizations associated with the RSS and BJP, participating in the electoral battle, was seen for the first time in 1999. The strategy for such fringe outfits was to rake up peripheral but emotive issues, through advertisements.

For instance, the Lok Abhiyan which was run by a Delhi MP, Vijay Goel, issued an ad with a picture of a solider, asking, 'What wrong did this man do?' and followed it up with one by Purva Sainik Sewa Parishad (PSSP) in NOIDA, Uttar Pradesh, attacking the Congress for not allowing proxy voting for soldiers—'The

Congress is ready to allow soldiers to die for the country. But not ready to allow them to vote for the country.'

Compared to the costs of elections today, the 1999 campaign was cheap. From the information I gathered those days, the BJP had apparently spent around seven crores on its print campaign, of which approximately 1.5 crore worth of ads were released by organizations such as the Lok Abhiyan, PSSP and the All-India Kashmiri Pandit Conference.

Meanwhile, the dirty war went beyond words. With the mode of campaigning shifting from cars to aircrafts and helicopters, both sides began a mad scramble to get ahead of each other. The Congress party, not exactly flush with funds, had booked an aircraft each from India International, Asia Airways and Millionaire Airline on the understanding that the payment would be on actual use. However, the BJP, aware of the Congress's financial position, used its official and financial clout to 'steal' the bookings and Sonia Gandhi was forced to use the slower Beechcraft. In an age when the Congress domination of politics had ended, and the BJP was in the game, politics was indeed turning out to be a war in every sense of the word.

* * *

As was apparent, the BJP had managed to create a lot of hype around its campaign, and the opinion polls projected that the party would win forty extra seats from the last time. I remember writing that the greatest challenge for the BJP was that it had already peaked. Hard-nosed internal assessments put the seat projection at 215–220, which meant a gain of thirty or more seats. Even back then, the BJP's winning strategy depended on ensuring that the Opposition vote was split between two parties. In 1999, they hoped to use this to their best advantage in both Maharashtra and Uttar Pradesh—the former because Sharad Pawar had formed the NCP, and the latter because there were expectations of a Congress revival in the state where the post-Mandal era parties, traditionally opposed to the BJP, had also struck bases.

Prakash Javadekar, then still a state player, later a Union minister who would be dropped from the cabinet in the second term of the Modi government, had claimed vis-à-vis Maharashtra that, 'The vertical split of the Congress will benefit us.' Also from Maharashtra was Pramod Mahajan who believed that the biggest gains will be made in Rajasthan and his home state, where the party had faced unexpected setbacks in 1998.

But what was also affecting the BJP were factions that were working at cross purposes, and huge rivalries between leaders in many state units such as UP and Madhya Pradesh. There was, for instance, a pro-Kalyan and anti-Kalyan Singh faction in UP, while sharp divisions of a similar nature were emerging in Madhya Pradesh and Gujarat.

At the end of an exciting, if ruthless, election campaign, the BJP got just one extra seat than the last time: 182, but the NDA won 306 seats and were safely in office for a full term. Despite 'Brand Vajpayee', Pokhran II, the Lahore bus ride, and the victory at Kargil, the BJP's vote share actually came down. But this could also be put down to the party allocating more seats to its allies.

Still, the numbers were nowhere near the pre-election hype. But the BJP sought consolation in the fact that the Congress actually lost twenty-six seats compared to 1998, and this happened after Sonia became party president. The party had plunged to 114 seats in Parliament.

It would be prudent to end this chapter with what Narendra Modi, then in charge of the organization, had said to me that year. His words come back to me as being verbatim of what party president Amit Shah stresses—the BJP's focus on managing elections and conducting training camps for its polling agents. 'We have evolved a thorough system down to the polling booth. We have the figures for every polling booth in a particular constituency. We are the masters of booth management,' Modi had said.

At that time, Narendra Modi was closer to L.K. Advani than to Vajpayee and this is how he described Advani in a comment that I would publish in my article in 1999. '*Hamare yudh ke rathi woh hee hain. Mahabharat mein Krishna ththe. Yahan Lal Krishna hain*' [Advani is the charioteer who is driving us out to battle. In the Mahabharata, it was Lord Krishna. The BJP has Lal Krishna].

14

FROM KARGIL TO KANDAHAR

Atal Bihari Vajpayee won the elections, but one of the planks which he had showcased during the 1999 Kargil war came back to haunt him. Till a few months ago, if he was seen as a man who had won a round against Pakistan, he was rather quickly accused of being a prime minister who had succumbed to terrorists.

On 24 December 1999 (a day before Vajpayee's seventy-fifth birthday), an Indian Airlines flight, IC 814, was hijacked from Kathmandu (Nepal) by five armed militants, with 178 passengers and eleven crew members on board, most being Indians.

The hijacked plane then began a convoluted journey. The hijackers first wanted to take the plane to Lahore, but were denied permission by the Pakistanis. Hence the plane, which was now running out of fuel, was brought to Amritsar airport across the border. Ideally, it is here that the plane should have been surrounded by Indian authorities and negotiations held, as it stood at the airport tarmac for forty-five minutes. However, before it could be refuelled, the plane again took off for Lahore, where the authorities had apparently had a change of heart and agreed to refuel it.

The plane then flew to a military airbase near Dubai, where the hijackers dumped the body of one unfortunate Indian passenger named Rupin Katyal, and released twenty-eight others. The plane was then ordered to fly to Kandahar in Afghanistan, that was under the control of the Taliban.

The year 1999 therefore ended with big breaking news and although I was heading towards the end of my time at *India Today*, and the new year break had begun, all reporters were summoned back from leave. I shall forever recall that last week of December 1999 and beginning of January 2000 in my journalistic career as a phase when I learnt a few lessons about Intelligence agencies and the narratives they offer. It was also the end of my innings in a magazine that then carried real weight, where I had learnt so much about journalism and got some big breaks into political reporting.

So, my last assignment at *India Today* was to work on the many stories we were doing on the Kandahar hijack. Eventually, the hijack ended with Jaswant Singh boarding a special flight to Kandahar on 31 December 1999—India set free three high-value terrorists in Kandahar, and got the passengers and crew back. I recall how all of us were running around in the newsroom that day. I had given inputs to the lead story which was done by the then editor, Prabhu Chawla, even as I filed a separate one on the Taliban (sitting in Delhi, of course).

My story for *India Today* was a joint byline effort with another reporter, titled, 'The Inside Story of the Negotiations at Kandahar', highlighting what had gone on before the hostages were released and brought back to India.

It's necessary here to recap the events. India had succumbed to the demands of the hijackers who were clearly backed by the Taliban in Afghanistan, and some elements in the Pakistan establishment. The BJP at the time had claimed that it had scaled down the demands of the hijackers. They had originally demanded the release of thirty-six persons in Indian jails but eventually agreed to just three. But the three were high-value terrorists, who would inflict further damage on India, and the rest of the world, after their release. Indeed, it would turn out that the motive for the hijacking was to secure the release of precisely these men, and therefore, the hijackers had succeeded in their mission.

The hostage crisis ended after seven days when India released Ahmed Omar Saeed Sheikh, Masood Azhar and Mushtaq Ahmed Zargar.

It's interesting to digress briefly into the stories of the three men in order to understand the network of global jehad that operated those days. Of the three, the sole Indian national was Ahmed Zargar, who was from Jammu & Kashmir and was raised in downtown Srinagar. He was originally from the Jammu Kashmir Liberation Front (JKLF), later migrating to hardcore militancy and was reportedly involved in the 1989 kidnapping of Rubaiya Sayeed, the daughter of a former Home minister of India, Mufti Mohammad Sayeed (who later became chief minister of J&K; Rubaiya was also the sister of Mehbooba Mufti, who would also be chief minister).

At the time of the hijacking, Zargar was leader of the pro-Pakistan Al-Umar Mujahideen, and proclaimed guilty of forty murders. He was arrested in 1992 and seven years later, in 1999, was flown to freedom. He has since then reportedly operated from Pakistan occupied Kashmir or PoK, though there were also reports that he was arrested by Pakistan authorities in 2002, but has been free since 2007.

Masood Azhar was probably the biggest catch for India, and still continues to defy Indian Intelligence with great impunity.

Born in Pakistan's Punjab, he is the founder of the Jaish-e-Mohammad (designated a terror group by US state department), and arguably one of the most dedicated anti-India Islamists who operates from across the border. He was arrested in India in 1994 when he had come to Srinagar to make peace between two warring factions of militants. Five years later, the key purpose of the IC 814 hijack was to get Azhar out, and it was achieved. It was said that one of the hijackers was his brother.

A few days after his release in Kandahar, Azhar was sighted in Karachi where he told a cheering crowd that, 'Muslims should not rest in peace till we have destroyed America and India.' He remains active in jehad against India and operates openly from Pakistan, although every now and then some restrictions are placed on him. According to Indian Intelligence, Masood Azhar was involved in both the 2008 Mumbai terror attack and the 2016 attack on an Indian Army base in Pathankot.

The third terrorist was possibly the most fascinating figure of the lot—British citizen Omar Sheikh (born in 1973) who went to Forest School in the UK and briefly attended the prestigious Aitchison College in Pakistan, from where his family originated. After a year at the London School of Economics, he dropped out, went as an aid worker to Bosnia, and then headed off for international jehad, with his base in Pakistan. He first came into limelight as a criminal who had kidnapped three British travellers and one American in India in 1994, and had sought the release of hardcore jehadis in exchange, including Masood Azhar. He was arrested and was serving his sentence in India, when the IC 814 kidnapping happened.

After his release in Kandahar, Omar Sheikh was back to using his British origins to lure Westerners, which led to the kidnapping and gruesome death of Daniel Pearl, the journalist from the

Wall Street Journal, in 2002. Omar Sheikh was said to have planned the kidnapping of Pearl, although there was a controversy over whether he had slit the throat of the American journalist. Sheikh was however arrested and sentenced to death in Pakistan, which was later commuted to life.

At various points, it has been suggested that Omar Sheikh was a MI6 agent who later became a double agent. At some point therefore, he may have been an asset for Pakistan's ISI. There can be little doubt that he was linked to jehadi organizations such as Al Qaeda, Taliban, Jaish-e-Mohammad, Harkat-ul-Mujahideen, many of which were at some point or the other linked to Pakistan's complex military-Intelligence apparatus. A senior US official had also claimed that it was Sheikh who, under an assumed name, had sent 1,00,000 US dollars to Mohammad Atta, one of the men who had flown the plane into the World Trade Centre in September 2001.

As I said earlier, of the three terrorists, Omar Sheikh was most intriguing because he came across as a man who was raised with all the privileges of a comfortable middle-class life, had access to Western education, but still opted for a life of blood-soaked terror. Numerous documentaries have been made to get an insight into the life and mind of Omar Sheikh, and film director Hansal Mehta has also made a film on his life titled *Omerta* in which the award-winning actor Rajkummar Rao plays Omar Sheikh.

* * *

These were the men that Jaswant Singh flew to freedom in Kandahar. It was something that the Vajpayee dispensation in general, and Jaswant in particular, could never live down as it did not sit easy with the idea of being tough on terror. In his book, *A Call to Honour*, Jaswant Singh writes:

> For 3 terrorists, 161 men, women and children. Is it right? Wrong? A Compromise? What? Between two moral rights: saving the lives of the innocents and a fight against terrorism falls this hollow, unfilled space of the undetermined.[1]

It was an act that had made the BJP deeply uncomfortable, and therefore in the immediate aftermath, some bogus narratives were also spun. As a young reporter on the beat, I was caught in a very confusing but troubling series of events to which I have never got the answers.

As I mentioned earlier, it was my last assignment for *India Today* where I worked with Prabhu Chawla and Deputy Editor, Swapan Dasgupta, both of whom had deep contacts within the ruling party and government.

After the hijack drama was over, I attended a press conference called by Home Minister L.K. Advani, which was meant to be a briefing about what the agencies had discovered after the plane had returned home. Advani basically read out from a sheet of paper, presumably prepared with Intelligence inputs, about how the captain of the hijacked aircraft had given details about the code names that the hijackers had used between themselves and identified the five after being shown photographs of known terror operatives. The code names the Home Minister provided were as follows: Chief, Doctor, Burger, Bhola, and Shanker. The 'real' names of these terrorists were also provided with details such as 'Bhola' aka Mistri Zahoor Ibrahim from Karachi, who had used Mumbai as the base to plan the operation; 'Burger' was Sunny Ahmed Qazi from the posh Defence area of Karachi and so on.

Later, through one of my own editors, I would get information that suggested that no such details had been gleaned, but the Home minister had read out a dossier given to him. It was an awkward moment: a young reporter had information that challenged the narrative being offered by the authorities at a time when feelings about national security were running high. I was told it would be foolish to expose or contradict Advani at this time so just go along with whatever dossier has been read out. Let me state here that Intelligence and security are not my areas of expertise. But that was a quick lesson on how narratives can be cooked up and embellished as facts, because there is often no real information to go by.

But basic rule of thumb: the next time you hear about an elaborate Intelligence dossier detailing an event, do question why the agencies were clueless about it before its occurrence, and how had they managed to gather so many details in a span of twenty-four hours! In hindsight, it sounds implausible that the hijackers would have been identified in such a short period of time. I'll never know the answers to many questions, but something did not sit right with me.

15

MY JOURNEY IN THE BJP

The next five years would be turbulent and eventful. The century would begin dramatically for the BJP because in the first quarter of the year, US president Bill Clinton came calling on a five-day visit to India that signalled a partial lifting of sanctions after Pokhran II. As was expected, the media went hysterical as Clinton was a charmer, besides being the most powerful man in the world at that time.

There were big changes afoot for me as well. I shifted from *India Today* to *Outlook*, that was edited by the late Vinod Mehta, and was assigned to continue covering the BJP. I had moved from a publication that was not inimical to the BJP, to one which was run by a brilliant and maverick editor like Vinod who made no secret of his strong disdain for the BJP.

My apprenticeship in *India Today* had stood me in good stead. When I was put on the beat, Swapan Dasgupta was overseeing the political coverage, and the doors just opened up because of his image as the 'English-speaking Hindutva' ideologue. By 2022, he has finished a term in the Rajya Sabha as an MP and lost from the Tarakeshwar seat in the 2021 West Bengal Assembly election.

Prabhu Chawla was a hard-nosed editor who had risen through the reporting route and had contacts across the political spectrum.

But the point I am making is that it was possible at that time to work with editors with clear Right-wing leanings. There were, however, pressures that began once the BJP actually came to power as opposed to my coverage of the rise to power, that eventually led to my departure. But that problem was not ideological; it involved being required to also fix things for editors/owners and also operate as someone who gets appointments with the powers that be. I was never cut out for that.

But back then, it was normal to have excellent relations with people whose politics you did not agree with. Swapan in particular was a good editor to work with, if one were interested in understanding the inner workings of the BJP, as I indeed was. The point I am making is that in my journey as a journalist, I did not want my ideological preferences to stand in the way of developing long-standing contacts, some of which have become friendships.

There is a funny anecdote involving Swapan Dasgupta. It followed my first interaction with Giriraj Kishore, the VHP leader who has now passed away. I was taken to him by Uma Bharti, then the most prominent firebrand sadhvi, who kept up friendly equations with women journalists in particular. Giriraj Kishore was seated on a bed and looked me up and down and examined my name card and then held forth about Hindus and Muslims.[1]

The encounter became hysterical as Kishore then moved to the wonders of cow urine. He spoke with pride about a clock that kept ticking in melas (fairs) organized by the VHP on the 'electricity' generated by *gau mutra* (cow urine). He suggested that cow urine would be the 'Bharatiya' (Indian) solution to the energy crisis (the mind boggles at the thought of a nation collecting enough bovine pee to fuel its cars!).

He then summoned one of his flunkies to give me a gift of cow urine churan (digestive) and soap. He promised a healthier digestion and complexion if the products were used regularly. Even as I was bewildered, I promised to follow the VHP beauty regimen.

I returned to the office and presented the gifts to Swapan, and said: For you, since this is your ideology. In those days, we would manage to have a laugh together over this experience.

The media scene today is very different. It has deteriorated into a ghastly cycle of screaming anchors obsessed with raising Hindu vs Muslim issues, singing peans to the prime minister and BJP, yelling at Opposition spokespersons and often inciting hate. Newspapers that struggle financially, in order to keep a balance, are compelled to carry opinions of ministers and BJP members. The independent online media faces a constant onslaught through orchestrated social media campaigns and is often slapped with criminal cases.

Post 2014, the atmosphere in the BJP media room is also very different. There are few inside stories that any of them can access and they just report after the facts are known. The current prime minister has not had an open press conference and only given carefully vetted interviews to a handful of outlets, channels and agencies and in one instance to a movie star from Mumbai, who basically asked how one could be as amazing as the PM is! The media scene today is actually a disgrace to any democracy.

16

THE ADVANI–VAJPAYEE
PUSH AND PULL

In the year 2000, the power equation between Atal Bihari Vajpayee and L.K. Advani was the dominant theme in the BJP. Even as it was established that Advani commanded greater loyalty of the cadre and younger generation of leaders, almost as soon as Prime Minister Vajpayee was safely ensconced in office, there was talk of a 'post-Vajpayee' era.

One of my first assignments at *Outlook* was to attend a BJP National Council meeting in Nagpur—which was significant, considering it was being held in the town where the RSS headquarters is located.

Vajpayee was a bit off-colour that day and abruptly left the meeting. No sooner there were murmurs of doubt and dismay. 'Did you see his face, it looked puffy and swollen?' 'And his voice sounded cracked and strained. How will he cope in the US when he can't even stand up here?' 'The last weekend, he'd cancelled a trip to his constituency, Lucknow, and instead sent Arun Jaitley. Now he couldn't even cope with a party function,' and so on and so forth was heard in the aftermath of the prime minister's departure.

Then came the most important question: with four years still left of his term, how long can the seventy-six-year-old pull on? Related to it was the other imponderable: who will succeed Vajpayee if ill-health compels him to demit office? For the BJP, this was a foregone conclusion because if there was one leader who could have replaced Vajpayee, it was Lal Krishna Advani.

Therefore, the debate over his candidature at that time was strictly confined to whether he would be acceptable to the coalition partners in the NDA. Since L.K. Advani had many loyalists and he had groomed an entire generation of BJP leaders, there were enough people to speak about the excellent rapport he enjoyed with NDA leaders like M. Karunanidhi, Mamata Banerjee, Parkash Singh Badal and Naveen Patnaik.

His only problem was Chandrababu Naidu, who was sensitive to the secularism question and had chosen to give outside support to the government. Naidu's party colleagues in Parliament would say that Naidu would never support a man who was facing charges for the Babri Masjid demolition in December 1992. The world was indeed different back at the beginning of the century. Today, Chandrababu Naidu is a spent force in Andhra Pradesh after the state has been divided with the city of Hyderabad going to Telangana and is keen on an understanding with the BJP in order to fight the ruling party in Andhra Pradesh, the YSRCP led by Jagan Mohan Reddy.

* * *

By 2000, Bangaru Laxman, a Dalit leader from Andhra Pradesh and a life-long member of the RSS, had become president of the BJP. His appointment was a radical move in keeping with the party's social engineering approach, yet his tenure was cut short when he was caught on camera during a sting operation conducted by *Tehelka* magazine, accepting bribes for lobbying in defence deals. He would eventually be convicted in 2012 and while out on bail, he died in 2014.

Bangaru was a pleasant man and I always felt a little sorry for the manner in which he was shamed, especially as we knew that there were others dealing in far bigger and damaging deals, but who were not foolish enough to get trapped in the manner in which Bangaru was.

For a year following Bangaru Laxman's exit, Jana Krishnamurthy, another little-known RSS man from Chennai, was made party president. He was also a pleasant man, avuncular and open to conversation. A typical RSS worker, Jana was a man who respected the cadre-based ideology of his organization and like the rest of them at the time, also forcefully made a case for Advani as Vajpayee's successor. In an interview with me, he'd categorically stated that the Ayodhya issue had made Advani a mass leader. 'After the Ayodhya stir, he also became a mass leader. Till then, Atalji was our only mass leader.'[1]

But did he see L.K. Advani succeeding Atal Bihari Vajpayee as prime minister? I asked him.

'Right now, Vajpayee is hale and hearty,' he said. 'The BJP will meet whatever contingency may arise in the future.' He then asked me, 'How many parties supported Vajpayee in 1996? But they supported him in 1998 and 1999. Another leader can similarly end his isolation. It will be much easier for Vajpayee's successor.'

Meanwhile, it became apparent that Advani was walking a tightrope. He consciously began to tone down his image as a hard-liner, an effort that would ironically see him challenging the RSS more openly than Vajpayee ever did. But that would happen some years later. At that given moment, he was caught somewhere between a rock and a hard place. There was Vajpayee, the quintessential pundit, being all things to all men. There was also Dr Murli Manohar Joshi, a former BJP president and later HRD minister, who was known to be closer to Vajpayee. Whenever the ideological purists felt that Advani was being too moderate, as he was in his new avatar, they would go to Joshi, who would also be open to acting in tandem with Vajpayee, in order to encircle Advani in a pincer-move strategy.

* * *

K.N. Govindacharya, the most brilliant of RSS pracharaks, and infamous for his mukhauta comment, would soon disappear from the formal structure of the party, now that Vajpayee was in for a full term. Three things happened to this talented man. First, as mentioned earlier in the book, Vajpayee made his dislike for him public; he was also isolated by Advani whom he was close to, and once even confessed to feeling betrayed by him, but the Home minister did have the burden of getting along with the prime minister; thirdly, even Murli Manohar Joshi, who agreed with Govindacharya's views on swadeshi economic policies (that promoted protectionism), wasn't comfortable around him as he was perceived to have been a master strategist for Advani.

I once remember asking Govind about all this and he had put up a brave face and told me with a smile that, 'After all, my goal is ideological. I have always worked for a cause. I am not ambitious for power.' On 22 March 2000, Govindacharya wrote to former BJP president Kushabhau Thakre, seeking to be relieved of his charge of Uttar Pradesh and requesting two years' sabbatical from any organizational responsibility. His resignation was accepted;

if the party had really wanted him to stay, he would have been simply ordered to do so.

Beyond the personalities, the Govindacharya episode also revealed to me the divide between the government and an ideology that once sustained the ruling party. A known votary of swadeshi, it was the Vajpayee government's pro-reform policies that irked Govindacharya no end. Conceding that 'Every government has its constraints,' he told me at the beginning of the century that there will be 'chaos on the horizon because of globalisation and the unemployment it will cause.'[2]

Post his resignation, although he appeared defeated and side-lined, he put up a brave front and said that he planned to travel around the country and forge the 'third way'.

'I want to see if we can charter a third way between absolute stateism and absolute marketism.' But the next moment, his natural sarcasm rose to the fore and he could not resist a dig: 'Are Montek Singh Ahluwalia, N.K. Singh and Swaminathan Aiyar the only people who should tell the government what to do?' Amongst other things, I believe that the departure of Govind also signaled the burial of swadeshi as a policy within the BJP.

The Govindacharya episode notwithstanding, because the BJP came from an ideological movement, there was churning and debate over what was happening. Kushabhau Thakre also had his moments when he let go of restraint and told me on the record: 'Ideology is one thing. It is a necessary guiding principle and framework for all our policies. *Lekin jab chalanewale log idealistic nahin hain, toh hum kya karen?* [But what can we do if the people running the show are not idealistic?] *Hum kya apne ghar ke andar bhajan gate jayen?* [Should we keep singing bhajans inside our homes?]'[3]

17

GURU DAKSHINA

At 8 a.m. on 4 August 2000, away from the media glare, a clutch of BJP leaders had assembled at the residence of HRD Minister, Dr Murli Manohar Joshi. A guru dakshina ceremony was underway, and a few men were seen making a ceremonial offering to the RSS flag, the *bhagwa dhwaj*. Among those present were Prime Minister Atal Bihari Vajpayee, L.K. Advani, and senior RSS and BJP leaders pledging their allegiance to the Sangh.

But amongst the crowd was a man who was relatively low-profile, whose only claim to fame was that he was the son of a former Indian prime minister. His name was Sunil Shastri and he was the son of Lal Bahadur Shastri. On that August morning, the son of the Congress leader placed his offering in a vessel and saluted the saffron flag. The BJP was expanding and years later, Lal Bahadur Shastri's grandson, Siddharth Nath Singh, would become a spokesperson for the BJP during the prime ministership of Narendra Modi and eventually become a minister in the government of Yogi Adityanath in Uttar Pradesh. But we still have many years to travel before we get there. Sunil Shastri did not last long in the BJP and faded away after the 2004 defeat.

The induction of Sunil Shastri was however an unusual event in the Vajpayee era as other parties still held their own. In the Modi era, members of other parties do head to the BJP that is ready to absorb anyone who brings some value to the electoral math. The limitless financial wealth of the BJP and the fear of ED no doubt speeds up the process in many cases, but the BJP is now the go-to destination for individuals who wish to be with a successful ruling party. Today, a recruit from the Congress, Hemanta Biswa Sarma, is the chief minister of Assam and so the unspoken rule about high office only being held by those who came from RSS backgrounds, has gone. Once in the party, however, the entrants are expected to cater to the ideological orientation of the party and promote Hindutva vigorously.

* * *

Back in the Vajpayee era, the prime minister was more concerned about palace coups than ideology. Atal Bihari Vajpayee's persisting health problems made him hyper-sensitive about other power centres. In September–October 2000, I landed some juicy details about a meeting between Vajpayee, Brajesh Mishra and L.K. Advani through a source in the PMO.[1]

Apparently, Vajpayee had complained to Advani that a journalist who had access to the inner circles of the BJP, had told a powerful industrialist that the prime minister was in such poor health that he was no longer fit for office; the journalist had proposed that the industrialist use his influence to persuade the prime minister to step down and anoint Advani his successor.

For Advani, it must have been a very embarrassing moment. He wouldn't have been associated with such a ham-handed effort to dethrone Vajpayee and install himself, so he merely replied that they should ask the journalist in question. The call was made right there and then; the journalist, naturally, denied the charge. But the fact that Vajpayee was ruffled by the little backroom gossip, allegedly spread by a hack, indicated that he was sensitive to moves and manipulations against him. By raising the issue, Vajpayee was also making it amply clear that he would not brook any challenge to his leadership.

By then, Atal Bihari Vajpayee had already set a record of being the country's longest-serving non-Congress prime minister. He had completed thirty months in office and there was no immediate threat to his prime ministership.

As mentioned earlier, throughout his prime ministership, Vajpayee was frequently stonewalled from within his own party and, of course, the Sangh Parivar. There was opposition to the government's economic policies, mounted with the blessings of the RSS; worse, he once again believed that the persistent rumours about his ill-health and deteriorating faculties also emanated from within RSS ranks. By the time he finished a year of his second successive term, he was confronted with a well-orchestrated whisper campaign that he was suffering from Parkinson's disease—a debilitating neuro-degenerative disorder. Vajpayee loyalists described it as the same old ploy to undermine the leader. The beauty of those days was that as a journalist, one could just walk into the PMO and ask, which I did. An aide had responded as follows: 'This is not the first time rumours about his health from within the party have been used to damage him.'[2]

However, we had information that the prime minister's biggest health challenge were his knees and that he was scheduled for a knee replacement surgery. Subsequently, as Vajpayee went for a UN General Assembly meeting and put up a rather lack-lustre performance, several questions were raised about his health yet again. We were told that the US-based NRI physician, Dr Chitranjan Ranawat, who was to operate on Vajpayee, had specifically asked the prime minister not to use any anti-inflammatory drugs before he examined him. Vajpayee was, therefore, in excruciating pain when he went on the public stage in America. Sudheendra Kulkarni, who was then attached to the PMO as a speech-writer, said, 'It was an exercise in courage to see the PM go on in spite of the continuous pain.' (Kulkarni is now a member of the Observer Research Foundation and since 2019 has proclaimed support for Rahul Gandhi. He is very critical of the policies of the Narendra Modi government.)

Atal Bihari Vajpayee would eventually be laid up for three weeks after a knee replacement surgery in Mumbai's Breach Candy hospital that the NRI doctor had flown in to perform. But even in that condition, Vajpayee had made it clear that power would not be delegated to anyone and had left instructions that unless there was a national emergency, no Cabinet meeting should be conducted in his absence.

18

THE TUSSLE BETWEEN THE BIG TWO

That longish period of Prime Minister Vajpayee's convalescence would set inner-party politics into motion and reveal the deep-seated insecurities and personal ambitions of two men who were credited with bringing the BJP to national prominence.

Lal Krishna Advani had always been a frontline strategist, helming the BJP's march from a dismal two seats in Parliament to its commanding position in 2000. As mentioned earlier, his own strategic line had led him to cede primacy to Vajpayee and 'graciously' take on a subservient role. In the first heady days of power, the party faithfuls would refer to him as the 'real' number one, the 'true leader' who'd plucked Vajpayee out of political lethargy and handed him the top job. Henceforth, Vajpayee would be viewed as a compromise to the pressures of coalition politics, while Advani was projected as the man who would not be prime minister. He was the kingmaker, said many loyalists, who always put the party before personal ambition.

But in the two-and-a-half years in power, the pursuit of personality-centric politics may have brought in rich electoral dividends for the BJP, but it also spawned the larger-than-life

Vajpayee persona, eclipsing all rivals. Vajpayee emerged as the pivot of BJP's politics; Advani paled in comparison.

This was never brought into such sharp relief as when Vajpayee refused to appoint a 'stand-in' while recuperating in Mumbai post his knee-replacement surgery. This wasn't just an ailing prime minister resenting the question of succession; in party circles, this was read as Vajpayee's insistence on not paving the way for L.K. Advani.[1] Therefore, a buzz began to do the rounds (possibly to test the waters) that Vajpayee was grooming External Affairs Minister Jaswant Singh for the top job. Some high-profile columnists had speculated that Jaswant was the only BJP leader with adequate liberal credentials to be prime minister. (I always believed it was not in the realm of possibility.)

The result was the biggest, and most transparent, display of mutual attrition, posturing and jockeying for control that the BJP had ever seen at the top. The media was deluged with well-aimed, albeit off the record, barbs.

I recall speaking to some people in the Advani camp who felt that some individuals around the prime minister were going all out to checkmate the Home minister. One loyalist called it the 'scorched earth' policy where every move would be made to keep Advani out, even if that meant destroying the BJP. There was also a feeling that the prime minister was perhaps being unfair to his old political associate. For instance, a prominent Union minister once told me that on the one hand, there was Advani who had gone all out to ensure that Vajpayee became prime minister, and on the other, there was this strong feeling that the prime minister's inner circle was doing everything in its power to undermine him. As always, Advani loyalists insisted that he was anyway functioning as the second-in-command in both the government and party, and it was now the turn of the prime minister to show generosity and make it official.

The 'Race Course Road circle' was likewise bitter about Advani seeking media attention, while the prime minister was laid up in Mumbai. Advani, meanwhile, made it a point to visit an RSS camp in Agra and issue statements praising the Sangh, possibly to reinforce his position in the party. It was openly said that in making statements about the Sangh's authority over the BJP, Advani was ensuring the organization's backing in the succession sweepstakes. As a consequence, a few BJP leaders began issuing statements about Advani being the only possible successor to Vajpayee, even as the latter was recovering in hospital. It must be stated here that the level of paranoia in the PMO appeared to increase several folds every hour, even as Vajpayee's health problems mounted.

Nor did L.K. Advani help matters by giving a series of TV interviews, ostensibly on the BJP completing a year in office. It was in one such interview that he lit into Jaswant Singh on the IC 814 episode—a remark which was interpreted as a putdown for the prime minister's most trusted minister. The muted 'antagonism' between two most powerful figures in the country had clearly entered a more nervy phase.

As far as Jaswant Singh taking over the reins from Vajpayee was concerned, old-timers belonging to both the RSS and BJP dismissed this succession plan as a joke. I remember speaking to a party veteran who put it rather succinctly, suggesting that someone like Jaswant Singh was unacceptable in a cadre-based party like theirs and added that only those who were unaware of the BJP's culture were spreading such canards. While asserting that the BJP wouldn't ever allow Vajpayee to foist Jaswant on the party, senior leader J.P. Mathur had once remarked that the suave foreign minister may perhaps become the president of the US, but not India's prime minister. As far as Mathur was concerned,

'After Vajpayee there is only Advani for the BJP.' A preposterous whisper campaign began suggesting that Jaswant Singh was an agent of the US.

It was during this phase that I'd done a brief interview with Bangaru Laxman. Among other things, the BJP president had said:

> Advani is the undisputed leader of the party. Look at his contribution to the growth of the BJP. When he took over as party president, the BJP had just two MPs. When he laid down office there were 86 MPs.[2]

But contrary to what the Advani camp had been demanding, he saw no need to depute a second-in-command.

> Why should there be any such announcement when the PM was conscious during the surgery? But in India, such talk is inevitable. After Nehru, who? After Indira, who? But why get into names now when Atalji is hale and hearty.

Laxman, who was always considered to be a 'Vajpayee man', also tried to put to rest all speculation that he did not agree with Advani's point of view on the RSS.

> When Advani describes the RSS' position as being similar to that of Gandhiji's vis-a-vis the Nehru regime, he was quite right. But Gandhi's influence did not compel Nehru to impose total prohibition and the five-year plans continued. Similarly, we function independently of the RSS.

In all fairness to L.K. Advani, he had never challenged Vajpayee openly. On the contrary, for the first two-and-a-half years that the BJP was in power, Advani seemed comfortable playing second fiddle to Vajpayee, going out of his way to back the prime minister even on sensitive issues such as economic reforms on which, if he had so wanted, he could have exploited the sharp difference of opinion between the RSS and the government. Further, in deference to the prime minister, Advani had kept quiet when the rules about careful division of power between the organization and government were breached, as this one time when Vajpayee was perceived to have stepped on Advani's turf while pitching for Bangaru Laxman as party president.

It was clear that Lal Krishna Advani was trying to pull off a trapeze act—on the one hand, he was trying to maintain his closeness with the Sangh Parivar; at the same time, he was also trying to reinvent himself as more moderate and liberal to be acceptable in a post-Vajpayee scenario. He was also well aware that to set himself on a collision course with the prime minister would be the undoing of that project.

Eventually, L.K. Advani would give me an extensive interview to clear the air. I reproduce sections here, as they shall best explain what was going on between the two grand figures of the BJP.[3]

Q: After keeping a low profile, it's felt that you're asserting yourself and seeking the limelight.
A: Too much is read into my actions and words. Even when I don't seek attention, I get it. Ministers keep travelling abroad but when I decide to go to the UK and Israel, I am in the news. The visit is covered even before it takes place!

Throughout these two-and-a-half years, I've concentrated on my ministry. I've been trying to do my best.

Q: There is speculation over Vajpayee's successor and the fact that he failed to appoint a No. 2 for the time he'd be in hospital after the surgery . . .
A: There has been speculation only because some people believe Atalji is unwell. They do not realize it is essentially a problem in his knee. Once he recovers from the surgery, he'll be fine. There is no need to talk of succession.

Q: There is also talk about the Atal-Advani relationship.
A: We've been together right from the first day in Parliament. He and I lived together in Delhi at 30, Rajendra Prasad Road. In '57, when Atalji first entered Parliament, Deendayal Upadhyay viewed him as the crucial person on whom to build the party, then the Jana Sangh. Similarly, what I did in November '95 (announced Vajpayee as BJP's prime ministerial candidate) was based purely on my assessment. I took everyone by surprise when I made this announcement at a public meeting in Mumbai's Shivaji Park. But thank God, I made it then; two months later came the hawala charges. And that was a right decision. Atalji and I've been together for long. There are no differences between us.

Q: You recently criticized Jaswant Singh for accompanying the released militants to Kandahar . . .
A: I never intended to directly attack Jaswant. I rang him up even before the broadcast of that interview and told him I had said something which may be misconstrued.

He accompanied the militants as he felt someone with political authority should be there in case things went wrong and decisions had to be made. I felt it was unfortunate someone had to travel with the militants.

Q: Is it a deliberate strategy for the RSS to play the role of Opposition?

A: No. There is no such strategy. The swadeshi ideologues have their own views on economic affairs. But it does not mean we will follow whatever they say.

Q: But you recently described the RSS' relevance to the Vajpayee regime as akin to Mahatma Gandhi's to the Nehru regime and Jayaprakash Narayan's to the Janata regime.

A: How can we disown an organization with which we have been associated since our childhood? The RSS has a moral influence on the Vajpayee regime just as Gandhi had a moral influence on the Nehru regime. Nehru respected Gandhi but did not agree with him on everything. Similarly, I respected JP but did not agree with him on everything.

19

HEY RAM!

As the year drew to a close, it was Atal Bihari Vajpayee who did something stunning to place himself ahead of L.K. Advani. It was described by his critics as 'janus-faced', which means duplicitous, but he must have calculated that it was essential. On 7 December 1999, at an Iftar dinner hosted by the BJP's sole Muslim minister, Shahnawaz Hussain, Vajpayee suggested that a 'Ram temple could be built at the disputed site in Ayodhya, while a masjid could be built at an alternative site.' This is what is eventually happening after the final Ram temple Supreme Court court verdict given in November 2019, but at the time it was seen as a controversial statement by the leader of a coalition. It was also seen as a polite way of reinforcing the VHP–BJP's war cry of *'Mandir wahin banayenge'* [We shall build the temple only there] during the run up to the Babri Masjid demolition in 1992. Sanjay Nirupam, who was then a Shiv Sena MP, and now with the Congress party, had joked, 'What a great example of Indian secularism, a call for the Ram temple at an Iftar!'

After saying what he did, Vajpayee then resorted to ambiguity by saying, *'Maine kuch naya nahin bola'* [I have said nothing new].

But the point was that he'd said it and with great clarity. It may be recalled that over the years, Vajpayee had built the image of being the dove among hawks, partly by appearing to be out of sync with the agitational politics of the Ram temple movement. He had therefore stunned the NDA allies when he gave his support to the construction of a Ram temple at the disputed site on the eighth anniversary of the Babri Masjid demolition at the Iftar, which fell on the day after 6 December.

The question was asked: why did Vajpayee risk his carefully nurtured image by playing the Ram card? So far, the entire Opposition had trained its guns on the three charge-sheeted ministers—L.K. Advani, M.M. Joshi and Uma Bharti—in the Babri demolition case. They now turned their attention to the prime minister, and demanded his resignation. Chandrababu Naidu sharply reminded Vajpayee that his support was for a national agenda and it is 'unwarranted that someone should exploit an issue which is before the courts for their political ends.' National Conference MP and the then Minister of State for Commerce and Industries, Omar Abdullah, felt 'let down' by the prime minister's statements and added that, 'For a Muslim minister, Babri Masjid is certainly an issue,' while Mamata Banerjee, who was then a senior leader of the Trinamool Congress (now chief minister of West Bengal) went to meet Vajpayee along with TDP's Yerran Naidu. After her meeting, she said to waiting journalists, 'He explained that there are some issues which the BJP as a party has to raise.'

Atal Bihari Vajpayee had essentially passed on to Mamata Banerjee what the RSS leadership had told him just a week before his statement on the Ram temple. On 1 December 2000, the prime minister had hosted a dinner for the top RSS leadership, which included the sarsanghchalak, K.S. Sudarshan; general secretary,

H.V. Sheshadri; general secretary, Mohan Bhagwat (now chief of RSS) and the joint general secretary, Madandas Devi. Meanwhile, the BJP line-up was limited to its national presidents, both past and present: Bangaru Laxman, L.K. Advani, M.M. Joshi and Kushabhau Thakre.

Those days, if one was determined to get information, it was quite possible to do so. My sources would tell me that the RSS had told the prime minister that while the government should do its work, it shouldn't expect the party to act like its secretary; the BJP, they felt, must be allowed to raise its own issues. The RSS also let Vajpayee know that it was protecting him from the likes of Ashok Singhal and Giriraj Kishore of the VHP, and the swadeshi lobby within the Sangh itself. The supreme leader of the RSS, K.S. Sudarshan added that for the cadre, a hardline on Kashmir was an article of faith; yet the RSS leadership had supported the ceasefire in the Valley that Vajpayee was promoting after the Kargil war.

The Sangh leaders also mentioned a National Council meeting of the Swadeshi Jagran Manch in Bhopal in mid-November, where speaker after speaker had attacked first generation economic reforms. At the meeting, BJP leaders were warned that the economic reforms could well become the bugbear of the government: there were indications that many of the Sangh's network of small-sector businessmen were adversely affected and could turn against the party. The disgruntlement, they added, had even spread to the farming sector.

In the midst of this high-powered drama, there was another sub-plot to the drama. The Research & Analysis Wing (RAW) had accused J.K. Jain, the well-known media baron and owner of Jain TV, of having links with Pakistan's ISI. The RSS was livid, as Jain was a trusted RSS–BJP supporter, and had put his channel and television studios at the party's service several times. They were also convinced that the prime minister's powerful Principal Secretary, Brajesh Mishra, was behind this entire controversy. How could Mishra have labelled one of 'us' a 'deshdrohi', thundered the RSS. There were other complaints about Brajesh that the RSS made to the prime minister: that his juniors in the PMO were bad-mouthing the Sangh and its leaders, and that the Principal Secretary had allegedly described the RSS as being 'irrelevant'.

Vajpayee's political antenna picked up the signals. The Sangh was demanding Mishra's scalp; they were also letting him know that the cadre wouldn't work for the party, for instance, in Uttar Pradesh in preparation for the 2002 Assembly elections. Vajpayee realized that unless he acted fast, things could go terribly wrong for him and the party without the Sangh's cadre footprint.

The prime minister was being put under pressure and had obviously come up with the BJP's much-used Ram card. When push came to shove, the swayamsevak in Vajpayee knew when to heed the sarsanghchalak's command. His statement about Babri was an act of appeasement to the hard-line, made to protect a man he really relied on: Brajesh Mishra.

* * *

For the next couple of months, Prime Minister Vajpayee stuck with his line on the Ram temple. He stated this position strongly during a Parliament debate that followed. When it ended and was put to vote, the coalition partners in the NDA were shocked, but were forced to go along with the BJP. The ruling party was obviously exultant and several members were in a chest-thumping mood on core ideological issues. The late Lal Muni Chaubey, an MP from Buxar (Bihar), had said, *'Ram rashtriya bhavna ka prateek toh hain hee'* [Ram is certainly an expression of our national sentiment]; M.A.K. Swain, from Balasore (Odisha), was buoyant while commenting, 'After all it is the Ram Mandir which brought us to power. Now we know that Atalji is no different from Advaniji. If some of our allies are worried about the Muslim vote, they should remember that by leaving us they lose the Hindu vote.'

By refusing to backtrack on the floor of the House, Vajpayee had played hardball with his allies. He had sent out a clear message to them: Put up or shut up. Many had hoped that he would revise his position. But he stuck with it and went so far as to say, *'Janata faisla karegi ki maine sahi kaha ki nahin'* [Let the people decide whether what I've said is right or not], implying that nothing else mattered but an endorsement from the people. Mamata Banerjee, who that very morning had termed the Babri demolition 'a barbaric act', was forced to vote for the government; TDP's Yerran Naidu, who'd described the prime minister's remarks as 'unwarranted', had to meekly toe the line. In the circumstances, the only assurance that the prime minister provided his allies with was that 'he would abide by a court verdict'.

This was really the first big instance of the BJP playing Big Brother in the NDA alliance. The prime minister had sharply deviated from the joint manifesto and got his allies to endorse a BJP agenda.

It was also a victory of sorts for Home Minister L.K. Advani and the other two ministers charge-sheeted in the Babri Masjid demolition case. After the prime minister's speech on the Babri matter, the line was that the BJP leaders charge-sheeted over the demolition must never resign over the Ayodhya issue. The BJP also read the conclusion of the Parliament debate as an endorsement for building a Ram mandir at Ayodhya. As a Cabinet minister had then said, 'Even the CPI(M)'s Somnath Chatterjee had said on the floor of the House that no one is against building a mandir in Ayodhya. There is only disagreement about the exact spot on which it should be built.'[1]

Even as the BJP entered 2001, Lord Ram was back as the party's mascot.

20

ENTER: NARENDRA MODI

There were two serious political concerns confronting the BJP as it entered 2001. First, it wanted to recover lost ground in Uttar Pradesh where polls were due in 2002—there was a great deal of confusion about whether the Ram temple was an issue that could still reap electoral dividend in Uttar Pradesh.

The second worry was the loss of control in the party's citadel in Gujarat, where Chief Minister Keshubhai Patel appeared to be losing his grip, where factionalism was rife, and corruption charges flew fast and thick. In sum, both UP and Gujarat were in focus for the coming year, leading to dramatic events that would change the political story of India.

* * *

Meanwhile, January 2000 began with a BJP National Executive, where all the familiar ideological see-saws were again apparent. Even as Prime Minister Atal Bihari Vajpayee hailed Lord Ram, Home Minister L.K. Advani spoke about the North-east and Kashmir but said nothing about Lord Ram. Vajpayee kept the attention on himself by striking one of those positions that were characteristic of him, being both contradictory and open-ended. He first declared that it was the press which had compelled him to speak on the Ram temple issue. He then went on to say that there was a difference between the demolition of the Babri Masjid (which everyone condemns) and the movement for the construction of a Ram temple at Ayodhya (which was a national movement). At this point, Advani intervened to say that even the then RSS chief, Rajju Bhaiya, had condemned the Babri demolition in strong words. Vajpayee then added that he stood by everything he'd said during the last session of Parliament. To put it simply—there seemed a desperate attempt to rationalize every argument put out by the party in the past several months.

By then Vajpayee's 'Musings from Kumarakom'—two articles he had written from the Kerala resort where he had vacationed with his family over the New Year—were also in the public domain. In them, Vajpayee characterized the demolition of the Babri Masjid as a 'flagrant violation of the law' and an act 'totally at variance with the Hindu ethos'. He also went on to say that the government was committed to accept the court verdict on Ayodhya, 'whatever it might be'.

But there was enough in the 'musings' to keep the loyalists happy. For instance, when Vajpayee went to great lengths insisting that 'the movement for the construction of a Ram temple at Ayodhya struck a supportive chord in more than one political party'. Or that, 'Ram is one of the most respected symbols of our national ethos—respect for him transcends sectarian barriers.'

The articles were a masterly attempt to regain some ground with the liberal intelligentsia and keep the allies happy even as the usual incantation about Lord Ram was designed to give the Sangh cadres their adrenaline rush. It was all very well for a prime minister to share his thoughts, but to me personally, the contortions on the Ram mandir issue were getting very convoluted and a tad boring. Advani, on the other hand, appeared to have had already calculated that the Ram temple issue would not give electoral dividends in the political scenario that existed at the start of the new millennium (he would be right in thinking so). After all, he was always more transparent and straightforward than the prime minister.

* * *

On 26 January 2001, at 8.46 a.m., I was oversleeping on a national holiday (India's Republic Day) when I felt my bed shaking violently. I was feeling the tremors of the killer earthquake in Gujarat that had its epicentre in Bhuj. It killed 20,000 people and destroyed 4,00,000 homes. The next day, along with half the reporting staff of *Outlook,* I was in Ahmedabad, from where most of my colleagues fanned out into Bhuj. I covered the devastation in Gujarat's largest city where several multi-storied buildings had collapsed. Anything one writes is inadequate to describe the horror visited on human beings after a natural disaster. Most of us tasked with covering such things go zombie-like into the nightmare, try to help, control our tears, struggle to not throw up when mutilated body parts emerge.

After the Bhuj quake, a small political quake would hit the chief minister of Gujarat. The RSS (that had also made its presence felt by assigning its cadre to relief work) began the process of finding a younger and 'cleaner' replacement for the seventy-one-year-old chief minister of Gujarat, Keshubhai Patel. The change, they said, would happen in the next six months.

After filing my story on the earthquake, I began working on the political story that was unfolding in Gujarat. The core members of Sangh were convinced that Keshubhai had become a symbol of ineptitude, and as a senior functionary then told me, 'Remove him and a lot of anger against the BJP regime will evaporate.'[1] Ironically, they felt that even the relief work by RSS cadre wouldn't be enough to repair the BJP's image.

Gujarat was struck by twin disasters of gigantic proportions, one natural and the other, political. The initial problem in replacing Keshubhai (who was chief minister for a year in 1995 before a rebellion forced another BJP candidate; he was again chief minister from 1998 onwards) was that there were many hopefuls. There was the amiable Surat strongman and the then Union Textile Minister, Kashiram Rana, who was close to the Vajpayee camp; Suresh Mehta, who had replaced Keshubhai as chief minister after Shankersinh Vaghela had revolted in 1995; and the then Minister of State for Heavy Industries, Vallabhbhai Kathiria. Besides, Keshubhai Patel himself was a Jana Sangh stalwart who had powerful backing both in the state and at the Centre.

There was also an entirely new face now in the reckoning, most notably, Narendra Modi, the powerful BJP general secretary in charge of organization at the national headquarters in Delhi. Modi had, in fact, been shifted to Delhi after the Shankersinh Vaghela revolt that had led to a split in the BJP in 1996. At the time, Modi was a strong Keshubhai supporter, and was believed to have played a role in alienating Vaghela. As a result, he was virtually banished from the state and ordered to stop meddling in Gujarat's politics after Vaghela formed a new party.

Four years and many disasters later, Keshubhai now saw Modi as his biggest threat in 2001 and openly said that he was fanning discontent against him. The battle lines were drawn and soon events took a nasty turn.

After the earthquake, Modi tried to get back to state politics and wanted to head the Gujarat Rehabilitation and Reconstruction Fund, but Keshubhai spoke to the high command and took over the chairman's mantle instead. The chief minister's political antenna obviously sensed the greatest threat from this quarter and he therefore used all his power to keep Narendra Modi away from the state.

In fact, just to explain the lay of the land that Modi entered, factionalism was so rampant in the state, that after the quake some of his visits to Gujarat ended in embarrassment, with workers boycotting his functions at the behest of their leaders. I quote from a story I wrote at that time about this man who was seen to be unsettling the established BJP leadership in Gujarat.

> Modi, with his designer glasses and watch, is a new-age pracharak reportedly keen to join electoral politics. Partymen feel Modi is projecting himself as Keshubhai's replacement. But the BJP/RSS high command is categorical that an organization man can't suddenly jump into electoral politics.[2]

I was wrong. On 3 October 2001, the fifty-one-year old Narendra Damodardas Modi managed to break new ground when he became the first serving sangathan man in the Sangh Parivar to occupy high public office. He had promised the party and parivar leadership that he would pull off what then appeared to be an impossible task—of stemming the slide of BJP's fortunes in the state.

As we have seen, he arrived in Gandhinagar after facing stiff opposition from most of the old-timers. The outgoing chief minister, Keshubhai Patel, kicked up a huge fuss before demitting office, because he held Modi singularly responsible for fanning dissidence against him since the Gujarat quake earlier that year. It was to Modi's credit that in a caste-driven Gujarat (like the rest of India), he as member of a backward caste that was numerically small, was breaking into the BJP leadership that had been dominated by Patels. And Keshubhai was doing everything to undermine him, even suggesting that he had been humiliated. 'The high command has forced me to quit at the cost of my self-respect,'[3] he'd said publicly.

I recall speaking to local Gujarat leaders who told me that Keshubhai's plans of an open rebellion against Modi were summarily nipped in the bud. It was apparently conveyed to him that if he stoked the flames, certain underhand deals involving his close relatives and associates would be made public.

Yet Keshubhai continued to sulk stubbornly. He was not the only one. The number two man in the outgoing regime, Suresh Mehta, even went to the extent of saying that he would never work under Modi, but he later accepted the high command's diktat. The other party heavyweight opposed to Modi was of course the late Kashiram Rana, considered to be close to Vajpayee.

I will never forget one of my interactions with the jovial new general secretary in charge of organization at the BJP headquarters in Delhi. I had gone to Narendra Modi's room with other journalists, when someone mentioned Kashiram Rana's name. Narendra Modi responded by saying, '*Woh maans khane wala*' [He is someone who eats meat]. I felt strange as I knew that with my Muslim name, I would also be seen as a meat-eater, and was there a problem with that? However, I don't think Modi was being nasty; it was just an unguarded casual remark that he thought nothing of at a time when he was less sophisticated (plus, in parts

of Gujarat there is a greater taboo on eating meat than anywhere
else in India). Still, I never forgot that remark and would write
about it years later in a profile of Modi.

* * *

From the RSS, the most significant voice that spoke against Modi
was Sanjay Joshi, the powerful organizing secretary of the Gujarat
BJP. He was in favour of elevating Vallabhbhai Kathiria, who he
argued had a clean image and would help retain the backing of
the powerful Patel community, while Modi, who belonged to
a backward community, had far too many enemies. The central
leadership of the RSS was however firm in its decision to give
Narendra Modi a chance. To an extent, Modi also became the
beneficiary of the RSS' belief in social engineering: in the past,
they had projected OBC leaders like Kalyan Singh and Uma
Bharti, and were now encouraging Modi to manage Gujarat.

Despite facing opposition from different quarters within the
state unit of the BJP, Narendra Modi eventually managed the
backing of the national leadership of the party. It was well known
that Home Minister L.K. Advani was in any case supporting
him, and Modi had been cautious not to get on the wrong side
of Vajpayee over the past year. Although Vajpayee first kept the
issue hanging by arguing that 'all sections should be consulted,' he
finally allowed himself to be persuaded. Modi's project to move
from back-room management to mass politics was executed with
tact, diplomacy, and a great deal of determination.

While analysing the reasons for the elevation of Narendra
Modi, senior functionaries of the RSS would say that the BJP
was in such bad shape in Gujarat that sulking leaders and petty
factionalism was the least of their problems. They argued that

there was only one man, a fine public speaker and a real go-getter, who would go to any length to pull the party out of the doldrums.

As they were eventually proven to be right, the choice of Modi prevailed and, in the process, many old hands of the Gujarat BJP, like Keshubhai Patel and Sanjay Joshi, were relegated to history. Narendra Modi would in the same period go on to make history, first in Gujarat and then in the entire country.

But before all that would happen, other dramas were unfolding in Atal Bihari Vajpayee's government.

21

OPERATION CORRUPTION

On 5 March 2001, *Outlook* magazine came out with a cover story titled 'Rigging the PMO',[1] by my former colleagues, Ajith Pillai and Murali Krishnan. The story, in a nutshell, was about the PMO taking certain decisions that were beneficial to select business houses, notably the Hindujas, and Reliance Industries. The lengthy cover story was accompanied by an interview with a senior bureaucrat and former Power Secretary, E.A.S. Sarma, who'd accused the PMO of not respecting Cabinet decisions and granting economic clearances with impunity. The story specifically pointed at three individuals in the PMO: Principal Secretary Brajesh Mishra, Officer on Special Duty (for Economic Affairs) N.K. Singh, and Atal Bihari Vajpayee's foster son-in-law, Ranjan Bhattacharya.

Although I had no role in the story, it created huge problems for me. Let me share the details from the account given in my late editor Vinod Mehta's memoirs titled *Lucknow Boy*:

Vajpayee summoned me home for tea. It was an unhappy meeting. N.K. Singh, Vajpayee conceded could if necessary be shown the door, Brajesh and Ranjan were another matter. I had got it wrong, Vajpayee mildly scolded, those two were pure as snow. Suddenly he changed the subject and launched an attack on *Outlook* correspondent Saba Naqvi. 'I don't know what has gone wrong with her lately; she is always writing against me.' He suggested she had been covering the BJP for too many years. Perhaps she needed a change of beat.[2]

A prime minister was actually asking the editor to get rid of me! With lesser editors, it could have meant the end of a career in political reporting. However, what Vinod Mehta did was ask me to temporarily stop covering the PMO but continue covering the BJP. As mentioned earlier, what was odd about the entire episode was the prime minister mentioning my name apropos a story which I hadn't even done. An officer in the PMO later told me that it could be because he probably had not even read the story! He may have just presumed that it was 'Saba Naqvi' because of *Outlook*.

Despite the prime minister's complaint, I must say that he continued to be pleasant with me and did not publicly show any resentment towards me. I remember once while walking in the lobby of Parliament outside the PM office, I'd turned round a corner and walked straight into his entourage. Vajpayee stopped, hit my hand in an avuncular fashion, and said to me in Hindi, that I was a very good girl, but the things I wrote! *'Kya kya likhti ho!'* That was it—my access to the prime minister was never curtailed.

What did happen in the interim was that *Outlook* began to be excluded from prime minister's trips abroad. Back in those days, a prime minister travelled with a press contingent in the same aircraft and besides the news agencies, invitations to other media, both national and regional, were also sent out. I must add here that not all magazines got invites, and *Outlook* less so after the stories against the PMO. It is to the credit of Vinod Mehta that he did make a point with some elan when *Outlook* actually got invited for an important trip that Vajpayee was making to China in June 2003. Instead of sending the foreign affairs expert, he chose to send me. It created resentment in the office, but Vinod was making a larger point about editorial freedom. Vinod was telling the PMO that thank you, but this is my candidate for the trip. Unfortunately, Vinod Mehta passed away in 2015, one of the last of the truly independent editors.

But back in March 2001, a far bigger embarrassment than anything *Outlook* wrote burst upon the nation. Operation West End was an audio visual-cum-print story run by *Tehelka* magazine that aimed at exposing corruption in Defence procurements. The biggest victim of this sting operation was none other than BJP president, Bangaru Laxman, who was caught on tape stuffing money into his pocket.

Meanwhile *Outlook* was not done with its 'PMO stories'. Its issue dated 29 March 2001 led with a cover story titled 'The PM's Achilles Heel'.[3] The story was written by the same duo—Ajith Pillai and Murali Krishnan—and focused on the same dramatis personae—Ranjan Bhattacharya, Brajesh Mishra and N.K. Singh, and yet again highlighted out of turn clearances granted to certain projects.

This time around the story stung harder because the day after the magazine hit the stands, Brajesh Mishra and N.K. Singh held a joint press conference and denied all charges. Without mentioning *Outlook,* they said that mischievous allegations were being made against them.

Apart from creating ripples within the Vajpayee government, what the *Outlook* stories also did was to give ammunition to a few men in the RSS who resented Brajesh Mishra and his stranglehold on the PMO. K.S. Sudarshan, the RSS chief, certainly did not take very well to him (the feeling was mutual) and used every opportunity to take pot-shots at the PMO. On his part, Brajesh Mishra did his best to keep RSS lobbyists out—men like S. Gurumurthy, the Chennai-based chartered accountant supposed to be close to the Sangh, and several smaller figures.

Eventually, Prime Minister Vajpayee again hosted one of his dinners for the RSS. When I ran into him that day, he actually told me that N.K. Singh, the controversial OSD in the PMO, who the RSS was gunning after, could be on his way out. 'He was only kept on till the Budget,' said Vajpayee. (N.K. Singh was eventually moved to the Planning Commission.)

I asked the prime minister if he believed that the feud within the Sangh Parivar had been settled? '*Abhi toh yudh shuru hua hai*' [The war has just begun], he said jocularly, referring both to the internecine battle and the larger war with a rejuvenated Opposition.

Meanwhile, sources in the RSS revealed to me that the prime minister had apparently told Sudarshan in no uncertain terms that there was no question of Brajesh Mishra quitting—'If Brajesh Mishra goes, I go.' The sarsanghchalak was also reportedly criticized in an RSS meeting for mounting a relentless attack on the PMO, at a time when they were reeling under corruption allegations. Hence, the RSS chose a temporary retreat.

A realisation began to dawn upon the BJP that they may be scoring self-goals by their all-too-frequent off-the-record complaints against the PMO. Till that point, few would rise to defend either Brajesh Mishra or Ranjan Bhattacharya, conveying the impression that the ruling party had serious problems with its own prime minister. What changed hereafter was that the party was now given instructions to rise to the PMO's defence. The newly appointed BJP president Jana Krishnamurthy told me how there was no basis to the charges levelled against Bhattacharya and Mishra. 'Is there anything against Brajesh as they showed against Bangaru? There are only indirect references.'[4]

Indeed, in one of his several interviews to me, Krishnamurthy also pointed towards what he described as a clear design behind both the *Outlook* and *Tehelka* disclosures. 'Look at the people they have targetted. Bangaru, who was considered PM's choice for president. George Fernandes, who is his closest NDA ally (he is mentioned by people in Operation West End), and Brajesh and Ranjan. Don't you see the pattern? The real target is Atalji whose popularity and acceptance is increasing. They can't defeat him electorally so they use these methods.'

There was a certain web of intrigue in and around the Indian prime minister. Although Vajpayee *appeared* to be powerful, he had to constantly negotiate and throw protective gear around himself. For some time after the magazine stories, the PMO retreated behind a wall of silence—Bhattacharya was asked to keep out of sight, while Brajesh was instructed to keep a low profile.

Yet, Vajpayee ruffled a few more feathers when he put his foot down over appointing RSS nominees in his office. Hence, the Sangh continued to smart over the fact that the prime minister did not allow it to run his office. Its real grouse, it was said in those days, was that RSS men had been pointedly snubbed by Atalji's household. Apparently, Namita had no patience with them and she was really the reigning deity in her foster-father's establishment.

The sub-text to what was happening all around was also the distrust, which had only increased manifold, between the prime minister's men and those who pledged their loyalty to the

Home minister. While the two leaders made no comments in the aftermath of the *Tehelka* story, both camps were buzzing with conspiracy theories. At the heart of the Vajpayee–Advani tension was an old issue—as mentioned earlier, the prime minister did not wish to anoint Advani his successor. In fact, in 2001, he also appeared to have stepped on Advani's turf by giving the former chief of RAW, A.S. Dulat, the charge of Kashmir affairs in the PMO.

Meanwhile, at that point in BJP's history, it was clear that although Advani knew that his greatest challenge lay in getting public acceptability on the scale that Vajpayee had, he, more than others, understood that discrediting Vajpayee amounted to cutting the nose to spite the face. The same party men who were busy fighting petty turf wars were told that the whole edifice could come tumbling down if Vajpayee was pushed any further. As it is, Vajpayee had been ruing post the *Tehelka* expose and had said, *'Pehli baar Parliament mein log mere muh per mujhe chor keh rahein hain'* [For the first time I've been called a thief in Parliament].

Finally, the *Tehelka/ Outlook* round of stories ended in a stalemate. The prime minister retreated behind the walls yet again, the RSS was still straining at the leash, wanting greater control over the spoils of power, and Advani was still waiting in the wings.

* * *

Then, in May 2001, a story appeared in the British press that once again embarrassed Brajesh Mishra. The *Outlook* story titled 'Rigging the PMO', had mentioned the PMO's proximity to the UK-based NRI business group, the Hindujas, who faced criminal charges in the Bofors payoff case. A leaked letter in the British press revealed that in the aftermath of the 1998 Pokhran nuclear tests,

Brajesh Mishra had sought the help of the Hindujas in getting an appointment with the then British Prime Minister Tony Blair. Even worse, the controversial Hinduja brothers, Srichand and Gopichand, who were being investigated by the Central Bureau of Investigation (CBI) in the Bofors gun case, had actually accompanied him to 10, Downing Street where he handed over a letter from the Indian prime minister to his British counterpart.

The Hinduja bombshell couldn't have exploded at a worse time for Brajesh—the Sangh had just about eased off its campaign against him.

It was a hot summer for Vajpayee as the RSS reared its head yet again. Several influential voices within the organization began to say that they should risk jettisoning the government as Vajpayee's leadership (and the economic policies of his government) were proving disastrous. At that time, good sources revealed that when the *Tehelka* scandal broke and the RSS upped its campaign against Vajpayee and the PMO, it was ready to throw its weight behind L.K. Advani if he would challenge the prime minister. At that time the minority view was that if the government goes, let it go, but the parivar could no longer back Vajpayee.

But such hotheads came up against an unexpected roadblock. The Home minister steadfastly refused to take on Vajpayee—he was convinced that any such attempt would be foolhardy. For, not only would it threaten the NDA government, it would also harm the party and the Sangh Parivar.

One of my best sources in the RSS had then told me, 'You people keep writing that Advani is taking on Vajpayee. Actually, Advani has inflicted Vajpayee on us and is now in the way of us taking him on.' The upshot was that the RSS continued its schizophrenic relationship with the Vajpayee establishment—on the one hand attacking it periodically, and on the other, rushing to its defence whenever his government felt threatened.

* * *

Then on 29 May 2001, at 8.30 a.m., the proprietor of *Outlook*, Rajan Raheja, was raided by the income tax department. A posse of 700 officials swooped down at the magazine's office in different cities and began search and seizure operations. In his book, *Lucknow Boy*, Vinod Mehta describes the humiliation he faced at the hands of Brajesh Mishra when he approached him to stop the harassment. Brajesh is supposed to have feigned ignorance of the raids and said, 'Really? You know how Atalji and I believe in press freedom.' Vinod writes: 'Listening to him I nearly vomited. He then lectured me on the importance of free press in a democracy.'[5]

So let it be said that the Vajpayee era, for all the romantic depiction as being liberal and tolerant, came down hard on media perceived as unfriendly. They too used agencies to get the point across. The impact on me was that I had to lie a bit low and the number of stories that found their way into the magazine went sharply down. It wasn't as if *Outlook* had transformed into a pro-BJP publication overnight. We were just putting our heads down and trying to survive.

I continued doing the routine stuff that involved pure party news as opposed to the personality-driven stories that dominated BJP coverage. It was during that time that I covered the changes in Gujarat, culminating in the end of Keshubhai's innings and the emergence of Narendra Modi.

22

DOVE VS HAWK: THE FALSE BINARY

Atal Bihari Vajpayee genuinely believed that only a Right-wing formation like the BJP could bring enduring peace to India and Pakistan, and also to Kashmir. Therefore, he had made up his mind that India–Pakistan–Kashmir was the primary theatre in which he wished to perform.

Hence, despite the bitterness of the Kargil war, which he had clearly said was a betrayal, he was ready to take another shot at peace. This entire scenario was unfolding in the background of US exerting pressure on the two countries to sort out their differences. Nawaz Sharif had been deposed, and General Pervez Musharraf was now President of Pakistan.

In 2001, India sent an invite to the General in Pakistan; it was accepted and the much-hyped Agra summit was scheduled for 14–16 July. The intent behind this meeting was to initiate a dialogue with Pakistan, while keeping the superpowers out. It was also widely speculated in the Indian media that the summit was designed to deflect public attention from domestic debacles that had dented the image of the NDA government.

The summit took place amidst what was initially viewed as convivial atmosphere—after all, the General had his roots in India and the common cultural backgrounds between the two nations was given a lot of coverage. I did not cover the summit per se but reported extensively on the politics that followed. In brief, the General came to India with a great swagger and when he found the negotiations with the Indian team not to his liking, he decided to do some grand-standing on Kashmir and used an interaction with Indian editors to get the word across that Kashmir was central to initiate progress on other fronts. The private interaction between General Pervez Musharraf and top Indian editors was recorded and subsequently broadcast on an Indian channel.

Frankly, having reported from Pakistan, I could well imagine the kind of individual Musharraf was: one of those stereotypical military generals who was used to giving orders, with a deep-rooted hatred for India, and with a near racist view of Indians as being somehow inferior and Hindus as being 'cunning' (the sort of remark members of the military establishment make about India to a visiting Indian journalist if he or she had a Muslim name). I was actually asked at one point at *India Today* whether I would like to cover the foreign affairs beat and I refused, partly because we have an obsession with Pakistan, and frankly, with a Muslim name, I did not like what Pakistanis were saying to me.

I have done the rounds of Rawalpindi where Pakistan's military is based. Many Indian journalists claim familiarity with the military-Intelligence apparatus in Pakistan and are overwhelmed by the hospitality and access they get so easily. But let me stick my neck out here and say that if they had Muslim names, then the contempt that this class of Pakistanis has for Indians in general, and Hindus in particular, would make them cringe.

Not so with Pakistani civil society and intellectuals who appreciate the deep roots of democracy in India. Even Nawaz Sharif, with whom I travelled for a day covering an election campaign, came across as an individual with genuine awe and admiration for Indian achievements, particularly our political process. On a lighter note, I remember him talking a lot about Indian films, certain film songs, and saying how Dharmendra was his favourite actor!

Indeed, a book is an opportunity to make revelations. So let me reveal what a journalist-turned-key aide to both Nawaz and Musharraf said to me when I first met him in 1997, seeking to accompany Nawaz on his chopper. He called me to his house, gave me a cup of tea in the lawns and said, 'You must have been so happy after the Bombay blasts? It was punishment for the Babri demolition and riots.' I froze and recognized instantly that this was a fishing expedition because of my Muslim name. No matter how I felt about Babri and the riots, I was damned if I was going to say anything to him. I responded firmly to him objecting why would I be happy over such things, adding that terrorism of any sort would only put Indian Muslims in a bigger spot. I then asked him if he was admitting to Pakistan agencies helping the underworld pull off the blasts in Mumbai? He just laughed off my response saying how this was all a joke and quickly switched the topic to a well known Urdu writer from India to whom his wife was related.

I make these digressions just to underline the point that Musharraf perhaps presumed he was this big General with medals pinned on his chest having to deal with some Indian wimps. I found it hugely hypocritical on his part that even as he did not want to include cross-border terrorism in the joint statement, he unequivocally demanded that Kashmir be seen as central to resolving outstanding disputes.

When the visit came to nought, Musharraf went on to suggest a 'hidden hand' which had sabotaged the summit. In subsequent interviews and, some years later, in his autobiography, *In Line of Fire,* he presented the matter as Vajpayee sitting 'speechless' while he, Musharraf, gave him a dressing down about 'someone who had the power to over-rule us'. He further wrote how he had said this to Vajpayee 'briskly' and left for Pakistan.

Therefore, the story I had to work on after the famous visit from the General was, whether L.K. Advani had sabotaged Agra. Was it the invisible hand of the Home minister that had abruptly brought down the curtains on the summit? Let me state here that not only many in the Pakistani establishment had suggested this, but even a section of the Indian press seemed to believe this version at the time.

Let's now examine the background for this story—much before the summit had even begun, Advani had gone on record to say that one should not have 'high expectations' from it.

> Animosities between the two countries have existed over decades, and over the past few years we have not even been talking. The meeting of the two heads of government is not going to resolve all the differences instantly.[1]

He then added for good measure, 'Please don't create any false euphoria around the talks which can't solve problems instantly—though engagement is essential.'[2]

But it was by no stretch an Advani agenda to up the ante on Kashmir to ensure that the talks failed. It was clearly a unanimous policy line, backed fully by the prime minister. A PMO source, usually keen to present Advani as the villain of the piece, told me: 'How could Atalji have gone back to our people or faced

Parliament and said, 'Okay, we have been so generous to the
Pakistanis that we have accepted that Kashmir is a core issue—
even though they do not wish to acknowledge the existence of
cross-border terrorism.'[3]

As for the 'hawk Advani' versus 'dove Vajpayee' speculation,
the two men at this time were like two sides of the same coin—
especially on issues that were overtly considered 'nationalistic'.
The difference lay in their styles, not in substance.

Meanwhile, the BJP and the Sangh Parivar, always skeptical
about peace noises towards Pakistan, were delighted with the
failure of the summit. Though party leaders had stopped short
of making contrarian noises, they had expressed grave doubts
about the entire initiative. One BJP leader had told me: 'If the
Congress was leading this summit, we would be on the streets,
chest-thumping against shaking hands with a man who spilt
Indian blood in Kargil.'

There was a deeper psychological aspect to the complex
attitude towards Pakistan. Hardliners in the BJP feared that
sorting out issues with Islamabad would inevitably involve diluting
its core identity. The rank and file are uncomfortable with peace
and possibly know that any issue with a Hindu–Muslim subtext
comes in handy for whipping up passions overtly and covertly.
As a party ideologue put it to me at that time, 'If all the Hindu–
Muslim conflicts were to be solved overnight, our entire identity
would be threatened.'

I was told that contrary to the media hype, India had decided
not to budge an inch on its Kashmir position. The exercise was
intended to get a measure of the enemy, and to showcase Indian
democracy and reasonableness to the world. According to Home
ministry sources, the tough position on Kashmir at the summit was
not scripted by L.K. Advani alone. Yet, senior Pakistani officials

continued to insist that they were on the verge of a breakthrough which was scuttled by the invisible hand of the Home minister. They said the hand struck when their President left to change for the formal signing ceremony. At that point, the only debate in the Pakistani camp was whether the ceremony would be before the cameras or not. There was even talk of a combined press conference where both leaders would field only two questions each.

But things were thrown off kilter when the Indian Foreign Secretary informed the Pakistani team that they had objections over two key issues—cross-border terrorism and Kashmir. When it became clear that the summit wouldn't make any headway, Musharraf gave instructions to prepare for his departure. His aides quoted him as saying, 'I now believe that Mr. Vajpayee is hostage to the hardliners in his government. We will get nothing from the Indians.'[4]

In fact, contrary to Musharraf's dressed-up memoirs, Vajpayee's aides claimed that he had ticked off the General for the remarks made at the meeting with Indian editors that was telecast in such great hurry. 'Aap ne toh mahaul hee kharab kar diya hai' [You spoilt the atmosphere], Vajpayee told Musharraf.[5] In fact, weeks before the run-up to the summit, the Home minister's office had been forewarned that the Pakistani delegation, led by their President, would attempt to exploit the perceived differences between Advani and Vajpayee. For once, the Indian Intelligence had got their facts straight. As it turned out in the end, the Pakistanis returned home with the General in a huff, empty-handed and a mite confused about why their hawk–dove assumptions hadn't work.

23

WHEN TERROR STRUCK

The world was reeling in shock. The sight of planes flying into the twin towers, followed by balls of fire and smoke, would henceforth define global terrorism. Just a few months after the 9/11 attack on New York City, on 13 December 2001, five men made an attempt to enter the Indian Parliament. Fourteen people died including the intruders: six Delhi police personnel, two Parliament security personnel and a gardener.

I reached Parliament that day but found it under siege and stood outside the security cordon, hearing distant gunfire and watching the huge security build-up.

The government swiftly blamed terror groups, Lashkar-e-Taiba or LeT and Jaish-e-Mohammad (the one led by Masood Azhar who had been released in Kandahar), and demanded that Pakistan act against the leaders operating from that country. On its part, Pakistan claimed that the attack on Parliament was an operation mounted by Indian Intelligence agencies to defame the legitimate movement for freedom in Kashmir.

Within two days of the attack on Indian Parliament, there were indications of a war-like situation between India and

Pakistan. The Cabinet Committee on Security (CCS) met and initiated the biggest mobilisation of troops on the border since the 1971 war with Pakistan. Operation Parakram was launched on 15 December 2001, and lasted ten months. The result: over four hundred Indian soldiers were dead, many in landmine explosions, even as the world watched helplessly, dreading a full-blown war between two nuclear-armed nations. Subsequently, the government stated in Parliament that Operation Parakram had cost the nation a whopping 800 crores. Most military and defence experts would critique the Operation as a costly misadventure that served no real purpose.

This, therefore, was the backdrop to the politics that unfolded in 2002. By the time Operation Parakram had been initiated, Narendra Modi was chief minister of Gujarat for over two months; the US had begun its 'War on Terror'; every Indo–Pak peace initiative had failed spectacularly; and Atal Bihari Vajpayee continued to dodder between poor health and moments of lucid wordplay.

The BJP found itself facing two state elections—first, in Uttar Pradesh at the beginning of the year, a state that had catapulted the party to national prominence at the time of the Ram temple movement, but where it had subsequently lost ground.

The quick sequence of events that followed is known. The BJP fared very poorly in Uttar Pradesh, down to seventy-seven seats in a House of 403; the party was in the third place after the Samajwadi Party (SP) and Bahujan Samaj Party or BSP.

The poor results were seen as a personal drubbing for Vajpayee. Uttar Pradesh has the highest percentage of Brahmins in the country, about ten per cent of the electorate of the state. Much was made of the fact that the Brahmin prime minister had failed to draw in the pundits of the Hindi heartland. Simultaneously, the verdict was also the rejection of the Ram mandir card, which the VHP had continuously worked on, even as the BJP was ambiguous about its efficacy. Given the backdrop, it was also the rejection of a Hindu–Muslim binary that was in theory meant to work for the BJP; in contrast, parties that highlighted caste did much better in UP back in 2002.

Then events took a bloody and dramatic turn. On 27 February 2002, two days after the UP results, more than a hundred kar sevaks were returning to Ahmedabad on the Sabarmati Express, after taking part in a religious mobilisation in Ayodhya. When the train stopped at Godhra, it was alleged that a few kar sevaks had got into an argument with Muslim vendors on the station. Suddenly, a few bogeys of the train were set on fire, resulting in the horrific death of fifty-eight passengers. What followed thereafter is known as the Gujarat riots: Muslims in the state were systematically targeted and killed. India, and particularly Gujarat, wasn't new to communal violence, but what was different in 2002 was live television. It was the first televised communal riot.

There is no purpose served here to get into the details of the riots on which several books have been written, documentaries made, and cases fought. But the riots had implications for Prime Minister Vajpayee whose entire image was built around being a moderate man who worked for peace. Horror upon horror was unfolding in Gujarat, and Vajpayee was looking increasingly helpless. He did make a few initial efforts to express his discomfort over the violence, but it wasn't enough to stop the dam that had burst.

On 4 April 2002, Prime Minister Vajpayee visited Gujarat and went to the Shah Alam camp in Ahmedabad, where displaced Muslim riot-victim families were given shelter. At a joint press conference with Modi at the end of the day, Vajpayee made his famous remark about 'Raj Dharma'.

'I have just one message for the chief minister. Follow Raj Dharma. I also adhere to it. For the king and ruler cannot differentiate between people on the basis of birth, caste and community.' Modi responded to the prime minister in a soft voice, 'I am following it,' to which Vajpayee remarked, 'I know you are.' The prime minister typically left matters a little open-ended, but his speech was perceived as giving the chief minister a public dressing down.

By then, Vajpayee had made up his mind that Modi must go and a BJP National Executive in Goa a week after his 'Raj Dharma' remark would be the occasion when he would be asked to put in his papers. But Vajpayee had clearly misread the mood within the rank and file of the party. He shared his thoughts about Modi with his second-in-command, Lal Krishna Advani, who was tactful enough to not contradict the prime minister to his face, but later wrote in his biography that he was opposed to Modi being removed as chief minister. Eventually, Vajpayee was managed and circumscribed by the smart tactics of Modi's defenders. Even before Vajpayee and Advani landed at Panaji airport, Modi pre-empted the move and offered to resign, but as was planned, it was not accepted by the rank and file of the party.

Narendra Modi then made a stirring speech to the National Executive and with the strong backing of the RSS, emerged triumphant: he was advised to seek a mandate from the people, the argument being that if the people supported him, he would have done no wrong. (It must be remembered that Narendra Modi was till then an appointed chief minister, not an elected one.)

Even at that time, many had felt that as prime minister, Vajpayee could have stood his ground and insisted on Modi's resignation. He, however, blinked rather easily and retreated from any confrontation. Later, in private conversations, his family pointed towards Arun Jaitley as being one of the principal strategists who had managed the National Executive in a manner that it appeared to tilt favourably towards Modi and against Vajpayee. The truth, however, that I had gathered from excellent sources, was that even Pramod Mahajan, who appeared to be close to Vajpayee, was actually batting for Modi at that Goa meet because he recognized that the cadre strongly supported him.

Going forward, Narendra Modi and the Gujarat riots would cast a shadow over the remainder of Atal Bihari Vajpayee's prime ministership. When the NDA was defeated in the 2004 polls, the prime minister's team held the Gujarat riots as one of the factors for the drubbing.

* * *

Immediately after his 'victory' at the Goa National Executive, Narendra Modi was ready to face the first electoral battle of his life. The internal assessment was that the so-called anti-incumbency against the BJP had been forgotten in the heightened communal atmosphere, and the sooner Modi went to the people, the better it would be for the party in Gujarat.

There was, however, a problem. The Election Commission of India was then led by James Michael Lyngdoh, who travelled in Gujarat to assess the post-riot situation on the ground and came up with a report which contradicted what was being said by the Gujarat government—that there was complete normalcy on the ground. The BJP, aided ably by the lawyer-turned-politician Arun Jaitley, took on James Lyngdoh contesting his position of deferring elections.

In August 2002, I was working on a story on the 'turf battles' being fought in the BJP between young leaders. In the meantime,

Outlook had hired a young reporter called Arnab Dutta who was said to have the inside track into the prime minister's household. Vinod Mehta reveals in his autobiography that Ashok Saikia, a bureaucrat in the PMO, who was close to the first family, had called him to hire Arnab, and this was post the income tax raids on the magazine:

> I was flattered that Vajpayee's PMO was recommending journalists. I also spotted an opportunity. Our access to the PMO, post the raids, had been severely curtailed and Ashok Saikia was perceived to be close to the family. Having a journalist who could walk in and out of the PMO as well as the household was something we needed. Arnab was hired pronto.[1]

Soon after, Arnab delivered a sensational story that went without a byline, but as a boxed special in the cover story written by me. It was headlined as follows: 'Unhappy Atal thinks of quitting'. I'll quote directly from the story.

> The prime minister is particularly upset at his party's continuous campaign against the Election Commission . . . And it is with Jaitley's role in the entire Gujarat fiasco that the PM is particularly unhappy. A cabinet minister reveals: 'The PM has told some of us that Narendra Modi would never have tried to pull off this stunt of resigning in between assembly terms if Jaitley had not advised him to do so.' Every time the Gujarat issue is put to rest, the PM feels that it is at Jaitley's insistence that it is again revived. A highly-placed source says: 'The PM is wary of the entire Gujarat issue whether it is defending Modi or challenging the EC.'

The story created huge problems for me, even though I hadn't done it. Yes, yet again! I recall Arnab coming to me looking panic-stricken—his sources were unhappy with the story, he said. I told him not to worry as the story hadn't carried his byline and that he could always attribute the box item to me. I also added for good measure that I was used to getting flak and giving it fully back!

Then just as suddenly as he had come, Arnab Dutta quit *Outlook*. Vinod Mehta later told me that Brajesh Mishra had called him and said, 'Saba has done it again!' Aware of how I'd been blamed the last time and mindful of the fact that I was still doing all the heavy lifting in covering the party and government, Vinod had actually sacrificed poor Arnab by informing Mishra that I had no hand in the story. If one had to draw a conclusion from the episode, then it was just that the principal secretary was uncomfortable projecting the prime minister as taking on Modi and openly targeting Arun Jaitley.

Vinod writes in his book that Jaitley asked him the source of the story. But I think he always knew, being very well informed on media gossip. When I met him next, he made a characteristic joke about the 'household' as he referred to the Namita-led establishment. What was shocking to my mind was the blatant manner in which this so-called 'household' now denied a story that they had themselves planted on poor Arnab.

24

ATAL AND JAWAHARLAL

Comparisons are often odious, even downright ridiculous. But it was no secret that Atal Bihari Vajpayee had a certain admiration for India's first prime minister, Jawaharlal Nehru. The BJP too played along in this image-building exercise, offering Vajpayee as the moderate Nehru-like consensus-builder, with L.K. Advani acting a perfect foil and playing the part of the more ideologically rigid Sardar Patel (though a section of the parivar, post 2002, considered Narendra Modi the 'real' Sardar).

Vajpayee was actually disarmingly open about his Nehru 'adulation'. I recall how during a trip to Laos, he'd made it a point to follow Nehru's itinerary of forty-eight years ago and like him, visited the same pagoda, Vat Sisaket, in Vientiane. Veteran journalists recall an incident soon after Atal Bihari Vajpayee was appointed the External Affairs minister in Morarji Desai's government in 1977. As a Jana Sangh MP, he had made many speeches criticising India's foreign policy. Therefore, his taking over the External Affairs ministry had sparked apprehension about his marking a break with tradition. But Vajpayee surprised everyone by toning down his views on several contentious issues, including Tibet. When he was asked about the change of heart, he had said, 'Then I was in the Opposition. Now I am occupying Nehru's chair.' Throughout his seventeen-year-tenure as prime minister, Jawaharlal Nehru had retained the foreign affairs portfolio; although Vajpayee always had a foreign minister, foreign affairs was his area of interest as well.

On a more serious note, much like Jawaharlal Nehru, Atal Bihari Vajpayee was also very humane. By no stretch of imagination was he ever described as being ruthless, and even critics would concede that he operated within a democratic framework, and respected the parliamentary traditions of India. Indeed, Parliament is where the young Vajpayee made his mark.

Vajpayee entered the Lok Sabha from Balrampur, Uttar Pradesh, in the 1957 election. His maiden speech in Parliament was excellent and Nehru graciously (and famously) introduced him to a foreign dignitary saying, 'This is a man who will be prime minister one day.'[1]

The most useful insights on the Vajpayee–Nehru comparison that was frequently made in those days came from the late journalist, Inder Malhotra, who had covered both prime ministers. In 2003, in the course of a detailed conversation full of memorable anecdotes, he told me that although Vajpayee may have been driven by the same instincts, he lacked Nehru's stamina or intellectual brilliance. 'Regrettably, the same application is not there. Even during the Janata days, Vajpayee lacked the concentration to go through a brief thoroughly. He has always been too laid-back. Now, he does not have the physical capacity to take on his opponents.'

On the other hand, Nehru not only wrote most of his speeches, he fought massive battles within his own party with the sole intent of pushing his vision of a secular and socialist India. 'In those days, India mattered because Nehru mattered. That is not the case with Vajpayee,' Inder Malhotra had said categorically to me.

Certainly, Vajpayee held out promise, but he never really lived up to it. For instance, Nehru was not only firm about his ideological vision, he would do everything to push it forward. As we have seen, Vajpayee would vacillate as he did on the Ram temple issue. 'Instincts alone do not take you far. They have to be backed up by hard work, something beyond Vajpayee. For instance, he is a good orator, but there is not one speech of his since becoming PM that is worth mentioning. But I can still remember so many brilliant speeches Nehru wrote himself,' said Inder Malhotra.

I began this chapter by saying how comparisons are odious, and they indeed are even if Vajpayee compels us to compare him with Nehru. But it shouldn't be forgotten that he himself encouraged this sort of rumination. Vajpayee couldn't leave a legacy even in his party possibly because he did not have the nerve to follow his instincts to the very end, something that Nehru did brilliantly.

The manner in which Vajpayee capitulated in the face of support for Modi, inspired me to write a story that began with a quote: 'There go my people and I must follow them for I am their leader.' I thought it was perfect to describe Vajpayee.

* * *

The most sensational assertion of Atal Bihari Vajpayee's might over Lal Krishna Advani happened in 2003. By then Venkaiah Naidu was BJP president and had landed himself in a mess by saying that in the next general elections, the party intended to posit both leaders.

Over the years, the BJP had made much of the duo—variously describing them as Ram and Lakshman, the new-age Nehru and Sardar Patel, and finally, Vikas Purush (Development Man) and Loh Purush (Iron Man). This somewhat funny description, coined by Venkaiah Naidu, along with the revelation that the party intended to project both leaders in the next elections, led to high-voltage theatrics and low-level politics in the summer of 2003.

In June that year, Atal Bihari Vajpayee returned from a three-nation tour of Germany, Russia and Switzerland. Venkaiah's statement had been made while Vajpayee was out of the country (as had happened with Govindacharya's mukhauta remark). Even as several party members and Cabinet ministers gathered at a small auditorium inside the premises allotted to the prime minister, Vajpayee went on stage and suddenly declared that although he was neither 'tired or retired', the BJP should march to victory in the next elections under Advani's leadership—'*Advaniji ke netritva mein vijay ki ore prasthan*' [Towards victory under the leadership of Advani]. Vajpayee's missive shocked the audience that included journalists. L.K. Advani quickly understood the implications of what Vajpayee was saying (that he would not be leading the party in the general elections next year), and looked visibly shaken and refused to say a word to the press. The next day, I was present at a media dinner at the prime minister's residence and noticed that while Vajpayee sat quietly eating appam and stew, Advani was also rather quiet, even to media queries. That upshot of the prime minister's loaded words was that the BJP rushed to express its confidence in him; the Cabinet reaffirmed its faith in him; and the hapless Venkaiah Naidu went blue in the face declaring how, '*Vajpayeeji ka naam aur Vajpayeeji ka kaam*' [Vajpayee's name and Vajpayee's work] would be the party's pitch in the next elections.

He further clarified the party's stand by reiterating that Atalji was 'our leader number one' with Advani being 'leader number two'.

Vajpayee had landed the BJP in a soup and the party tied itself in more knots in trying to interpret the prime minister's statement, which was another rebuff to the idea of equality between Advani and him. After a few days, it finally 'decoded' what the prime minister was saying and came up with this explanation: all that he meant was that Advani would handle the election campaign, while he (Vajpayee) would remain the public face of the party. It was fun covering the voluble BJP in those days!

But that one question remained—what had led Venkaiah Naidu to issue a statement that in the next general elections, both leaders would be projected with equal prominence? Highly-placed government and party sources would say that Naidu misread cues that came from the Advani camp. At the same time, they believed that Advani was indeed seeking to up his profile before his crucial visit to the US at the invitation of Vice-President Dick Cheney, and the UK, where he was also meeting Tony Blair. Advani eventually left for his two-nation tour two days after the prime minister's statement, apparently 'in a deeply disturbed state of mind,' sources close to him said.

If there was one thing Vajpayee was not known to either forget or forgive, it was insult to self-respect or what he described in Hindi as 'swabhiman par chot'. Former BJP general secretary Govindacharya, and former chief minister of Uttar Pradesh, Kalyan Singh, had learnt this the hard way. Govind had supplied the word mukhauta, but Kalyan Singh, whose government was dismissed because the Babri demolition in 1991 took place under his watch, had famously used the phrase 'tired and retired' to describe Vajpayee as tired and Brajesh as retired, from the IFS. Vajpayee never forgave him. So when he wanted to hit out at his detractors in the party, he had used the phrase 'neither tired nor retired', but march towards victory under Lal Krishna Advani.

* * *

Just two months before this episode, Atal Bihari Vajpayee had showcased his natural talent and desire for peace. He had gone to Kashmir and made a fabulous speech appealing for equanimity. On 18 April 2003, at the Sher-e-Kashmir stadium in Srinagar, Vajpayee in his debut performance in the Valley stood in front of an estimated 30,000 people and spoke about spectacular policy initiatives. He offered to engage with Pakistan, initiate a dialogue with secessionist groups, create jobs and work towards restoring peace. This was big news after hostilities between the two countries in recent years.

The positioning was a bolt from the blue. We were told that he even caught some of his team unprepared, and it was him alone again acting from instinct. That day he came up with a line that moved audiences in Kashmir, always cynical about Indian initiatives. The prime minister said that the Kashmir issue should be guided by the three principles of *insaaniyat* (humanism), *jamhooriyat* (democracy), and Kashmiriyat (Kashmir's centuries-old legacy of amity). That speech resonated to such an extent that when Prime Minister Narendra Modi went to Kashmir years later, he also made a reference to those famous three words.

* * *

Towards the end of June 2003, Atal Bihari Vajpayee made an important five-day visit to China. As mentioned earlier, *Outlook* was invited and Vinod Mehta had chosen to send me.

It was my first experience of travelling with the prime minister. As it was a significant trip, several top editors of national dailies were also in attendance, and it was amusing to watch them compete to show who had greater access to the prime minister's family that was also travelling with him.

Narendra Modi has ended the tradition of taking journalists along on foreign tours, but while travelling with Vajpayee and later with Dr Manmohan Singh, I realized that such trips were very useful. There were regular press briefings on the aircraft and many off-the-record interactions with key people in the PMO and security establishment.

Besides the significance of what was achieved with China at that time, the media's interactions with Brajesh Mishra and others in the PMO suggested that a consensus was building in the government to agree to the US request to send Indian troops to Iraq, where the superpower was getting bogged down in its so-called 'War on Terror'. The Bush administration was putting pressure on India to send a full army division of 17,000 soldiers— making it the second-largest contingent—or more, to serve in the Mosul region of Iraq. Some influential members in the BJP were convinced it was in India's interest to be on the right side of the war. The gains, they argued, would not only forge a stronger bond between the two nations, but there was also an opportunity of procuring huge contracts in the post-war reconstruction of Iraq. It may be relevant to state here that Advani had then recently returned from the US and was reportedly tilting on the side of agreeing to the US request. More interestingly, from the signals Brajesh gave on the aircraft, it seemed that he was not ruling out India's direct involvement in the war in Iraq.

Meanwhile, Prime Minister Vajpayee said nothing and appeared to drag his feet on the issue, even as some people in his team were telling journalists that there were preparations afoot to send troops to Iraq.

* * *

Some years later, the CPI general secretary, the late A.B. Bardhan (whom I frequently visited at the party's central office, Ajoy Bhavan), told me a delicious little story about how Atal Bihari Vajpayee had ducked the pro-war voices in his own party. Soon after he returned from China, but before the monsoon session of Parliament, Vajpayee summoned Bardhan and the CPI(M)'s general secretary, the late Harkishan Singh Surjeet, to his office. He chatted in generalities and then told them in a few carefully chosen words that their protests against the Iraq war were *kamzor* (weak), and they should pick up the momentum.[2] The two Communist veterans understood what was being asked of them. At that time, the Communists were an important block in Parliament. After getting the signals from Vajpayee, they raised the pitch against US action in Iraq very high. Therefore, by the time Vajpayee formally refused the US request to send in Indian troops, it appeared quite reasonable for him to do so.

I had repeated this entire anecdote to Vinod who used it as one of his diary items in his column in *Outlook*. But let's be clear that by outwitting his own party, and by refusing to get enmeshed in a long drawn US war, Vajpayee had certainly saved India from a disastrous engagement.

25

THE FEEL-GOOD DISASTER

On 4 December 2003, the mood at the BJP's national headquarters in Delhi was electric. The party had won three Assembly elections in Rajasthan, Chhattisgarh and Madhya Pradesh. A large gathering of party workers at the Ashoka Road office were seen celebrating both Holi and Diwali on a date that had no relevance to either festival! There was loud bursting of crackers, even as people smeared each other with gulal (colour powder), and loudspeakers blared songs about the blooming of the lotus (the BJP symbol).

A few miles away, the telephone rang non-stop at Pramod Mahajan's residence, who was in-charge of the poll campaign and was particularly credited with pulling off a miracle of sorts in Rajasthan. Similarly, Arun Jaitley was also congratulated for overseeing Uma Bharti's campaign in Madhya Pradesh, marking the tradition of BJP central leaders managing Assembly elections.

A buoyant Pramod Mahajan told me that day, 'Just wait and see the grand strategy we shall have for the Lok Sabha elections. It's a new type of election management, and it has worked beyond all our expectations. This will set a trend for the general elections and the months in between will give us a breather to make up in Uttar Pradesh and Bihar.' The clock began ticking—Pramod set about convincing Prime Minister Vajpayee to advance the general elections to April 2004 from September that year. Others chipped in seeing great merit in the argument, and eventually the election was advanced.

Here are the reasons why the BJP went in for early polls, firmly believing in their campaign tagline: 'India Shining'.

- According to Pramod Mahajan, the BJP had won comfortably in three Assembly elections without raising the spectre of mandir–masjid or orchestrating communal riots. As a result, a leader like Pramod saw it as an opportunity to propagate what was by then the line of both Vajpayee and Advani: to move beyond divisive issues. They believed infrastructure had improved and the BJP should go with the development pitch. They even came up with a clever little acronym—BSP, which stood for Bijli, Sadak, Paani (electricity, roads, water). I remember Prakash Javadekar calling this BSP (not to be confused with the political party) our new 'ally'.

- The BJP was taking great delight in Sonia Gandhi's predicament, who was then viewed as a vulnerable queen whose best knights had fallen in the battlefield. The suave Digvijay Singh, the clean and earnest Ashok Gehlot, and the controversial but talented Ajit Jogi, were all strong chief ministers (of Madhya Pradesh, Rajasthan and Chhattisgarh, respectively) who were considered the backbone of the Congress. All of them lost the elections.

The BJP at that time viewed Sonia in much the same way they claim to see Rahul Gandhi today. As a weak leader, who was not a match for their prime ministerial candidate who would be seeking re-election. Mahajan described 2004 as 'a semi-presidential US-style election for the whole country that will pitch Vajpayee against Sonia.'

• With Vajpayee playing the great helmsman, there was yet another round of initiating talks with Pakistan because the party believed that it made for good optics. Equally, just before the polls, there was another go at 'solving' the Ayodhya dispute by involving Shia clerics this time. (The reason: the Babri Masjid is actually a Shia mosque.)

* * *

The BJP entered the campaign in 2004 feeling supremely confident. Its members began to chant that there was a 'feel-good' factor, claiming they would cruise to easy victory by pitting the charismatic Atal Bihari Vajpayee against a 'cipher', which was the BJP's new 'name' for Congress president Sonia Gandhi.

I remember writing a piece in which I had raised questions about the great display of certitude being projected by the BJP:

Now that the BJP-led NDA government has initiated the process of advancing the general elections from September to April, the big question is whether the going is really so good for the BJP. Is the party poised to improve on its 1999 haul of 182 Lok Sabha seats? Will the other NDA parties hold on to their ground in their respective states? Is there an Atal wave in the making, particularly after the SAARC meet in Islamabad, that will gather momentum as the BJP heads towards an April-May poll? Do BJP netas really have good reason to repeat ad nauseam, 'from feel good to feel great'? Yet, a good hard look at the numbers and reality on the ground in many states beckons the question: where can the BJP possibly make gains?[1]

I further wrote, 'Claims of crossing the 200-seat threshold appears unrealistic. Given the realities on the ground, the BJP would have done well if it retains the current haul of 182 seats.' *Outlook* kept up the tradition of conducting opinion polls (that went horribly wrong) and predicted a win for the NDA; the magazine had done one during the Gujarat Assembly elections in 2002 and after predicting defeat for Modi, got copious amounts of egg on its face. I however stuck to my assessment that did not dovetail with the opinion poll.

Meanwhile, so far as the BJP's new campaign was concerned, it must be mentioned that right from the beginning, the RSS and BJP leaders from the Hindi heartland were sceptical about it. They never bought into the 'feel-good' slogan. 'It is a phrase that will only be understood by the urban middle class. We can't even translate it into Hindi—it means nothing to a large number of Indians,' a prominent BJP leader from Bihar told me.

Yet the party persisted: India was shining and everyone was feeling good. Venkaiah Naidu told me how from feel-good, 'we will feel great very soon.'

* * *

The day before the results of election 2004 were to be declared, the air-conditioning in the media briefing room at the BJP's national headquarters in Delhi stopped working. Wiping his brow in the May heat, party spokesperson Mukhtar Abbas Naqvi lobbed a feeble joke, 'India is still shining—but if there is a temporary breakdown, it is because of the Congress party,' so sure was he of his party's glorious victory.

The next day, 13 May 2004, the usually garrulous BJP was shocked into silence. The BJP had slid by forty-four seats from its last tally of 182, down to 138. The Congress party was up by thirty-one seats, winning 145. There was a difference of seven seats between the two national parties. Today, were we ever to even see such a result, rest assured institutions would be used and back-room moves made to keep incumbants in power.

The old BJP just accepted the defeat. The task was handed to Pramod Mahajan to admit that he was 'half-stunned and half heart-broken.' There was nothing less than utter shock and despair that hit the national leadership of the BJP. I recall the then party president Venkaiah Naidu refusing to concede that the 'feel-good' and 'Bharat Uday' (India Shining) campaigns were far removed from reality.

The defeat was of epic proportions because it had left the BJP confronting a major crisis about its core identity. For not only had the moderate Atal Bihari Vajpayee lost the prime ministerial battle to a mere 'foreigner', even the great 'Hindu Hriday Samrat' Narendra Modi felt the ground shifting from under his feet in Gujarat, where the BJP's performance was below expectations.

* * *

Narendra Modi was reportedly not comfortable with the way Prime Minister Vajpayee was projected in 2004. At an internal party forum he had said, according to good sources, that wooing Muslims was a fruitless exercise as they would never support the BJP.[2] Moreover, in his perception, chasing Muslims alienated Hindus. The prime minister's speech at Kishenganj in Bihar, when he had offered to create jobs for two lakh Urdu teachers, had in particular invited Modi's criticism.[3]

The Himmayat (meaning, support in Urdu) Committee in Uttar Pradesh, set up to sell Vajpayee to the community, also came up for severe criticism after the poll debacle from certain sections of the party and the RSS. For instance, one of the buses used by the Himmayat had a picture of Vajpayee and Musharraf. 'When you use a picture of a Pakistani to sell a Hindu party like ours to the voter, you should know that the BJP has lost its way,' said a former MP from UP who was badly trounced in the elections.

In retrospect, the so-called wooing of Muslims in 2004 was indeed taken to ridiculous levels. There were also sniggers about a publicity film starring Delhi's Imam Bukhari—famous for issuing fatwas that Muslims ignore—appealing to the community to vote for the BJP.

In the end it was clear that this forced wooing of Muslims, which was nothing but a side-show of the India Shining campaign, had failed miserably and given more ammunition to the hardliners within the party to go back to the original agenda—focus on ideology, and forget everything else. The BJP's defeat in seats that included Kashi, Mathura and Faizabad (Ayodhya) was particularly humiliating.

At that time Ram Madhav was the most savvy spokesperson of the RSS. Following the 2004 defeat, as RSS spokesperson, this is what he said to me:

> In these polls, there was not much of the ideological element and the focus was on development and leadership. Perhaps the softening of the ideology and the attempt to project a secular face did not enthuse party workers or core voters. We have to ensure that our core doesn't get put off or demoralised, and stays with us.[4]

The 'pro-Muslim' or 'Hindu' debate notwithstanding, the BJP had lost its core urban support base. The India Shining pitch had come a cropper because it failed to address the concerns of rural India. A closer scrutiny of the results, however, revealed that the BJP was rejected even in those parts of India that should have benefited from economic reforms and logically 'felt good' about their glittering new malls promising consumer nirvana.

In Delhi, where the party had held all seven seats, it won only one. The results from Mumbai, the industrial capital of India, were perhaps even more shocking, where the BJP had a pre-poll alliance with the Shiv Sena. Several high-profile members of the Vajpayee government, including the then Lok Sabha Speaker, Manohar Joshi, lost. An even bigger upset was actor Govinda of the Congress, un-seating Union Petroleum Minister Ram Naik from Mumbai North, which he had won five times with record margins.

In all, twenty-six members in the Vajpayee council of ministers were defeated. While most of the star speakers of the BJP—Arun Jaitley, Sushma Swaraj, Pramod Mahajan and Jaswant Singh—were in the Rajya Sabha, veterans like Yashwant Sinha and Murli Manohar Joshi who came through the Lok Sabha were defeated. It was indeed an epic defeat.

And then began the free fall.

26

THE BJP BURLESQUE

A tal Bihari Vajpayee did not shape world history the way the late Mao Zedong of China did. But much like Chairman Mao, known as the helmsman of China, Vajpayee acquired some impressive titles despite the defeat in the 2004 general elections. He was left with no desire to do the hard work that came with being Leader of the Opposition, and hence he decided to settle for the title of chairman (he was also partial to being called a helmsman). The BJP, in deference to the grand old man, amended its constitution forthwith to create the post of chairman of the parliamentary party for him; the same evening, he was also given the title of chairman, NDA. He was now chairman 'twice'.

When BJP president Venkaiah Naidu was asked about the exact definition of the role, and whether it involves power without responsibility, he retorted sharply, 'It involves responsibility with respectability.'

Subsequently, a theatre of the absurd began in the BJP. Even as the 'foreigner' Sonia Gandhi handled the big moment with grace and dignity, the two ladies who projected themselves as symbols of Indian womanhood in the BJP, Sushma Swaraj and

Uma Bharti, in a me-first haste to hog the limelight, ended up looking quite silly, adding to the party's embarrassment. As the Congress and its allies moved towards government formation, these ladies of the BJP kept up a political burlesque on the side where they competed for stakes that seemed sublimely ridiculous.

First act was Sushma Swaraj's, who had sworn to tonsure her head, don white robes, sleep on the floor and eat roasted gram, if Sonia became prime minister. If the arch exemplar of Indian womanhood threatened to play the anachronistic role of a Hindu high-caste widow, could the original sanyasin of the BJP be far behind? The shloka-reciting child prodigy-turned-politician came charging to Delhi from Bhopal, handed her resignation as chief minister of Madhya Pradesh to BJP President Venkaiah Naidu and called a press conference to announce that she was off to Kedarnath and Badrinath. While there were sniggers at the unfolding drama (and BJP workers joked Uma needed a vacation), there was relief that she had not threatened to tonsure her head—again. The nation had been subjected to a bald Uma immediately after she won the Madhya Pradesh Assembly polls in 2003. After the 2004 defeat, BJP President Venkaiah Naidu too had donated his locks at Tirupati. I went to Arun Jaitley for a comment, someone who rarely loses his sense of humour, and told him people were calling the BJP the Bharatiya Mundan Party, in an oblique reference to the sacred tonsuring ceremony for young children in certain communities. With a straight face he said: 'I wish people in our party would realise this is the age of 24-hour news channels.'[1]

* * *

Two months after the defeat, the BJP leadership headed to Goa to participate in a *chintan baithak*, traditionally a quaint Sangh

Parivar tradition, where leaders congregate for a few days to introspect and plan for the future. I remember having great fun writing satirically about the thirty leaders who had arrived for the chintan baithak—while chintan means introspection, chinta means worry in Hindi, and that is what was writ large on their faces!

For four consecutive days, the leaders shut themselves in a huge hall and listened to many lectures—so deep were they in thought that there was no time even for excursions to the fabulous beach in Goa. A security warning also kept the thinkers far away from the sun, sea and sand. There was also added worry about the media highlighting the growing five-star culture in the party. There was such a heightened sense of caution, that a short cruise which had been planned was subsequently cancelled for fear of media criticism.

Therefore, from 9 a.m. to 8 sundown, the core group remained immersed in 'chintan'. One participant who emerged to meet a handful of us journalists joked about their own predicament. He said that, 'One evening we asked Vijay Kumar Malhotra (senior leader of the BJP) to sing us a song, but he said he had lost his voice!'

The only bit of entertainment came at the end of the meet when Murli Manohar Joshi, who did not have the warmest equation with BJP President Venkaiah Naidu, moved a resolution praising him for his 'dynamic and effective leadership'.

'Some of us almost fell off our chairs,' said a party general secretary to me.

Many of the younger leaders came away from the meeting with the impression that the two veterans, Atal and Advani, were badly hit, so much so that when delegates spoke of attempting toppling games against the Congress-led coalition by wooing regional parties, they actually heard such plans out. The two veterans were also confronted with criticism, one of the healthy traditions in the BJP of those days. At the Goa chapter, the Vajpayee government was accused of abandoning ideology and being 'unmindful' of 'unsuitable' social groups that supported it. Advani was told that the feel-good slogan was all wrong and his Bharat Uday Yatra, which he had undertaken to promote India Shining, had achieved little and had prevented him from paying attention to candidate selection.

Meanwhile, some of the NDA allies such as the JD(U) and TDP blamed the Gujarat riots for their defeat and warned against reverting to a hardline agenda. It was an analysis that Vajpayee agreed with.

Eventually, the four days of soul-searching in Goa did little in terms of establishing a paradigm for the future. The leaders returned home and spouted the same old inanities about Hindutva, nationalism, minority appeasement, and so on. It was the allies who seemed to recognize the challenges the BJP faced going forward and it wasn't looking good.

* * *

Three months after the Goa chintan baithak, on 27 October 2004, the BJP anointed the seventy-seven-year-old L.K. Advani as president and also Leader of the Opposition. This was his fifth term as president and it was clear that with that, Atal Bihari Vajpayee was finally in a semi-retirement mode. The party that had exploded on the national scene fifteen years ago was very low on morale. Venkaiah had to quit the president's post mid-term; a rather facile explanation was offered. The press was told that he was 'emotionally shattered' by his wife's prolonged illness and had therefore taken time off.

However, sources close to the party were saying something else. Apparently, his departure was a well-orchestrated plan by a section of second-rung leaders in the party, along with a few RSS nominees in the BJP, the outgoing General Secretary (organization) Sanjay Joshi, and Vice-President Bal Apte. The two key players who had a role in persuading Advani to take up the post were Ananth Kumar and Arun Jaitley.

It wasn't as if there weren't other contenders for the post—Dr Murli Manohar Joshi was seen as a potential BJP president and stories were planted by a section of the RSS that both its chief, K.S. Sudarshan and Vajpayee wanted Joshi to succeed Advani. There was no doubt that Sudarshan shared an excellent rapport with Joshi, and Vajpayee too had used him as a stalking horse in the past. But with Advani still around, it would be highly unlikely that Dr Joshi could become president again.

As it happened, Murli Manohar Joshi was in Allahabad when Lal Krishna Advani took over as BJP president. He wasn't even summoned to Delhi for the crucial meeting when Venkaiah quit office. The outgoing president did, however, make a telephone call at 5 p.m. to inform Joshi of the dramatic developments.

Also missing from all the action was the sulking sanyasin, Uma Bharti, then an important figure in the BJP, as an OBC woman with Hindutva credentials. Despite repeated pleas from her colleagues to come down from her refuge at the temple of Lord Shiva at Madhmaheshwar in the Uttaranchal hills where she had gone (she had by now been replaced by another BJP candidate as chief minister), there were no clear answers from her.

L.K. Advani spoke to *Outlook* on the issue and said that he wasn't certain whether she would join them at the National Council meeting which was scheduled for 27 October 2004, when his takeover was to be formally ratified. Yet, he confirmed that some sort of a role shall be found for Uma as she was at the time one of the few backward caste faces in the BJP, whose second-rung was otherwise dominated by upper-caste leaders.

During his interview with *Outlook*, Advani spoke rather openly and focussed on the big gap that his party had to negotiate in the Hindi heartland. At its peak, the BJP had fifty-plus Lok Sabha seats in Uttar Pradesh. In 1991, which was the post-Ram mandir agitation period in UP, it won fifty-one seats in the state; fifty-two in 1996 and fifty-seven in 1998. The real slide however began in 1999 when the BJP claimed just twenty-nine in UP, down to a dismal ten in the 2004 polls. The recovery would only happen a decade later when the BJP would win seventy-one of the eighty seats in the 2014 Lok Sabha election under the leadership of Narendra Modi.

* * *

Finally, on 27 October, a National Council meeting took place at Delhi's Talkatora stadium to ratify L.K. Advani's presidentship. The out-of-tune music at the venue was curiously in sync with the tone and tenor of the gathering—'*Himmat kabhi na haro*' [Never lose courage], sang a group sounding more like a gaggle of schoolkids morphed on the spot into a marching band. As they struck another off-keynote, Atal Bihari Vajpayee presented a garland to Lal Krishna Advani.

Besides the size of the monster garland, there was nothing special about Advani's 'Kodak' moment, this being his fifth coming as BJP president. A sense of deja vu hung heavy in the air; the leader and his party were struggling to strike the right note. As if that wasn't enough, then came the boring and long-winded speech of the outgoing president, Venkaiah Naidu, who was, unfortunately for the audience, in his elements! 'People say

Advaniji is 77,' (as if his real age was a well-guarded secret) 'but I say he is like a 37-year-old. He has the energy to handle two jobs (BJP president and Leader of the Opposition).' Then were some plum lines by the outgoing president to scotch charges of ideological vagueness in the BJP—*'Koi hardware-software nahin hai',* by which he meant that there was no confusion in the party ideology.

Soon, it was the 'Iron Man's' turn to rise and address the 2500 faithful who had gathered in the packed stadium.

L.K. Advani spoke for over an hour, the nuances of his speech somewhat at variance from the prepared text that was released to the press later. It soon became clear that Advani was walking on a balance beam—it was unclear whether he was addressing the BJP or the RSS–VHP hawks who had of late been openly expressing their displeasure about the direction of the party. As I would write in *Outlook,* 'In trying to be all things to all men, Advani could fall between the stools.'

For instance, the prepared text was deliberately vague about the Ram temple issue, only saying that the BJP was committed to building it, without getting into any specifics. Yet, the manner in which Advani spoke that day, it seemed as if he was all set to revive the agitation. Still, Ram mandir was the only issue that seemed to excite the crowd, and it was significant as Advani had spoken about it after six years. As if on cue, party men sprang up and a roar of 'Jai Shri Ram' rent the air. One overenthusiastic young man even yelled an old favourite, *'Jo Hindu hith ki baat karega, wahi desh mein raj karega'* [Only he who espouses the Hindu cause will rule the country]. That done, the crowds settled again into a listless indifference.

Advani was never a great political orator. But his words, carefully measured as they were, carried weight in the party at that time. During his speech, he said that, 'The government of Shri Vajpayee will be remembered as the most performing administration since Jawaharlal Nehru.' The logical question to ask was—why then did the voters reject BJP–NDA? Advani addressed that as well, saying, 'We assumed that there is a direct correlation between good governance and the electoral outcome. But we have found a disconnect and now realise that good governance must be combined with prudent politics.'

Was prudent politics a brand that was being practiced by Narendra Modi? I would write in my report for *Outlook:*

> The most political speech that carried a vital clue on the future was made by Gujarat chief minister Narendra Modi. The biggest challenge, he said, was not the *dal* (party) but the *desh* (nation). And this nation would again be destroyed if reservation is given to Muslims. 'The Congress is determined to bring about another partition by playing votebank politics,' thundered Modi. With the nose of a bloodhound, Modi has already seized on the issue that is likely to provide the next ideological battleground for the BJP. If Muslims get reservation and if the Congress does not nuance it carefully, then it will not be rash to predict that Narendra Modi could be the post-Advani face of the BJP.[2]

In the midst of a day which began with a lacklustre speech and progressed in fits and starts, it was still Vajpayee who got the biggest applause. Advani, he said, 'was like the party president even when he was not the president.' That remark made everybody wonder whether the ex-prime minister was paying his colleague a compliment or taking a mischievous dig at him! The next moment, he was back to being the elderly statesman, 'Advani can always show the way. *Mein nishchint baith sakta hoon*' [I can sit back content in that thought], he said. Then again came the humour—'Once Advani and I both lost the elections and didn't know how to spend the evening. So we went to see a film (*long pause*). It was *Phir Subah Hogi*.' (He was making a reference to the 1958 Hindi film, which when translated means, There Will be Dawn Again.) Everyone clapped and after many months, there were smiles on the faces of party workers.

The other veteran in the party, Dr Murli Manohar Joshi, displayed none of Vajpayee's grace and tact. Halfway through Advani's speech, Joshi walked out and never returned. There were others firsts which were noticed at the meeting—Pramod Mahajan and Arun Jaitley sat next to each other and exchanged pleasantries; Uma Bharti sat next to Pratibha Advani and waved at the press to establish that she had returned, both from her retreat in the hills and also to the party. It was just another regular day in the BJP, then full of colourful and dramatic personalities.

27

JINNAH'S GHOST SPOOKS THE BJP

In June 2005, Lal Krishna Advani set off for a visit to Pakistan. He was born in Sindh in undivided India and was one of the Partition refugees on both sides of border who would rise to political prominence. Advani's Pakistan visit began a strange sequence of events where the ghost of Muhammad Ali Jinnah, Pakistan's founder, impacted the careers of two BJP notables: first his own, in 2005, and later Jaswant Singh's, in 2009.

The minute L.K. Advani set foot on Pakistani soil, in an act almost akin to a magic realism novel, the Indian Right-wing hawk suddenly transformed into a Muslim-loving dove. Peace with Pakistan, he said as one of the first things; the demolition of Babri Masjid was the saddest day; Partition is irreversible; there is a Pakistani in every Indian. And then remarkably, from the president of a party whose members openly referred to Muslims as *Jinnah ki aulad* (Jinnah's offspring), Advani came up with a complex formulation that presented Jinnah, the creator of the Two-Nation Theory as a 'great man' who had promoted Hindu–Muslim unity.

This was nothing short of heresy for the party of the faithful. Their ideological guru had just debunked an entire body of beliefs.

A lesser leader would have been shown the door. But the man at the centre was the chief architect of Hindutva, who had groomed all the second-rung leaders who were now so well trained in critiquing Jinnah. The mismatch between the party and its leader had never been so stark. The BJP was plunged into what they called a *dharam sankat* (conundrum) of epic proportions.

The VHP leaders lost no time in labelling Advani a 'traitor'. The RSS was angry and stunned at Advani's transformation. But the more crucial battle was being waged within the BJP where even his loyalists were unwilling to endorse his statement. Even the moderates within the party saw Advani's revisionist attitude vis-à-vis Jinnah as too bizarre to be viewed as a genuine battle for the middle ground. Pragmatists like Pramod Mahajan watched silently from the sidelines; Sushma Swaraj had a minor altercation with Advani's aide, Sudheendra Kulkarni, who had scripted his Pakistan speeches. When Kulkarni demanded that the party release the Jinnah statement (the party eventually did not issue a press release, but uploaded the statement on its website), another senior leader snapped at him, saying, 'We aren't contesting elections in Pakistan!' For once, even an Advani acolyte like Venkaiah Naidu didn't find the words for a robust defence of his leader. Many leaders went public with their misgivings. Murli Manohar Joshi was categorical that 'there is no question of compromising with ideology and supporting Advani's words on Jinnah.' Yashwant Sinha even went as far as demanding that Advani quit as Leader of the Opposition, and then backtracked. In an internal meeting, the ex-chief minister of UP, Kalyan Singh, allegedly said that the party should be saved the embarrassment of a debate on Jinnah in Parliament by requesting Advani to resign from the post. 'It is impossible for us to defend his words about Jinnah,' he said. One of the few Muslim members of the BJP, Shahnawaz

Hussain, declared, 'Jinnah is not a hero for any Indian Muslim. He is communal, not secular. We joined the BJP to fight Jinnah's legacy not to defend it.' Vinay Katiyar, hero of the Ram temple movement and a man who is known for his incendiary speeches, said: 'Jinnah first partitioned India. Now he has partitioned the BJP.'

The real mystery lay in understanding what Advani hoped to achieve by his statements in Pakistan. Did he believe that praising Jinnah was the key to softening Indian Muslims? If so, then it revealed a very stunted understanding of Indian secularism. I was also vaguely insulted as it suggested that Jinnah was an ideal for Muslims!

The drama got more and more bizarre, even as Lal Krishna Advani refused to backtrack. He was also reportedly upset that his party colleagues had toned down the welcome reception on his return and were reluctant to release any statement hailing his visit to Pakistan. Many second-rung leaders who later called on him were told in no uncertain terms that he was 'deeply hurt' at their inability to defend him.

L.K. Advani would then use the entire force of his personality and authority to try and make the party fall in line. But he was met with a stubborn resistance fuelled by the 'no compromise over ideology' stand of the RSS. When everything else failed, it was eventually left to Atal Bihari Vajpayee to defend the man with whom he had such a complex working relationship. But the prudent man that Vajpayee was, he is believed to have told his small band of loyalists that if Advani lost this round, the party would go into the hands of hardliners and that would signal the end of the NDA in its current form.[1]

Advani then made it clear: he was ready for a showdown with the Sangh. By then, the RSS chief, K. Sudarshan, had publicly humiliated him and Vajpayee by saying they should make way for younger leaders.[2] Advani began telling his loyalists in private that the RSS needed to be fixed. A few months later, in September 2005, at a press conference after a BJP National Executive meet in Chennai, he said, 'The impression has gained ground that no decision can be taken by the BJP without the consent of RSS functionaries . . . this will do no good either to the party or the RSS.'[3]

That Chennai press conference was a result of Advani losing RSS support after the Jinnah remarks. After all, the ideological implications of what L.K. Advani had said after his visit to Pakistan were huge for the BJP. The party was, in one stroke, being asked to give up its pursuit of identity politics, and the Pakistan–Islam–Muslim pyramid was being demolished by the very man who had constructed it. Even if Advani had set out with the noble intention of changing the BJP, the manner in which he did so placed a question mark on the entire enterprise.

Besides, the question that bothered liberals was why should Jinnah be praised by an Indian political figure? Of course, he had ambiguities, but his legacy is fundamentally an anti-thesis to everything that India ideally stood for. He was behind the Partition which was based on the premise of 'different religions, different nations' and the name of the country he founded literally translates into Land of the Pure, implying others are impure. I wondered if the fascination with Jinnah had something to do with the fact that at one level, BJP leaders also identify with a nation founded on the basis of religion.

I also believe that if a Vajpayee had set out to praise Jinnah, he would have made poetic, open-ended statements and perhaps pulled it off. The methodical Advani was trapped in the precision of his carefully chosen words. As mentioned earlier, the blame was also placed on his speechwriter, Sudheendra Kulkarni, who continues to be an advocate of the Indo–Pak peace process even today when he is out of the BJP and a strong critic of the Modi regime.

While working in Vajpayee's PMO, Kulkarni had shown a penchant for quoting Jawaharlal Nehru, Sufi saints, and Urdu poets. With Vajpayee, it worked perfectly well, particularly because the ex-prime minister often departed from the written text. But he went horribly wrong with the Jinnah quote. However, many were of the opinion that shooting the messenger was not going to wash—it was Advani who should have shown more caution.

The RSS's Ram Madhav issued a terse statement and it seemed as if for the time being, the matter was over.

> Advani's statements on Jinnah and the Akhand Bharat concept
> is irrelevant as it does not jell with our ideology. We cannot
> accept that Jinnah was secular. The BJP has mature leaders who
> understand the implications of all these things. We don't need
> to tell them what to do. Advani knows what the RSS wants. He
> will do what is appropriate. We hope tomorrow it will be over.

Alas, there was no tomorrow. Muhammad Ali Jinnah cast a long shadow on what remained of Advani's political innings. His relations with the RSS never recovered. In 2009, he was nominated, if half-heartedly, as a prime ministerial candidate, but this was more due to his great role in bringing the BJP to the political forefront and at that time, the BJP had no other options.

Six months after the Jinnah episode, I was told by Pramod Mahajan that the party was hugely relieved that Advani's presidentship was coming to an end. Rajnath Singh became BJP president in 2005 and continued till 2009. He would again be president from 2013–14 at the critical time when Narendra Modi needed backing for his pursuit of power in Delhi.

* * *

Jinnah's ghost did some more damage before that. At the time of Advani's Pakistan trip, Jaswant Singh was the only BJP leader who had sprung to his defense. Four years later, in 2009, Jaswant Singh came out with his long-in-the-works tome on Jinnah titled *Jinnah: India-Partition-Independence* and even he did not portray Pakistan's founder as all evil. By then, defeated twice in general elections, the BJP was a desperate cabal of individuals hanging onto their little turfs. The seventy-one-year-old Jaswant, who had been with the party since its inception, was expelled for having written a book, without even the civility of a handshake.

There were many reasons why the top leadership of the BJP acted so harshly with Jaswant Singh, taking the extraordinary decision to expel him for writing a book. First, the 'Oracle' had spoken just the day before. The new RSS sarsanghchalak, Mohan Bhagwat, in an interview to a TV channel, had openly expressed his discontent with the goings-on in the BJP—'It must stop immediately, it is now too much', adding that 'The BJP should look beyond these four . . . there are more than 70 to 75 leaders who can take up the top job at any time.'

Second, Gujarat Chief Minister Narendra Modi was particularly upset with the political fallout of Jaswant's book. Gujarat was, after all, the home state of Sardar Vallabhbhai Patel, who was deified as the Iron Man whose legacy the BJP was trying to appropriate in spite of him having been a leading member of the Congress party. Now a BJP leader had gone and criticized the Sardar, besides praising Jinnah, which, for Modi, was sacrilege.

What also worked against Jaswant Singh was the timing of the release of his book. Gujarat was readying for by-elections, and the Congress party wasted no time in making the Jinnah book an issue. The Gujarat unit of the Congress started referring to the BJP as the Bharatiya *Jinnah* Party, while the Youth Congress planned protests to burn copies of the book.

Meanwhile, the Chhote Sardar (younger Sardar, in a reference to Sardar Patel) of Gujarat had to better his previous performance when the BJP's tally in Gujarat had gone up by just one seat—fifteen out of twenty-six—in the 2009 Lok Sabha polls. This was the backdrop against which Modi exhorted the national leadership to send out a stern message to Jaswant and finally, his government banned the book.

Sadly for Jaswant Singh, no one in the BJP came to his defense. President Rajnath Singh unceremoniously expelled him.

L.K. Advani's conduct was particularly disappointing. He did not show any inclination to defend his long-time colleague and friend who had been the only BJP leader to defend him publicly when he had stunned everyone in his party and the larger parivar with a sudden rediscovery of Jinnah in 2005. When Advani was being attacked by the entire BJP and RSS, Jaswant had declared in that famous baritone: 'I completely stand by Lalji. You are all misunderstanding his position.'

The sole explanation is that by then, Lal Krishna Advani was a pale shadow of what he represented. Presumably still the only leader in the party who would actually read the book, but at eighty-one, Advani had to constantly ignore hints about retirement.

The treatment of Jaswant Singh was unfair by any standards. Advani too had made complex points about Jinnah, but then his arguments had never been accepted or gone down well with the public or party. Jaswant was a soft target and it was argued that the real target was Advani and, strategically, this episode was also intended to make his position more untenable in the party. Jaswant was dispensable; Advani (and not Jinnah) was embedded in the DNA of the BJP. That is why the BJP and entire Sangh Parivar revealed such double standards on dealing with the ghosts of Jinnah. Meanwhile, Jaswant's book was considered an authoritative and well-researched work by those who read, and not merely critiqued.

28

THE BARITONE

Atal Bihari Vajpayee's fondness for the well-turned out, English-speaking, suave Jaswant Singh wasn't a joke. The man who wrote and sometimes even fixed the ex-prime minister's speeches may have invited criticism from some quarters within his own party, but there was no doubt that Jaswant Singh was an erudite man with impeccable taste. His room in Parliament stood testimony for his taste in high art and high-minded books.

Before his controversial book, *Jinnah: India-Partition-Independence*, Jaswant had been reading up on the man for several years and was aware that his book would create a measure of controversy. But he was both shocked and hurt by the consequences. Given the Jaswant persona, it is entirely possible that the critique of Sardar Patel was derived from his own memories and understanding of the past. He was after all a feudal from Rajasthan, and Patel, ably aided by V.P. Menon, had foisted the Instrument of Accession on the erstwhile rajas to join the Indian Union. Therefore, Jaswant pointedly asked, 'What part of the "core belief" has been demolished by my book? What is core about Patel? He was the first leader to ban the RSS and imprison its leaders . . . but he didn't ban the Muslim League.'

Jaswant Singh had courted several controversies in the past—his party could never live down the Kandahar hijack. Then another furore had erupted when in his book, *A Call to Honour* (2006), Jaswant had alleged there was a mole in the office of former prime minister P.V. Narasimha Rao. Two years later, a minor scandal was reported when he was charged with illegal drug possession in October 2008 for offering *kesar*, a traditional opium-laced drink in Rajasthan, to guests at his ancestral home.

Around the time Jaswant Singh was expelled, two BJP leaders who are still around and have made news in recent times, also found themselves excluded from the direction the party was headed. After the 2009 defeat, Yashwant Sinha had written to Rajnath Singh saying that he wanted the party to fix accountability for the poll debacle and in order to set an example, he quit from all party posts. The result: he was neither made chairman of any Parliamentary Standing Committee, nor was he invited for the chintan baithak in Shimla that followed shortly.

The former editor, author and Disinvestment Minister in the Vajpayee regime, Arun Shourie, too, was being kept out of the loop. (He created a scene that wouldn't be forgotten, described in the chapter, 'BJP Burlesque: Part II'). But suffice it to say that their equations in the BJP began to unravel after Pramod Mahajan's death, when both Sinha and Shourie began an attack, both overt and covert, on Arun Jaitley. Shourie too was excluded from the Shimla meeting.

Soon after his expulsion, in March 2016, Jaswant Singh granted me a lengthy and detailed interview. This was the only time in my career when a stand-alone interview was made the cover story[1]:

Q: Arun Shourie has defended your book in an article and attacked the BJP leadership in much harsher words than you have ever used . . .

A: I greatly appreciate my friend Arun Shourie's integrity, both intellectual and otherwise. Naturally, everyone will use the language they opt to use and we have to accept that the 'harsher words' are his style. But the substance of what he has said is really not that different from what I have been saying. What has happened as a consequence really of my being as they say 'expelled', I find very insulting. Because I must tell you, my dear Saba, that as gentlemen cadets in the academy, if you were found unsuitable to continue your training, you were withdrawn from training. You were not expelled. I don't want to dwell on it too long because every time I do, I find it wounding. Am I a criminal that you expel me? I wish they had a greater sense of the nuances of language and the courtesy that is the foundation of interpersonal relationship in a political party.

Q: You mentioned to me on the phone that you were particularly hurt with Advani's failure to defend you . . .

A: Do you know the function of leadership? To me, it's a matter of great sadness that Advaniji has singularly failed in his function as a leader to lead. A leader will have to lead by example. Not through diktats, not through vague and unspecified insinuations and fears. And in the army, the leader takes the flak. If you transfer responsibility, and if you do not stand up for those who are colleagues, then you are not a leader. There are numerous examples of how Advaniji, on the occasions that trouble him and where he is likely to come under fire, either keeps quiet or immediately transfers responsibility to somebody else. This is not the trait of a leader.

Q: Are you driven by any sense of revenge?

A: Actually, it's not revenge. It's a great sense of pity for Advani. Here was a man who was consumed by an ambition to be prime minister, and that desire made him commit so many mistakes. Do you know this whole wretched thing of money for votes is a classic example of wrong decision-making, and it's extremely troubling that he did not stand up and say no? Advaniji was at the centre of this whole drama. The facts are clear. I stumbled on to the whole thing when a very strange-looking fellow was brought here to my house by Sudheendra Kulkarni. I was not consulted but I was appalled that Advaniji was giving the MPs the go-ahead to display money in Parliament. Advaniji said they had two choices. They could take the money to the Speaker or into the House. But Advaniji told the MPs to display the money in Parliament.

Q: You recently went to see Atalji. Did you get any signal or message from him?

A: I went to see him. It was Ganesh Chaturthi. He is able to speak though a voice box here (points to his throat). So he speaks. But you know the voice box speech is always very guttural. His mind is clear. I went really to wish him well. I said, '*Aap ka ashirvaad lene aaya hoon*' [I have come to seek your blessings]. He said, '*Kya ho gaya, kya ho gaya?*' [What happened, what happened]. It's enough actually. I asked for no comments about the furore after the book. He just said *kya ho gaya, kya ho gaya*. That was all.

Do you know that Advaniji is using the party to which he belongs for his various book launches. Every book launch he goes to in whichever part of India (for language editions of his autobiography, *My Country My Life*) is actually organized by the party. Please, this should be asked of the party. The party congregates for his launches. This is a demonstration of sycophancy. Misuse of the party. It's sickening. You go there because the party has organized everything. Marathi, Telugu, Urdu. How many have read even his English book? But people are compelled to go there, demonstrate sycophancy.

Q: You must have read his English book. As a fellow author, how do you rate it?
A: It is written in a variety of styles. It is as if one person has written one chapter. Another chapter has been picked from some speeches. That sort of thing. You know they hate me. I don't want to hit below the belt.

Q: You are being most polite, Mr Singh. Now Mr Shourie has called the BJP president Humpty Dumpty, Alice in Blunderland, Tarzan . . .
A: (*smiles*) That is Arun's style, you know.

Q: Do you agree with the suggestion that Rajnath Singh is like Humpty Dumpty?
A: No, no, he is President (*smiles*). President! You know he is just a provincial leader who should never have been pushed up. He is a UP state-level leader who has been prematurely pushed up without sufficient preparation or thought.

There's lots more in the interview but the fundamental point was the war of words that had been unleashed. Jaswant was expelled; Shourie was a rebel who used colourful language; while Yashwant Sinha was also a rebel, but till then a cautious one.

In September 2012, I got a call from Jaswant Singh asking me to moderate the launch of his new book titled *The Audacity of Opinion*. I accepted saying I would be delighted to and have preserved a signed copy in which Jaswant thanks me. Two former editors of mine, Swapan Dasgupta and M.J. Akbar, both now in the BJP, were also on the panel. That turned out to be the last time I met Jaswant Singh. In 2014, he had a fall in his home after which he was in a state of coma for six years till his death in 2020.

Indeed, as I write this, my mind does go to the fact that Vajpayee himself, his great NDA enabler, George Fernandes, and, of course, Jaswant Singh, are all gone. But they had at least lived full lives. What happened to the much younger Pramod Mahajan was truly shocking.

29

THE TRAGIC END OF
PRAMOD MAHAJAN

Cain rose up against his brother Abel and killed him. And when the Lord said to Cain where is Abel your brother, he said, I do not know; am I my brother's keeper?

—Genesis, Old Testament

The first sin recorded in the Bible is the murder of a brother by a brother. Cain, the son of Adam and Eve, slays Abel in a fit of jealousy. Contemporary crime seems sordid, less grand. Yet, the emotions that drove Pravin Mahajan to pump three bullets into his famous elder brother may have been the same deadly mix of blind rage and bitter jealousy.

On 22 April 2006, Pramod Mahajan was shot thrice by his forty-six-year-old younger brother at point blank range, and died thirteen days later. The reasons for this tragedy were never adequately explained, although there was a rumour that Pravin (who died in 2010) was mentally unstable. What happened thereafter to Pramod's son and personal assistant was shocking, to say the least, but more of that later.

But first the political cost. Pramod Mahajan was literally the lynchpin of the system that had propped up the BJP in the Nineties. He was the go-to man to get things done, be it the Ram rath yatra that he organized for L.K. Advani, or the India Shining campaign that he oversaw from his home at 7, Safdarjung Road. (I recall it being planned and executed from porta cabins that were built on the lawns.)

At the time of his death, Pramod Mahajan was also the most effective fundraiser in the BJP. He came from the financial capital of India, Mumbai, and had links to big and small industry. He was following a tradition of Mumbaikars in politics: in the Sixties, there was S.K. Patel, followed by Rajni Patel during Indira Gandhi's days, and then Sharad Pawar, initially with the Congress and now NCP, and finally Pramod Mahajan for the BJP. All of them could make elections happen on the ground.

Therefore, one of the problems the BJP faced after his death was how to retrieve the funds that were parked with him? There is after all an overall lack of transparency in political funding and even opposing political parties have joined hands to ensure that the Right to Information (RTI) Act does not cover this area. An MP who spoke to me on promise of anonymity, explained what the BJP confronted after Pramod's death: 'Trust is key to the art of raising funds in politics. Money is placed with different individuals and businesses and then given during an election or a party function. Many of the biggest funders dealt only with Pramod.'

When this MP first got a ticket to stand for elections, he was asked to raise money from local supporters of the party and other candidates, which he did successfully. The MP then proceeded to tell me that Pramod Mahajan had later given him an envelope as a good luck wish from the party's side! That is precisely how

Pramod built his network, especially as Atal Bihari Vajpayee and Advani preferred to not deal with money directly.

With India's economy having opened up in the Nineties, the process of raising funds by political parties also underwent a major change—for instance, there was a time when local traders would make small-to-medium contributions that created a corpus for Jana Sangh and later the BJP, and that is why the labelling of the former as a 'traders' party'. In the early 1970s–80s, one of the men who kept the party financially irrigated was none other than Nanaji Deshmukh and, as mentioned earlier in the book, he could make it happen because of his close association with industrialists. But back then, nearly 70 per cent of the money was still raised by the cadre. Pramod himself told me that once the BJP came to power in the late Nineties, 90 per cent of the money came from big corporates.

However, in the post-2004 scenario, with the BJP out of power at the Centre, the states became the financial lifeline of the party, and this also marked the genesis of Narendra Modi's rise in the party as a man who delivered on promise. With Pramod Mahajan gone, the prosperous state of Gujarat put the money on the table for several election campaigns in other states, particularly Bihar. Although chief ministers like Arjun Munda of Jharkhand, Raman Singh of Chhattisgarh, and Vasundhara Raje of Rajasthan added to the kitty, they could never match Modi's financial clout as Gujarat was and remains one of India's most prosperous states.

* * *

The saddest part of Pramod Mahajan's macabre murder was that a man who had supported several loyalists and retainers, had failed to notice the darkness build up in his own brother's soul.

Pramod Mahajan may have become the financial nerve-centre for the BJP, but he had come up the hard way, taking care of his siblings even as he earned to support himself as a student. All of that came to naught on that fateful Saturday morning, when the forty-six-year-old Pravin Mahajan walked into Pramod's Worli residence in Mumbai and pumped three bullets from a .32 Belgian pistol. All of that is well documented.

What is less known is that just before dying, he had apparently forgiven his younger brother and told his brother-in-law and fellow BJP traveller, Gopinath Munde, 'Pravin ko chhodo' [Let Pravin be]. I'd met Munde when he next came to Delhi and he told me what Pramod had apparently said to him. That of course was not to be, as the police took Pravin into custody and thereafter began a tragic sequence of events. (Pravin Mahajan died in jail in 2010.)

Pramod Mahajan was given a state funeral at the iconic Shivaji Park in Mumbai. I recalled how just five months before his death, he had taken to playing emcee at a high-tech function at the same venue, the likes of which neither his party colleagues nor reporters like me had ever seen. It was the National Council meeting of the BJP to ratify its new president, Rajnath Singh, and a glitzy public spectacle had unfolded: large plastic lotuses, whose petals opened and closed in perfect synchronisation, were placed at the venue even as firecrackers lit up the night sky.

Pramod Mahajan had also organized a spectacular show of Marathi theatre's classic, *Jaanta Raja*, complete with horses and elephants. That evening he introduced his daughter Poonam to me and a colleague from *The Hindu,* and was delighted when we told him how we loved the show. 'I will bring it to Delhi as soon as I find a way to transport the elephants,' he had joked.

There was also a minor scandal witnessed at the meeting when some BJP members and journalists found a CD anonymously delivered to them. It was a recording of pracharak Sanjay Joshi having sex with a woman, very much his private matter except that pracharaks are ideally meant to be celibate. It was obvious that scores were still being settled in the BJP; many prominent BJP leaders wanted to get even with Sanjay Joshi who had once been in charge of Gujarat. No one ever knew where the CD came from, but there was a lot of speculation. The BJP and RSS suggested that the Congress had recorded and distributed it. Joshi on his part kept saying it was fake. Like I said earlier, none of us shall never know, but let it be said that the 'sex scandal' was the biggest in the Sangh Parivar and overshadowed the BJP meeting.

* * *

I remember my first meeting with Pramod Mahajan soon after the BJP came to power in 1998. He looked at my visiting card and commented, 'Look, you're a Muslim, and you may be apprehensive. But let me tell you something. After the Mumbai riots (of 1993), I feel this rioting is pointless. Muslims kill five, the Hindus kill 5,000! How is that an equal battle?'

Four years later, at a BJP National Executive after the Gujarat riots, when he saw me go past Narendra Modi, he had said, 'Saba, you have to survive with everyone.' I liked Pramod and saw him as a pragmatist who was not obsessed with ideology. That was one reason why he could maintain long-term relationships with journalists even if they were opposed to the ideology of the BJP. In the nine years I knew him, he never once showed any rancour towards me despite my frequent run-ins with the Vajpayee administration.

I recall how on several mornings, I would get a call from his man Friday, Vivek Moitra, saying, 'Pramodji has given you time from 11.15–11.45 p.m.,' and despite the short interaction, his briefings were most useful because as long as there was an understanding that his 'off-the-record' statements wouldn't be reported, he was willing to speak and share information.

I remember this one time when Moitra unusually summoned me at 7.45 p.m. The reason: Pramod Mahajan was extremely angry about something and would I come to meet him, asked his secretary. I did, and found him sitting alone and looking livid because of the constant in-fighting among the second-rung of leaders within the BJP. He spoke of stories being planted against him, and used some unprintable words against a high-profile colleague. After venting, he shrugged it away a moment later. That was classic Pramod, who mostly insulated himself from petty rivalries by adopting an independent style of functioning.

Even at the height of power, when he was Vajpayee's most trusted minister, Pramod remained accessible. But as mentioned earlier, he was particular about mutual trust and if one changed one's mind and wished to quote him on a controversial subject, it was prudent to check. He would often call back at night and, more often than not, agree to be quoted. Just a month before his death, he had called me late in the night while campaigning in Assam and complained about a news snippet in my magazine. When I explained, he readily accepted my premise, cracked a few jokes and then went on to chat about the next round of Assembly polls. Unlike some BJP leaders who on being criticized would waste no time in complaining to editors, Pramod reposed his trust in correspondents and didn't go over their heads.

Again, after L.K. Advani's infamous Pakistan visit in 2005, he summoned me for a one-on-one, and then produced an article from which he believed Advani's speechwriter had copied the speeches. He was seething because he genuinely wanted Advani to continue at the helm of party affairs. But being the ultimate pragmatist, he knew it was no longer feasible and went along with consensus.

As Union Communications minister, he wasn't half as good as he was as minister for Parliamentary Affairs. Again, it was his ability to reach out beyond the ideological brotherhood, which made him popular with MPs across party lines. He had a great rapport with many of the Left MPs and is still rated as one of the better Parliamentary Affairs ministers of the past two decades.

* * *

Exactly a month after Pramod Mahajan's death, his secretary of fifteen years, the forty-one-year-old Vivek Moitra died of a drug overdose on 3 June 2006. On the night of 31 May, he, along with Pramod Mahajan's son, Rahul, and a twenty-one-year-old student, was said to have imbibed a cocktail of alcohol and drugs, and was declared dead on arrival at New Delhi's Apollo hospital. Rahul Mahajan was taken into police custody.

This reckless party had taken place the night before Rahul was to immerse his father's ashes. Eventually, the remains were sent by a courier service to Guwahati where the Assam unit of the BJP organized a small ceremony on the banks of the Brahmaputra.

The entire sordid episode exploded in the face of the BJP—the India Shining slogan was ridiculed as 'India Snorting' and a vicious SMS campaign ensued suggesting BJP's name be changed to Bharatiya Janata 'Let's Party'.

Atal Bihari Vajpayee was away on vacation in Manali, and on his return made a generic statement about the incident: 'Sometimes our youth get misled. They have to be shown the right way.' At both a personal and professional level, Vajpayee owed it to Pramod Mahajan. Among several other things, when Atal Bihari became prime minister and shifted to Race Course Road, it was Pramod who had hosted his foster grand-daughter's birthday party.

Meanwhile, various people who were beholden to Pramod began making sinister allegations and the rumour mills began churning one sordid tale after another. Even as it was getting tough to sift chaff from grain, I was told that an influential relative of a senior BJP leader had visited the Mahajan residence on that fateful night of 1 June and had allegedly promised to help settle some financial disputes for the powerful secretary of Pramod Mahajan. It was said that the revelry that had followed at the Mahajan household was in anticipation of the happy times that the person had promised would arrive shortly. There were other sources who subsequently suggested that the home, that would buzz with routine activity during the day, would transform into a dubious den by night. A man who had worked on the India Shining campaign for the BJP told me: 'There was a cloak of secrecy about the goings-on. Only Vivek seemed to know who was coming or going, and he was very secretive about it. Even Pramodji was very secretive about his dealings. He created several financial nodules which were independent of each other.'

It was well known that Vivek Moitra, the postgraduate in Law from Bombay University, who had joined Pramod as a young man, was the keeper of his secrets. Just before his death, Vivek had been complaining about how certain people had reneged on promises—after Pramod Mahajan's death, many refused to return the money that was parked with them. Given that Vivek was the only one who knew details of the complex financial matrix created by Pramod, it was suggested that many stood to gain by his death.

With each passing day, the Pramod–Vivek–Rahul saga sounded more and more like a popular crime novel. In my several meetings with Vivek Moitra, that took place while waiting for Pramod, I remember him as a young man who loved to brag and talk big. For instance, he would talk about the glamorous parties in Mumbai and once told me, 'When you come to Mumbai, I will show you what a real party is!' He proceeded to drop names of the best discotheques in town and starlets who he said would happily party with us humble journalists. No one really took him seriously, except when he set up meetings with Pramod Mahajan.

Lots of stories of murder by heroin or cocaine did the rounds after Moitra's death. One of them went like this: someone who knew that Vivek occasionally did drugs, played a dirty trick on him and passed on some spurious stuff to him. Since Vivek Moitra knew about the money, he was the real target, while Rahul the unintended victim.

In comparison, the second theory sounded rather staid—Vivek and Rahul felt orphaned and desperate in the wake of Pramod's death and took refuge in the mood-altering cocktail of alcohol and drugs.

For years after his death, I had Vivek Moitra's number in my mobile phone. It was a ghoulish reminder of this shocking episode in the history of the BJP.

30

THE FIERY SANYASIN

If there is one BJP leader who has survived in the BJP, albeit in a diminished role, despite several controversies, it is Uma Bharti. Her face shall forever be etched in BJP's history: the sadhvi who made long impassioned speeches for the Ram mandir at Ayodhya in the Nineties; who, on 6 December 1992, apparently said, '*Ek dhakka aur*' [One more push], as the Babri Masjid fell to the ground[1] (all contested and denied as she is still embroiled in the criminal cases along with L.K. Advani and Murli Manohar Joshi).

By the time I got to know her, she was in active politics. That the BJP is a party which attracts sadhus and sanyasins is well known, and that dovetails with its saffron agenda. This strand of the BJP is currently at its peak with Yogi Adityanath, the head of a religious order, being chief minister of India's most populous state, Uttar Pradesh, since March 2017 and winning a second term in 2022.

Therefore, it was in the natural scheme of things that the child prodigy-turned-ascetic from Madhya Pradesh should join the BJP. But Uma's projection, as that of Kalyan Singh and later, Narendra Modi, must also be understood as being part of the social engineering project initiated by the RSS to expand BJP's base to the OBCs. As we have seen, this line was originally pushed by Govindacharya to whom Uma was close.

In a sense, Uma Bharti was a unique figure in the BJP, because she appealed to two of the most potent political currents prevalent in the Nineties: Mandal, that was pegged on mobilising people on the basis of caste, and mandir, which was focussed on religious mobilisation. She did briefly live up to her potential and played the part of a political giant-killer. In 2003, she led the BJP to a two-thirds majority victory against the Congress in Madhya Pradesh, then led by two-term Chief Minister Digvijay Singh (the Congress had briefly returned to power in 2018 but its government collapsed after a chunk of MLAs defected to the BJP).

But after less than a year in office, in August 2004, some months after the BJP's defeat in the general elections, an arrest warrant was issued against Uma in connection with the 1994 riots in Hubli, Karnataka. On 14–16 August 1994, way before the Bharatiya Janata Party came to hold the reins of power at the Centre, Bharti had led an agitation and hoisted the Tricolour at the Idgah Maidan in Hubli, Karnataka. In the rioting that followed, ten people were killed. Since the ground was disputed, and the BJP activists had defied an order banning assembly at the spot, a criminal case was filed and charges included attempt to murder, rioting with deadly weapons, assaulting public servants and so on. Uma was therefore forced to resign, and she subsequently spent the next few years acting in ways that did not suggest any level of temperance.

For a sadhvi who should have presumably acquired some inner peace, she was remarkably volatile and egotistical. For a brief period, her rages and tantrums became the topic of derision, often followed by a disappearing act to holy sites in the

Himalayas, mostly Kedarnath or Badrinath, located in the state of Uttarakhand. She never got over the fact that she was replaced so quickly as BJP leader in her home state of Madhya Pradesh—first, by Babulal Gaur (August 2004–November 2005), and later, Shivraj Singh who would replace her, settling into a long and successful innings and several terms in office as chief minister.

As a person, however, Uma Bharti was a favourite amongst journalists whom she cultivated and invited over to her various homes and 'abodes' in Delhi. She was warm and funny in her own way and entertained us all by saying nasty things about her own colleagues. What I also noticed was Uma's collection of soft toys, including many teddy bears—rather incongruous for a woman who took to asceticism before her teens, but a manifestation perhaps of a lost childhood. She also nurtured relationships and one of the BJP's rare Muslim faces, former MP, Shahnawaz Hussain, was actually a protégé of Uma when she was in charge of the party's youth wing.

The big Uma entertainment that I witnessed took place at the BJP headquarters on 10 November 2004, a day when party president L.K. Advani was speaking. She stormed into the meeting, tore into Advani with her words and then challenged him to take action against her—all in front of the media.

This round of infighting in the BJP had taken a dramatic turn in full glare of national television cameras. What the finger-wagging sanyasin was complaining about was not just Advani, but some unnamed party colleagues whom she accused of orchestrating inimical media reports about her. She also demanded a discussion on her complaint at the first meeting of the party's newly appointed central office bearers.

Uma Bharti's outbursts had followed Lal Krishna Advani's admonition of party leaders for airing their differences through the media. 'There is a limit to how much departure from discipline can be tolerated,' a visibly angry Advani had said. But possibly because she was also named for speaking too much to the press, Uma blew a fuse. She was sitting in the front row and got up to demand that the meeting discuss the issue of 'off-the-record' briefings by a few leaders of the party.

L.K. Advani, who was flanked by Atal Bihari Vajpayee and Jaswant Singh on the dais, retorted by saying that there would be, 'no further discussion or explanation' on the issue of indiscipline.

Thereafter, when Advani refused to yield to her demand yet again, the forty-five-year-old Bharti got up and pointing a finger at him said defiantly, 'No, I am sorry, I want to discuss it here. I want you (Advani) to take disciplinary action against me,' and walked out of the meeting.

After the showdown, as was expected, she immediately departed for a pilgrimage in the hills.

* * *

This was however not the end of the drama. Then a leaked 'letter bomb' arrived, an exclusive for *Outlook* magazine's Hindi version, *Outlook Saptahik*.[2] The Madhya Pradesh correspondent from the magazine[a] had accompanied Uma Bharti to Kedarnath, and got hold of the letter written by her to L.K. Advani. To say it was incendiary would be putting it mildly! The letter spared no one, including the former party president, Venkaiah Naidu, the general secretary, Pramod Mahajan, the Madhya Pradesh *prabhari* (in charge of election), Arun Jaitley, the then BJP deputy leader in the Rajya Sabha, Sushma Swaraj, the former chief minister of Uttar Pradesh, Kalyan Singh, and senior leader from Karnataka, Ananth Kumar.

In the angry missive, she described the party's top leaders as 'power hungry, deceitful and conspiring'. (By then, Uma believed that no one had defended her when she was forced to quit as chief minister; simultaneously, she had begun to believe that both as a woman and a backward caste, she was not given her due and was slighted by other leaders of the party.) She claimed in the letter that Jaitley (who was handling MP) had conspired against her and, '"taken his revenge" because when she was chief minister, she had not paid heed to his suggestions.' She added that 'phoney telephone calls were made "in a systematic manner" to different State officials using the name of her relatives to give her a bad name.'

Uma exhorted both Advani and Vajpayee to lend her support to take on Pramod Mahajan, because according to her, both Jaitley and Venkaiah 'also wanted to get rid of Pramod,' who wanted power only to make money. She got personal and hit below the belt when she targeted Venkaiah Naidu for making his wife's menopause a 'national issue' (he had cited health concerns about his wife to quit as BJP president in order to make way for Advani).

She had indeed become the rampaging sanyasin and in the process alienated all her colleagues.

* * *

The year 2004 was turning out to be both bizarre and ridiculous for the BJP. By the end of the year, party president L.K. Advani had proclaimed, rather outlandishly, that his party was 'an instrument of the divine'. He said so at a time when his phalanx of soldiers were fighting it out in the public space. The year following the defeat in the general elections was turning out terribly for the party.

After her explosive letter was made public, Uma Bharti met Advani twice, and then like seers of yore, decided to travel across the country. She first went to the south of India, Vellore in Tamil Nadu to meet the jailed Shankaracharya of Kanchipuram, Jayendra Saraswathi (who died in February 2018); her next stop was in Hubli, Karnataka, followed by Hyderabad in Andhra Pradesh, after which she turned northwards and arrived at a temple in Mirzapur, a town famous for carpets and brassware, in Uttar Pradesh. The best quip for her journeys came from Arun Jaitley: 'She might take a train, a bullock cart, then a palki or she may climb on a donkey en route to Kedarnath!'

In November 2004, Uma Bharti was finally expelled from the BJP. She would be re-inducted in June 2011.

* * *

In her second coming in the BJP, the lady had mellowed down. Possibly she had no choice but to finally accept the reality that Shivraj Singh Chouhan would remain the BJP's chief minister in Madhya Pradesh till Narendra Modi and Amit Shah willed otherwise. At some point she must have done a reality check and come down from the high horse (and the mountains). Even in the course of her low profile life in the Narendra Modi government, she has been snubbed: she was first given and then removed from the ministry of Water Resources and Ganga Rejuvenation in 2017, and she got no post in the second term.

The last public sighting of hers that left an impression was in 2022, at a liquor store in Madhya Pradesh where she was throwing cow dung at the store and picking up bottles and smashing them. She wants total prohibition to be imposed in the state. She was in 2022 just sixty-three years old, relatively young in politics, but apparently all burnt out.

31

THE BJP BURLESQUE: PART II

A t one point in 2007, the great Hindu Parivar appeared to be out of sync with the great Hindu 'Hriday Samrat'. The reason: just when Gujarat Chief Minister Narendra Modi appeared to be riding across his state like a colossus, the national leadership took a calculated decision to bring him down a peg or two.

It's hard to believe this today, but the man who was instrumental behind this act was none other than Rajnath Singh, then BJP president, now Union Minister of Defence, who decided to make several changes in the team of office-bearers to the BJP. But the real bombshell was the stripping away of two crucial posts from Narendra Modi—he was dropped from the party's highest decision-making body, the parliamentary board, as also from the Central Election Committee which takes the final call on candidates to both houses of Parliament, besides state assemblies. At a time when Modi's performance was being showcased as the amazing 'Gujarat model of development', this move was unexpected. When asked then, Rajnath's team had offered some unconvincing explanation, such as no chief minister being member of these bodies, so why an exception for Modi?[1]

Why indeed? Except that Modi, as mentioned above, was the first among equals in the BJP. To add insult to injury, Arun Jaitley—his closest ally in Delhi—was also delivered a minor snub when he was removed as chief party spokesperson. On the face of it, this seemed like a petty and vindictive move. Arun Jaitley's briefings were far superior to those conducted by junior spokespersons. Besides, the quality of language of his press statements generally tended to be grammatically correct and better than the routine party handouts.

When journalists enquired into the reason for Arun Jaitley's removal, sources close to Rajnath Singh came up with a conspiracy theory saying they found it surprising that there were such few media stories against Arun Jaitley.

There was particular pique towards an article that had been published the day after Jaitley was divested of his media responsibilities. The story in a leading newspaper described Rajnath as a 'second-rater',[2] and then went on to state how, 'second-raters tend to hire third-raters at the cost of first-raters.' Despite the careful couching, it was more than apparent that the 'first-rater' alluded to none other Jaitley, while the spokespersons who'd replaced him possibly as third-raters.

For routine BJP-watchers, it soon became clear that Rajnath Singh wouldn't have acted alone without encouragement from certain sections of the RSS. Although Narendra Modi was a sworn RSS worker and had risen from the ranks, during his second-term as chief minister of Gujarat, he was clearly larger than the parivar and was not doing their bidding in all matters. Broadly, some people just wanted to take him down a notch or two, and the Sangh, in any case, would have preferred a more pliable Narendra Modi.

In all probability, the Sangh used Rajnath Singh to conduct a little experiment to see how far Modi could be shackled. Modi's style by then, however, was to get on with the task at hand and ignore those he did not like. He remained singularly focussed on the Assembly polls which were due in his state by the end of the year, in December 2007. I had written at that time:

> Indeed, given that the entire BJP and parivar establishment has allowed Modi to evolve in a certain manner over the last five years, it seemed a little late in the day to suddenly expect him to start taking orders from Nagpur or 11, Ashoka Road, the BJP's national headquarters.[3]

Rajnath Singh wouldn't have tried to cut Modi down without clearing it with the two veterans in his own party, Atal Bihari Vajpayee and L.K. Advani. Vajpayee by then was mostly inactive and would not have cared very much as he had been out-manoeuvred by Modi in 2002. On the other hand, Lal Krishna Advani may have had some trepidation over annoying Modi: Gandhinagar, the capital of Gujarat, was his Lok Sabha seat, and he needed Modi's support to win it in 2009. In retrospect, the entire Modi affair was curiously mysterious because in 2007, Gujarat was one of the safest and wealthiest states for the BJP.

* * *

After this entire controversy, I felt a little bad about playing a small role in landing Rajnath Singh in a mess at that time. I recorded an interview with him in which, amongst other things, he'd said that Narendra Modi's removal from the Parliamentary Board was '70 per cent decision of the Rashtriya Swayamsevak Sangh and 30 per cent his own choice', while the removal of Arun Jaitley as the national spokesperson 'was a 50:50' responsibility between him and the RSS.

The interview created a furore in party and Sangh circles. Rajnath Singh point blank denied it, but I was in possession of the recording. I think he expected me to not carry the controversial part as a courtesy, and was genuinely surprised and upset at what I had done. Problem was, I was a reporter first, and his words on the tape were too revealing to be ignored.

Meanwhile, the party decided to put out their view and the newly-appointed spokesperson, Ravi Shankar Prasad (later Union Minister for Law and Justice, as also Electronics and IT in the first term of the Modi regime who was later dropped), issued an official statement saying that the interview contained certain statements which the president had never made; his observations had been deliberately distorted and quoted out of context; and how there was a palpable and malicious attempt to convey a negative image of the BJP.[4]

The second act of this exciting drama featured a senior leader of the BJP calling and asking for the recording. I took up the matter with my editor, Vinod Mehta, who also asked me for the recording (then a small cassette in the sort of mini recorders reporters carried) and kept it in his drawer for safe-keeping.

'You say nothing, let them fight it out,' he'd said to me and rightly so, for I had done what was expected of me professionally. Frankly speaking, even I didn't want to get drawn into another episode of a contracted faction fight, hence I politely let the BJP know that Vinod had the recording. Finally, after all the contradictions, neither did Rajnath issue a formal denial, nor send a legal notice to my magazine, precisely because he knew the truth.

As a consequence of the interview, a crucial meeting of the BJP was postponed not only because it had caused the party president embarrassment, but it was temporarily viewed as evidence of a growing rift between Rajnath Singh and Narendra Modi.

However, during his next tenure as BJP president (January 2013–July 2014), Rajnath Singh more than compensated by reading the writing on the wall—Narendra Modi was the star on the ascendant and there was no point in going against the tide, as it were. He would later play a big role in enabling Modi overcome resistance to his national ambitions from the veteran, L.K. Advani.

The following extract from the controversial interview illustrates how divided the BJP, indeed the entire parivar, was at that time.[5]

Q: The next big battle for the BJP is Gujarat. But the VHP and large sections of the RSS are unhappy. There is open rebellion in the BJP state unit. How do you react to this?
A: All parties have problems. There will always be a few in every party who will be unhappy. It is the same with the BJP. But there is no vertical division in the Gujarat parivar. The party remains intact.

Q: When did you last meet Narendra Modi to discuss the problem of dissidence?
A: Over a month ago. We met for an hour and a half.

Q: On January 29 this year, you had removed Modi from the BJP's highest decision-making body—the parliamentary board. At the same time Arun Jaitley was removed as chief spokesperson of the BJP. Did you act under RSS pressure or advice?
A: The media made too much of it. These were routine changes. Okay, the RSS was consulted. In Modi's case it was 70 per

cent RSS and 30 per cent my decision. In Jaitley's case the responsibility was 50:50.

Q: Rajnathji, you know Modi is a strongman and he would have seen this as a slight.
A: No, no, no! Narendra Modi is not a dada. He is an asset for our party (*laughs*).

Q: And what about Arun Jaitley? Why make him an enemy who would then run you down?
A: (*Laughs*) You only run down rivals. As you all very well know, Arun Jaitley has no rivals in the party and he never runs down his colleagues.

Q: After the UP debacle, you gave him charge of the state and made it clear that he would be kept out of Gujarat. Now suddenly you have also made Jaitley the election-in-charge of Gujarat. Did Modi ask for Jaitley? How do you explain this change of mind?
A: It was quite clear that Jaitley wanted to work with Modi in Gujarat and I saw no reason to stop him.

Q: The old guard of Gujarat have been systematically destroyed by Modi. What will happen to them?
A: You are talking of people like Keshubhai Patel. Narendra Modi is not the only politician who cuts down his rivals. Everyone does this in politics. Modi has his own style of human management.

Q: Modi is believed to be trying to cut down the Sangh and the VHP . . .

A: From what I know of Modi, I don't believe it. He was a pracharak once.

Q: There are RSS functionaries who say Modi is too arrogant and won't share anything with even the cadre who worked for him . . .
A: There is no such thing. Narendra Modi has his own personality. I am sure he will lead BJP to victory in Gujarat.

Q: Advani sees himself as the future prime ministerial candidate of the BJP. How do you feel about this?
A: Advaniji has never discussed this with me. So why should I have a reaction?

Q: But it is quite clear he does not want to retire.
A: Why should Atalji or Advaniji retire if they don't want to?

Q: RSS chief K.S. Sudershan had said it is time for the old guard to retire and make way for younger people. He said that the next leader should be young . . .
A: (*Laughs*) I don't consider Atalji-Advaniji to be *buzurg* (senior citizens). Both of them work so hard for the party even today.

Q: Who do you trust the most in the party? Do you believe certain individuals are running you down because they want your job?
A: I trust everyone and I trust myself. *Ek se ek log hain party mein* (There are all sorts in the party). There are some people who tell lies. But most are honest. For me personally the biggest setback was the performance of the BJP in UP.

* * *

Down, down, down. Would the fall never come to an end!
I wonder how many miles I've fallen by this time?

—Chapter 1, 'Down the Rabbit-Hole',
Alice's Adventures in Wonderland

In the history of the BJP, 2009 was possibly the worst year that I'd witnessed. It is therefore appropriate to quote Lewis Carroll, as there was indeed a descent down the rabbit hole with no end in sight. And it would be a BJP figure who would quote *Alice in Wonderland* in memorable ways, after the party lost the general elections for the second time in a row.

The journalist-turned-politician, ex-Minister for Disinvestment, Communication and Information Technology and Rajya Sabha MP, Arun Shourie, savaged the BJP president Rajnath Singh in a television interview on 25 August 2009, calling him Humpty Dumpty and *Alice in Blunderland*. He also said that the RSS should bombard the BJP's national headquarters and take over the party. The party's other leading lights weren't spared either, in a more tangential fashion, through a somewhat incomprehensible three-part series of articles in a national daily.

A stunned BJP appeared pulverized after the Shourie mauling, particularly as it came on the heels of the furore over Jaswant Singh's book on Jinnah (see chapter 'Jinnah's Ghost Spooks the BJP'), and the latter's subsequent expulsion from the party. For five days after the Shourie outburst, the BJP went silent and abstained from holding any official briefing, which was really strange in an otherwise voluble party. Instead, on 28 August, Mohan Bhagwat, the RSS sarsanghchalak, held a press conference at the RSS office in Delhi's Jhandewalan. It was unprecedented that the chief of RSS should summon the national press to speak on behalf of the

BJP. I would attend the Bhagwat press conference and be inspired to write a spoof called the 'Final Solution' that argued, take direct control and stop the back-seat driving![6]

Those were incredibly bad days for the party. Although Arun Shourie had ridiculed Rajnath openly, the president who had been so swift to act against Jaswant, merely asked Shourie for a written explanation. To quote from Chapter 2 of Lewis Carroll's *Wonderland* saga, 'Pool of Tears', the intrigues in the party were getting 'curiouser and curiouser'! Meanwhile, a senior BJP leader joked, 'You pay to take your child to the circus . . . this is a free performance.'

Although Arun Shourie wasn't a product of the Sangh Parivar, he had written books and essays that give legitimacy to the Hindutva ideology. He had a successful career as an economist and later as a journalist starting with the *Indian Express*. As a writer, he was and remains prolific, tackling various complicated subjects from economics, governance and even philosophy and life.

Earlier, as part of the Vajpayee government, Arun Shourie had headed two critical economic ministries and was part of many controversial decisions, particularly those involving the disinvestment of public sector holdings.

Also, in the course of the 2009 campaign (an election that the BJP lost), it was Arun Shourie who had said that Narendra Modi could be projected as prime minister and also suggested that the Sangh take direct control of the party. He would later become a fierce critic and remains one of the figures who continues to relentlessly, and cleverly, attack the Modi regime.

The BJP, back then, off the record, tried to make light of the controversy. I recall calling several leaders for their reactions to Arun Shourie's transgression and even after a decade, I remember some nuggets—'Why are you calling? Is someone else abusing us?'

Or, 'We are as clueless as you are,' or the gem, 'We can't brief you because we are translating *Humpty Dumpty* into Hindi to explain the meaning of the insult to the party president.' That was Arun Jaitley, always ready with a joke.

It was clear that the BJP had briefly become the Mad Hatter's Tea Party. It would be a while before the ascent out of the mess would begin.

32

ARUN JAITLEY: THE ULTIMATE DILLIWALA

The ship therefore sank before it could set sail again. The script began to change only after Narendra Modi started his ambitious journey to shift from Gandhinagar to New Delhi in 2013. After years of fulminations, tantrums, murder, mayhem, old age, senility and so on, a few people would survive, whether well or not is another matter. But it must be mentioned that besides Narendra Modi, L.K. Advani and Atal Bihari Vajpayee, I would rate Arun Jaitley as the most important BJP leader who survived the long haul from the Vajpayee-Advani led BJP to the Modi era. He would pass away in 2019 from prolonged health problems, leaving a vacuum for the media that he cultivated so well, even individuals considered inimical to the party.

He would also be the individual that I could always access in the BJP and over the years developed a very warm, affectionate relationship with. He looked out for me and would often call after a heated TV debate and admonish me for taking certain positions. I would continue to take those positions and he would keep calling to critique and then chat and ask about my daughter, show great interest in her progress and suggest law as a profession. (It's another matter that she is indeed doing law now.)

I believe he was different from many Indian politicians for two reasons: first, politics was not the be-all and end-all for him and were it to end abruptly someday, he could go back to being one of India's top lawyers, a practice he built himself and did not inherit. Second, he was the only politician I knew who had genuine friends, a wide circle that included some who were clearly inimical to BJP's ideology. For instance, Rajeev Nayyar, the lawyer-son of late journalist Kuldeep Nayyar, very hostile to the BJP ideology, was devoted to Jaitley and I remember both father and son travelling to Amritsar as an act of solidarity when Jaitley contested the Lok Sabha seat in the 2014 election.

Jaitley would fail at electoral politics and in 2014 he lost the Amritsar seat to Captain Amarinder Singh, who served a term as Congress chief minister of Punjab. But in a political eco-system that had for decades been dominated by the Congress, he was an exceptional figure in the BJP as the primary connect to media, judiciary and bureaucracy of the old order. He also served as main communicator and spin doctor in the BJP and had multiple levels of contacts in the media, from reporter to editor to proprietor.

The man in the second hottest seat in the country during Narendra Modi's first term in Delhi, as finance minister, was temperamentally talkative, sociable and a great host, known for setting a fine table—and then proceeding to describe each food item in considerable detail. He could talk endlessly about his caterers, the kebabs they made, the Kashmiri cuisine that he loved serving. I remember once landing in Patna, and going to my regular hotel there called Chanakya. Jaitley was then in charge of Bihar and the point man for the BJP alliance with Nitish Kumar. He called and proceeded to have a hilarious conversation, first holding forth about people's habit of spitting, then he cracked some jokes about everyone in the local BJP and told me that the electricity supply was so bad that he had a meeting in a cold storage and finally he recommended that I try a dish called Chicken Mercury available in the hotel menu.

Once he took to certain individuals, be they from law, the media or politics, he would stick his neck out for them. He would also make a formidable adversary for those he fell out with and did not like and was said to be behind the blocking of the rise of individuals such as Arun Shourie and Yashwant Sinha in the BJP after Modi came to power in Delhi. Many colleagues in the media, some of them fine journalists, also suffered as a consequence of Jaitley reportedly complaining about them to proprietors and/or editors. In those days he was being referred to as the Super Chief of Bureau, and was indeed tasked with narrative creation. I was an odd fit but somehow kept up with him.

The reason my equation with him endured, I suspect, is because I was never looking for favours or a job/promotion through him (as some journalists did) and was a credible byline in the coverage of the party; I got his jokes and he could trust me to keep an off-the-record conversation confidential. I had also known him for years, from the time he was a young lawyer and I a student in St Stephen's college in Delhi University, where I once consulted him over a legal matter. He would some years later represent my mother in a case and refuse to take a fee, all before I got to know him as a reporter. When my first book, *In Good Faith*, was released at the India International Centre (IIC), Delhi, in December 2012 by Mani Shankar Aiyar and sociologist Ashis Nandy, Jaitley put in an appearance after a long day in Parliament where he was Leader of the Opposition in the Rajya Sabha.

Arun Jaitley's friendships went back to four or even five decades—his old college buddies, those who were in Tihar jail with him for nineteen months during the Emergency— lawyers, doctors, and even a newspaper proprietor. But the bonhomie visible around Jaitley was missing when it came to some of his own colleagues in the party of the same vintage. The late Pramod Mahajan and Sushma Swaraj were rivals from the same generation.

But nationally what defined the life and legacy of Arun Jaitley would be his equation with Narendra Modi. As mentioned earlier in this book, their relationship was cemented in 2002 during the post-Godhra riots phase when Prime Minister Vajpayee tried confronting Chief Minister Modi at the National Executive in Goa. But the rapport between the two had been established earlier.

In 1996–2001, as a result of infighting in the Gujarat BJP, Narendra Modi had been literally banished from the state as one faction saw him as a trouble-making pracharak. It was during this period when Modi lived in the party headquarters in Delhi, where he struck up an equation with Arun Jaitley.

In 2001, Jaitley was among those who lobbied with L.K. Advani to send Modi as chief minister to Gujarat—a major decision at that time as he was the first full-time RSS pracharak to be directly inducted into active politics. Ever since, Modi and Jaitley worked together comfortably, the former evolving into a charismatic public speaker who is described as being quiet in private, and a great listener, the latter loquacious in closed circles but not so great at mass contact.

Indeed, much before he shifted to Delhi, Modi ensured that Jaitley be the national leader in charge of the Gujarat Assembly elections in 2007 and 2012. The Modi–Jaitley equation progressively grew in strength. So much so that when Modi shifted to Delhi, he relied on Jaitley to recommend many names that would enter the council of ministers. Jaitley no doubt also established the necessary linkages to media and judiciary.

Jaitley would at one point serve as both Finance and Defence minister in Modi's first term. His legacy as finance minister was, however, disastrous. He was holding the portfolio when the PM announced the demonetization policy on 8 November 2016. There was speculation that the PM did not inform the finance minister but I gather from subsequent conversations with multiple sources that he did not 'consult' the finance minister although he did let him know what would happen that day. Through much of the first term, Jaitley's health was beginning to fail and after he read his first budget speech in Parliament, I was one of the visitors who went to his room in the House and saw an exhausted individual, who had somehow still told his staff to organize lunch for a few visitors.

In my view, the most flawed policy that Jaitley gave the nation was the electoral bond scheme, about which I elaborate at the beginning of the book. He kept insisting the scheme increased transparency in political funding but as we have seen, the reverse happened. I cannot say with any certainty if Jaitley had come up with a master-plan to gradually shift all political funds to the BJP, or he had just given India a very problematic scheme.

* * *

Jaitley and Modi made an odd pairing. But one reason that I suspect the two men could get on is also because as a successful lawyer, Arun Jaitley never had the time or inclination to be a durbari (hanger-on) of a prominent political figure. And Modi has never really required a coterie of people who just hang around him, although he has trusted aides such as Amit Shah and some bureaucracts.

In 2007, while covering Narendra Modi's second electoral campaign during the Assembly elections in Gujarat, I remember meeting Arun Jaitley in Ahmedabad. I asked him why he went out of his way to help the controversial chief minister in several legal and political wrangles, and got this reply: 'Why do you want to write about me? After all, I've known Modi for years. We've worked together in Delhi much before he came to Gujarat. I see him as an exceptional talent.'

Since no one knew back then that Modi would be prime minister one day, the question was asked: why was the suave Jaitley allowing his name to be repeatedly linked with Modi, who was associated with the Gujarat riots (it's another matter that he was exonerated by the courts subsequently)? However, then as several times later, I never got an answer for this question, although I presumed that it was pegged on common ideological moorings.

As a student, Jaitley was a member of the Akhil Bharatiya Vidyarthi Parishad (ABVP; students' organization affiliated to the RSS), and had risen to be president of the Delhi University Students Union (DUSU). It's therefore quite possible that he believed in the need for a strong Hindu leader who would be unapologetic about a certain ideological orientation.

Gradually, as Modi became a force to reckon with, many BJP leaders and sections of the Sangh Parivar grew to fear him. But Jaitley was steadfast in aligning himself with Modi, even if that invited the displeasure of Prime Minister Vajpayee. The balance of power between the two men also evolved: If at one time, the lawyer had patronized the pracharak from Gujarat, by 2007, the pracharak had transformed into a mass leader and Jaitley was tasked with being the backroom strategist.

Jaitley's friends in the media also began putting forward the argument that Modi alone had the dynamism to revive the BJP nationally, at a time when he was seen as too polarising a figure. My former editor, Swapan Dasgupta, was one of the first to begin promoting Modi in the editorial pages of big newspapers.

* * *

Many of Jaitley's friends were influential in their respective fields of expertise. Among the closest was the well-connected Delhi solicitor, Raian Karanjawala, who was Jaitley's junior at the Shri Ram College for Commerce (SRCC). Karanjawala told me, 'A lot of Arun's friendships go back to his days in the college debating society.' Jaitley and Karanjawala were in the SRCC team that went to debate in St Stephen's where they were up against Shashi Tharoor and Swapan Dasgupta (the latter would become another good friend). In the Hindi debating circuit, there was the journalist, Rajat Sharma, another member of the Jaitley group who now heads India TV. Among lawyers, Jaitley would count Maninder Singh as a very close friend and he was made ASG after the Modi win in 2014 just as another regular in the Jaitley household Mukul Rohatgi was made Attorney General of India in 2014. In the judiciary, Jaitley spoke highly of Rohinton Nariman who retired as a judge in the Supreme Court in 2021. I have heard Jaitley remark that in the Supreme Court, Rohinton could be the most brilliant legal mind. (Incidentally, neither he nor his father, Fali Nariman, are BJP loyalists.)

* * *

Curiously, it wasn't a BJP politician but former prime minister V.P. Singh who was instrumental in bringing Jaitley into national politics. The story goes that Ramnath Goenka, founder of the

Indian Express group, was served with a demolition notice for a
building in Delhi in the 1980s by the then Lieutenant Governor,
Jagmohan. Jaitley was one of the lawyers roped in to fight the case,
because as Karanjawala said, 'He was making a mark for out-of-
the-box, innovative solutions.'

After Jaitley, along with others in the team, won the Express
case, V.P. Singh would make him the additional solicitor general,
although at thirty-seven, he was considered young for the post.

I last met Jaitley on 25 June 2019, a month after the second
term mandate when he called and invited me to his home. He was
by then back in his old south Delhi residence having given up his
ministerial bungalow. He was weak and struggling to engage but still
wanted to. He told me that when he was diagnosed with soft tissue
cancer in New York earlier this year, he found the best way to cope
was to keep writing his daily blogs as the election kicked off in India.
But he said the treatment was more exhausting than the disease.

I said that when he got better he should write his autobiography.
He smiled but said he was struggling to read now. He survived
illness more cheerfully than anyone I have ever known. His
interest in life remained even as it was slipping away.

An article that I would write on Jaitley in the *Times of India*
after his passing just two months later would be among those
selected by his family for a book later released by the then Vice-
President.[1] I attended a prayer ceremony for him where I was
seated next to cricketer Gautam Gambhir. I recalled then that it
was in Jaitley's home that I met film star Shah Rukh Khan who
came to perform at the sangeet ceremony of his daughter who was
married off in style and lavish functions held over several days and
all the caterers busy serving every kind of cuisine.

He died at the beginning of the second term of Narendra
Modi. I have often wondered if things would have been different

if he were still around. Sensitive to media perceptions, would he have advised against policies that have sought to intimidate certain outlets through criminal complaints and cases? How would he have responded to India's slipping ranks in world press freedom indices? Close to big business, many of whom were his clients when he functioned as a lawyer, how would he have responded to the unbridled powers of enforcement agencies? Would he have been a sobering influence on the regime or would his influence have waned in time?

33

THE ABSOLUTE LEADER

In January 2007, I went to Ahmedabad and Gandhinagar to attend the Vibrant Gujarat Global Summit, that had by then become a big event in Chief Minister Narendra Modi's calendar. As we have seen earlier, at that point, the BJP appeared to be withering away nationally, the energy sapped by a spate of inner-party fights and tussles. Modi was a study in contrast as he emerged, step-by-step, the strongest leader in the party. The centre of gravity was clearly beginning to shift from both Delhi and Nagpur, to Ahmedabad. The year 2007 that began with the Vibrant Gujarat Summit, ended with an Assembly election, the second that Modi would win comfortably.

By then it had been five years since the 2002 Godhra riots. Narendra Modi, who was once cornered and attacked by both national and international media, was transforming himself into a global Hindu leader, friend of industrialists, supporter of a free market, and as he liked to put it, the protector of Gujarat. He had emerged as something of a colossus in the state, revealing, along the way, a talent for making critics irrelevant, reducing rivals to ciphers and working his mass appeal and public-speaking abilities to his advantage.

After taking the 'Hindu' identity to a fever pitch in 2002, the most interesting facet of Modi's evolution by 2007 appeared to be his unbridled pursuit of one-time RSS pracharak showed no adherence to the protectionist swadeshi economic rhetoric. Globalisation and the free flow of capital was the dream he began selling; this was also linked to Gujaratis' proficiency in business, plus the presence of a large Gujarati diaspora across the world.

He began forging strong relationships with captains of Indian industry, something that would remain a constant feature in his ascent to power in Delhi. NRI businessmen began to view him favourably and advanced economies like Singapore and Japan were now eager to ink deals with the business-friendly chief minister of Gujarat.

* * *

At a first glance, the Vibrant Gujarat Global Summit in 2007 appeared something like a regular trade fair, with sundry stalls of various countries, corporations and quasi-governmental outfits. However, the big difference was that the big guns of Indian industry were in attendance—Ratan Tata, Mukesh Ambani, Shashi Ruia and K.V. Kamath—besides NRIs. The meet I attended, announced it had notched up investments to the tune of Rs 2.5 lakh crore. Pharma giant Wockhardt's Habil Khorakiwala, who had just taken over as FICCI president, described Modi as a 'dynamic visionary'; Ratan Tata, whose small car project in West Bengal was then mired in a mighty mess, said, 'You are a fool if you are not in Gujarat.'

That said, the highlight of the 2007 Summit was Special Economic Zones or SEZs—I remember that day when Chief Minister Modi pointed out to the large gathering and said that

Gujarat was among the first states to enact a SEZ law in 2004, even before the Centre did in 2005. In a speech designed as much for the industrialists, as for a mass audience (it was also broadcast), he came up with one of those lines that make for easy headlines: the whole of Gujarat, he said, is a SEZ—S for Spirituality, E for Entrepreneurship, and Z for Zeal. The hall resonated with loud applause.

One must ask in hindsight: as was proven in 2004, if the India Shining campaign was counterproductive, why did Modi believe that Vibrant Gujarat would work in his state? After all, unbridled industrialization has often turned out to be poor politics in several parts of India. But then, Gujarat was different: it had the highest rate of urbanization at 40 per cent. There were of course sections of the population who were marginalized and poor, but there were large numbers who felt empowered and believed they had prospered during Modi's rule, even as their sense of belonging to the Hindu fold was heightened.

Additionally, there was a historical context to what was unfolding in Gujarat. In the course of the twentieth century, some of the most popular mass movements in the state were reactionary in nature.[1] For instance, one little known fact is that in 1986, the Bajrang Dal was established in Gujarat among other reasons, to attract the unemployed. Similarly, the Bharatiya Kisan Sangh, affiliated to the RSS, mobilized the community of Patels and had two million members in Gujarat by 2007. The Swami Narayan sect too had contributed to a heightened Hindu identity. This therefore was the socio-political milieu in which Narendra Modi first made his mark as a mass politician.

By 2007, Narendra Modi was also cultivating Gujarati sub-nationalism by cleverly turning the tables on his opponents. For instance, every time there were protests against constructing the

Sardar Sarovar Project (SSP) on the Narmada river, that had displaced villagers and tribals, Modi would seize the opportunity and announce a protest of his own, against the slow progress of the project in a state prone to water shortage. In speeches, he called those who opposed the dam 'five-star activists from Delhi and Bombay.'[2] He positioned himself deftly as a victim of a conspiracy, even as human rights lawyers, NGOs and members of civil society kept raising questions about the 2002 riots in Gujarat. Even that was worked to his advantage: I remember BJP members suggesting to me, tongue-in-cheek, whether certain well-known activists would do them the honour and arrive in Gujarat in the middle of the campaign? BJP strategists believed that the greater the attack on Modi by activists, the greater his popularity.

One disclosure: I wasn't *allowed* to cover the 2002 elections that followed the riots. The reason being that the identities of journalists were under scrutiny, and there were instances when television anchors were forced to 'hide' a member of the crew if he or she happened to be from the minority community. Vinod Mehta, my editor at *Outlook*, was clear that I wouldn't be sent, and I didn't argue with him.

After winning the 2002 elections, Narendra Modi held a press conference at Gujarat Bhawan in Delhi. I vividly recall that journalists on the BJP beat like me, who actually knew Modi, sat quietly as the campaign had been so polarized, while newcomers gushed and asked questions like Modiji, how did it feel to silence critics? There was no doubt that Narendra Modi was every inch the conqueror, despite the huge media critique.

Anyway, I felt it my duty to ask something beyond the 'how does it feel' kind of a question, and asked the victorious Modi about his equation with Atal Bihari Vajpayee. The answer was skilfully deflected. Then I asked him another, to which Modi replied: 'Let Saba do a one-on-one interview. But I want to tell her that I used to carry *Outlook* magazine to campaign, and I want to thank *Outlook* for the help they gave me.' That was sarcasm, the point being made that people were put off by the hostile English media. A reference was also made at the press conference about how many pollsters had got it completely wrong. That was the beginning of a divided press core in the media briefing room. The gushing loyalists and the traditional old-time journalists were both there. Either way, we were witnessing the beginning of a phenomena.

He was also right about pollsters getting the mandate wrong: Vinod Mehta had indeed commissioned one of those spectacularly wrong opinion polls and although this may seem like I am absolving myself, the protestations of a humble reporter like me were ignored. Anyway, that was the last time the once friendly pracharak responded to a question from me. I would subsequently track every campaign of his, both at the state and national level, but soon realized there was no point asking for an interview, despite the fact that I would put in a formal request each time till 2019 by when I had stopped being a political editor of a publication and functioned as an independent journalist and columnist. However, I must mention that I wasn't the only journalist who wasn't given access and, in hindsight, one must recognize that becoming aloof and impenetrable also worked well for Modi, and did in fact enhance his image.

* * *

In Gujarat, the BJP had grown organically through a network of strong leaders, each with a specific bastion. By 2007, it was apparent that Narendra Modi had succeeded in diminishing every local leader in the state—Kashiram Rana in Surat, Suresh Mehta in Kutch and, of course, Keshubhai Patel, the ex-chief minister. It soon became public knowledge that no minister in the Modi set-up really counted, as the files were eventually cleared by the chief minister.

Even more interesting to my mind was the manner in which Narendra Modi distanced himself from the VHP in particular, and sections of the RSS. It is in fact well chronicled that relations between Modi and the VHP leader Pravin Togadia soured soon after the 2002 riots. The section of the RSS that had opposed his rise were also ignored and they would eventually back some of the dissidents from the BJP. The reason: the RSS was said to be apprehensive of its ex-pracharak who refused to pander to their demands for favours; but then as chief minister, Modi was also furthering the ideological agenda efficiently.

In Gujarat, he evolved a system of governance that operated through a loyal group of bureaucrats, a method Narendra Modi continues with in Delhi. The question I therefore asked in 2007 was this: did the obliteration of other power centres mean that some of the cadres would refuse to work for him during the Assembly polls? I remember asking a few insiders who said that it would be a case of cutting the nose to spite the face. With the BJP out of power at the Centre, Gujarat was RSS' safest and most ideologically significant bastion. Besides, Modi was by then the main fundraiser for the party at the national level and therefore, at the time of elections, all saffron forces would indeed unite in Gujarat.

I would write in a story in 2007[3] in which I said, 'If Modi does indeed return with the same monster majority he today commands in the Gujarat assembly, there is no doubt he will cast his eye on the BJP throne in Delhi.' I do take credit for being prescient in my assessment, years before Modi headed to Delhi.

* * *

The campaign that began in the autumn of 2007 was fascinating. While listening to Chief Minister Narendra Modi's speeches in the 2007 campaign, one could've been forgiven for thinking that the 'Republic of Gujarat' had declared war on what he called the 'Delhi Sultanate'—how Gujarat doesn't spread its hands for alms before Delhi; Gujarat has so much money that he has locked it up, so that no one can touch a rupee that is meant for the welfare of his people; how he is the chowkidar, not the ruler of Gujarat; the guardian of Gujarat's prosperity and so on and so forth.[4]

That is what Modi told voters in rally after rally. When the man spoke, the urban middle-class Gujarati listened, enthralled. At a rally in Ahmedabad, the preceding speaker described him as 'hamara mard mukhya mantri' [our He-man chief minister]. I remember Modi entering the stage like a gladiator and roaring: 'Let there be a contest between Delhi and Gujarat,' and the crowd had roared back in excitement.[5] 'I tell Delhi, don't take a rupee from Gujarat and Gujarat will not take a rupee from you.' He followed it up with his achievements in the spread of irrigation and electricity in Gujarat, of his state having the highest growth rate in Asia, and more in a similar vein.

By 2007, many Gujaratis had elevated Narendra Modi to a demigod status. He was their messiah who would rid them of poverty, backwardness and every ill which made them feel less privileged than those who lived and ruled in New Delhi. And no one believed in his invincibility more than those who continued to oppose him unequivocally. I remember Gagan Sethi, an

Ahmedabad activist who'd worked amongst displaced Muslims in 2002, telling me, 'We may make Modi the villain and feel nice about it. But we have to accept that he has addressed that underbelly of Gujarati Hindu society. Modi has created his own cadre that is loyal to the leader.'[6] Achyut Yagnik, the political analyst called the phenomenon, 'Moditva', as the next phase of Hindutva personified in an individual.

Meanwhile, even as Narendra Modi was surging forward, there were certain BJP leaders in Saurashtra and in central Gujarat who were openly working with the Congress to topple him. In 2007, I met Somabhai Patel, the MP from Surendranagar who, after spending forty-seven years in the Jana Sangh, BJP and VHP, called Modi a 'fake Hindu'. In every speech, he made it a point to expose his ex-colleague and at times he went to the extent of attacking Modi's personal life. The aggression of Somabhai somehow pointed to the rage of a man who had been rendered redundant.

Simultaneously, the helplessness of the Congress party in the face of Modi became starkly apparent to me for the first time during the 2007 elections. The party that was in power at the Centre had no narrative of its own to offer in the state, and was piggybacking on the strength of BJP dissidents. Years of BJP rule in Gujarat, preceding even Modi's tenure, had somehow sapped the Congress. Take, for instance, the story of Ahmed Patel who was one of Sonia Gandhi's closest advisers till his death on 25 November 2020. Back in the Eighties, Patel was a popular Lok Sabha MP from Bharuch in south Gujarat and rarely identified as a Muslim. But an orchestrated RSS campaign reduced his standing in popular perception as a Muslim leader and effectively ended his Lok Sabha career (he would subsequently prefer the safer Rajya Sabha route to Parliament).

Yet, if viewed from the prism of pure numbers, the Congress's vote share in Gujarat always stood at around 40 per cent, and this even when the state was ruled by the BJP. (In the 2017 state polls, it was 41.5 per cent.) But once Modi appeared on the scene, India's oldest political party was unable to offer a viable counter-narrative to cross the gap. Back in 2007, the Congress claimed to be fighting the poll on the basis of arithmetic and anti-incumbency. For instance, it gave some tickets in Saurashtra to BJP dissidents; there were also some hard-core riot accused who fought as independents, but with the covert support of the Congress party. The idea, they said, was to take advantage of divisions in the cadre of BJP-VHP-RSS.

Therefore, it was in Gujarat that the Congress first came up with the formula of 'soft Hindutva', a decade before Rahul Gandhi went hopping from temple to temple in the 2017 Gujarat Assembly polls. But in the end, all of it came to naught and Narendra Modi won comfortably.

* * *

By the end of 2007, Narendra Modi had established himself as one of the most important figures in contemporary Indian politics. He was self-made, and in many ways, a loner. There are many examples in Indian politics of powerful political figures who chose to stay single—J. Jayalalithaa, Mayawati, Mamata Banerjee, and Naveen Patnaik. Modi stood apart from them because many of them ran parties that were said to be built around themselves. Historically, the BJP was deemed to be a party which was opposed to the culture of a cult figure; but eventually Modi would make the party bend to the will of 'The Leader'.

After the 2007 elections, I stayed on in Ahmedabad to work on a cover story that profiled Narendra Modi. I spoke to many people who were said to be close to him, party colleagues and other old associates, and the picture I got was of a solitary man— someone who chose to eat alone; didn't entertain any relatives, however close; wasn't emotional, except when faced with a large and live audience as a political leader.

By then, he had not only evolved a carefully cultivated sartorial style, but also gestures to suit his public persona. He was described as a workaholic, and election or no election, he apparently worked from 6 a.m. to 11 p.m. Arun Jaitley would tell journalists, 'Modi is like a man possessed when it comes to work. He's in office till 11 p.m.' The projection of him being a tireless worker began during his tenure in Gujarat.

The chief minister of Gujarat was creating his own cult of personality. For instance, he had authored an anthology of poems titled, *Aaankh Aa Dhanya Chhe* (Blessed Are These Eyes), and in a poem called, *Gaurav* in the collection, he had written:

I am proud that I am a human, and I am a Hindu Every moment I experience I am big, wide, I am Sindhu

If the verse was a reflection of the man, then the inner world of Narendra Modi was about *Narendra Modi*. He was a solitary reaper in Indian politics with a following that would be the envy of global cult leaders.

His home, I was told, spoke volumes about the man. I spoke to a few people who were invited in and was told that he lived frugally. He employed a personal staff of just three who lived at his official residence—a cook, and two peons. When the cook was on leave, one of the peons cooked dinner for the man who had become the toast of corporate India. Even the three official assistants at the time—O.P., Tanmay and Dinesh—who screened all the calls (when journalists like me would call for an interaction), didn't apparently have access to his living quarters. An old-timer in the Gujarat BJP, considered close to Modi, told me, 'People used to get hurt as they were unable to establish a personal rapport. But we realized he did not mean any ill. That is just the way he is.'

Modi therefore did not and does not enjoy a durbar. While many politicians run huge, rambling establishments with a retinue of staff, live-in retainers, and a regular flow of hangers-on, Modi is stoic at home and after a long day at work, prefers to eat his dinner in solitude.

The 2007 election was the first where I spotted 'Modi masks'. At every rally, there would be groups of boys bobbing up and down with Modi masks on their faces. He was not just a mass leader; he was acquiring dimensions where he appeared to be the central object of a cult.

* * *

I was back covering another Assembly election in Gujarat in 2012. By then, the UPA regime in Delhi led by Dr Manmohan Singh was caught in a swamp of corruption cases; Modi in contrast was going from strength to strength. If in 2007, the rest of India saw the curious sight of his fans bobbing up and down in Modi masks, five years later the props for the mega Modi show had changed. Swami Vivekananda was the motif of the campaign, and Modi was now showcased as a philosopher-thinker.

In rally after rally of his 'Vivekananda Yuva Vikas Yatra', the build-up to his arrival was akin to that of a rock star. I remember how a posse of stormtroopers on motorbikes, wearing bright orange t-shirts with Swami Vivekananda's image printed on the front and that of an introspective Modi on the back, stood behind a rath. Near the entrance of the stage, there were several youngsters dressed like Vivekananda in ochre robes and turbans. While girls with pots balancing on their heads waited in the wings, there was live singing on stage. Then the drums rolled, the sound technicians amped up the sound to a thumping beat and a loud cry of Bharat Mata Ki Jai went up, the crescendo building to a pitch!

Narendra Modi walked briskly to the stage, accepted a few turbans as mementoes and wasted no time in delivering a knockout performance. Animated faces looked up at him in anticipation. He made the familiar comments about 'Delhi Sultanate' and then posited himself as a man of peace, who loved his *praja* (people). He then evoked Swami Vivekananda. 'Has anyone tried to turn Swami Vivekananda's dreams into reality? The six crore Gujaratis will do that.' Modi used the technique of engaging his audiences by throwing questions at them: 'Do you get water now?' Yes, cried the crowd. 'Do you get electricity?' Yes. 'Are your roads any good?' Yes, yes! 'Are you happy and satisfied?' The crowds cried in unison—YES! 'But I am not. I imagine greater things and greater progress for my people,' he said at the climax of the performance. Real rock star stuff.

Naturally, he won. I would write a cover story for *Outlook*[7] comparing Modi to the Great Wizard Lord Voldemort of the *Harry Potter* series: in the cult novel, Voldemort is a wizard of great powers, referred to as He-Who-Must-Not-Be-Named. He sets out to conquer both magical and real worlds, and it is his personality and ambition that are pivots for the drama in the seven books that had an entire generation riveted. Harry Potter and his friends, teachers and helpers are relatively ordinary folk reacting to events unleashed by the Wizard, also named the Dark Lord.

In the real world, I chose the symbolism of magic to describe the moment when Narendra Modi would be viewed as a man who wove his spell to conquer Gujarat thrice and then cast his eye on the rest of India. By then, the Gujarat Congress seemed quite terrified of Modi; so much so that it was advised that they should not even utter his name unless strictly necessary and keep the campaign low-key and only about 'arithmetic'.

It was precisely during that phase when large sections of the media became spellbound by the possibility of not how, but when Modi would conquer India next. The middle classes were also getting in the thrall of the idea of a strong leader in an age of drift; the young saw Modi as dynamic; the women were overtly enamoured of this big, strong man; according to statistics reeled out by the BJP, even Muslims in Gujarat and elsewhere had come to accept him as the inevitable leader. A lot of it was hype that I did not believe.

There was of course much debate about this groundswell—many dismissed it as a structured narrative systematically being promoted by an overzealous band of Modi loyalists. In my view, Modi epitomized the union of Hindutva with big corporate funding that would propel him forward. Even before his candidature as prime minister was in the ring, loyalists fought for him on internet forums and media. In the cover story dated 31 December 2012, I wrote:

We must, therefore, ask now if 'Modi as PM' is an audacious plan by a man who has successfully executed many in the past? Even the prospect of Modi attempting it is significant and has become the single issue around which the politics of other players would be determined. Even if he were to remain the Man-Who-Could-Not-Be-PM, he will still make us stop in

our tracks, watch the man make his attempt and wonder if he
would stop and turn the history of the nation.[8]

By then it was clear that Modi's application to any task was
commendable. An army of human rights lawyers, activists and
riot victims had failed to get him in any legal trouble in spite of
a central government seen to be hostile towards him. No Indian
leader had faced the kind of censure he did in the West (when
many countries denied him visas), and still build a reputation
as a wealth generator of Gujarat. A section of India was by then
anxious to see him become the prime ministerial candidate.

* * *

In Narendra Modi's carefully constructed scheme of things, the
next step would be to rein in his ideological family. It was now
the question of handling the opposition within. His victory in
2012 certainly enhanced his power, but sections in the RSS, and
rivals in the BJP, were not going to allow him to walk over them.
They would fight back, mostly by hanging on to the coat-tails of
JD(U), the NDA ally, whose chief minister Nitish Kumar had
threatened to break rank on the issue of Modi. In 2013, Nitish
had said that if Modi was nominated as the prime ministerial
candidate, he would walk out of the alliance with the BJP (they
ruled Bihar as part of an alliance). He made Modi a prestige
issue and did indeed craft a separate path in the 2015 Bihar
Assembly elections where he fought in an alliance with the RJD,
led by Lalu Prasad Yadav; but he ditched Lalu by 2017, and
aligned with the BJP again (in violation of the people's mandate,
let it be said). Still, Modi certainly had the last laugh vis-à-vis
Nitish Kumar.

The BJP had begun a journey from 'untouchability' to acceptability in the era of Atal Bihari Vajpayee when the wishes of allies were given primacy, and figures like Nitish were ministers at the Centre. On the other hand, 'Project Modi' involved turning the Vajpayee model on its head. It placed a strong figure at the pivot, in an era when the BJP had actually become a viable force and the opposite pole to the Congress for regional parties to converge around. There were therefore strong arguments within the party against Narendra Modi being the prime ministerial candidate.

But by then there were also strong arguments being made within the BJP to turn inwards, and rebuild its core under a leader whom the cadres saw as charismatic. This was amply clear at every BJP gathering where Modi seemed to be the only chief minister to inspire the rank and file. Huge chants would go up every time he entered a meeting. His contemporaries, like Shivraj Chouhan in Madhya Pradesh, Manohar Parrikar in Goa, or Raman Singh in Chhattisgarh, just didn't have that carriage within the party. Modi, quite simply, had prevailed in the mind of the cadre.

There was another more complicated reason put out by some BJP strategists.[9] One argument was that in the age of a squabbling leadership, Modi was the only leader who could manage the backroom moves of the RSS. The Gujarat chief minister was also pushed to the forefront like a subaltern hero, the OBC who had little time or patience for the machinations of the Brahmins who dominated the RSS. Again, insiders argued that Modi was the right man to disrupt the carefully ordered world of the traditional elites in the brotherhood of the Sangh.

The favoured leader of a section of the RSS has always been Nitin Gadkari, who served as BJP president from 2010 to 2013 (that's when Rajnath Singh began another term). He is from Nagpur, where the RSS headquarters is located, and a Maharashtrian Brahmin, like most of the Sangh leadership has traditionally been. He is also a successful businessman in his own right and considered an efficient minister who had held the portfolio Road Transport and Highways since Modi's ascent in Delhi.

On top of it all, Gadkari is a very amiable personality, who would never make others feel threatened, be they non-BJP individuals or sections of the RSS. Every now and then his name is circulated in certain media circles as the man the RSS would like in the top spot, but this is wishful thinking as Modi has taken the BJP from coalition to single party rule and enabled the RSS to implement its agenda.

In the summer of 2013, after a victory in the 2012 Assembly polls, Narendra Modi visited New Delhi to attend the Chief Ministers Conference. The BJP was gearing up for the 2013 elections and was scouting for the right man to head its national election campaign committee. The president of the party, Rajnath Singh, had apparently made an offer to his predecessor, Nitin Gadkari, who turned it down and, in retrospect, he was wise in doing so. That Narendra Modi would be ideal for the position was a foregone conclusion, for the party cadre had made up their minds that they wanted him as the leader.

As mentioned earlier, Narendra Modi had assiduously built the cult of personality, prevailing over cadre, leaders, region and ideology. He had succeeded in juxtaposing Gujarat's development with his own image. He'd worked both on the notion of Hindu identity and regional pride, at times positing Gujarat against the Centre. In his home state of Gujarat, he had taken complete control over the state apparatus, running the state through bureaucracy. Most significantly, he presented himself as the wealth generator in a 'vibrant' Gujarat, a leader committed to basics—bijli, sadak, paani. A leader who meant business, in a post-liberalisation, increasingly urbanized, aspirational India.

* * *

It would eventually be L.K. Advani who would challenge the projection of Narendra Modi as prime minister.[10] He believed that after Atal Bihari Vajpayee, he was the seniormost with a stellar record of service to the party. But by then, the RSS had made many categorical statements about the need for the old guard to retire and younger faces to take leadership positions. Advani was however playing with a weak hand as he had been the prime ministerial face in the 2009 general election (there were no other contenders then) and faced an ignominious defeat.

It is said that to understand one's own limitations is a sign of great wisdom. In 1996, L.K. Advani had displayed it by putting aside his own ambitions to project Atal Bihari Vajpayee as the prime minister-in-waiting. In that regard, Advani was different from several other politicians in that he had once let go to conquer. But in 2013, he failed to do so and this time the party did not rally around him. Nitish Kumar's unhappiness with the Modi candidature helped him make an argument, but it was not adequate in the face of the support within the BJP for the chief minister of Gujarat.

Personally, I have some sympathy for L.K. Advani. Through his Ram rath yatra he had catapulted the BJP on to the national stage. But if the goalpost had shifted along the way to becoming prime minister or short of that, remaining in perpetuity the pre-eminent leader of the party, he was indeed thwarted. For the man who put the party on the political map, the final battle came too

late. Advani was eighty-six when he tried to take on Modi and be
the prime ministerial candidate himself.

He lost. By then, Modi supporters and a dominant section
of the RSS–BJP cadre were arguing that they could rebuild from
the core if they were 'left alone' to follow the Man from Gujarat,
who in their view was set to conquer India. They put forth their
argument as follows: L.K. Advani's primacy in the BJP was over,
and the allies should not dictate the direction of the party that was
not in power at the Centre, and therefore, the timing couldn't be
better for the 'coming' of Narendra Bhai. On 14 September 2013,
Narendra Modi was declared the prime ministerial candidate by
BJP president Rajnath Singh. It was an official decision taken
by the party's Parliamentary Board—Modi's anointment had
become inevitable. This time round, Rajnath Singh took great
care to facilitate Modi's elevation. The same RSS that had once
instructed Rajnath to clip Modi's wings, now directed him to
announce Narendra Damodardas Modi's candidature for prime
minister of India.

* * *

Meanwhile, India was witnessing a significant change in its body
politic: in April 2011, the anti-corruption movement initiated by
Anna Hazare and the subsequent emergence of Aam Aadmi Party
(AAP) in 2013, had inflicted serious damage to the Congress party,
and the prime ministership of Dr Manmohan Singh. UPA II had
been mired in one corruption scandal after the other.

I remember the large gathering of protestors at Delhi's iconic
Ramlila Maidan—working men, women, the aged, and even
schoolchildren who had arrived in hordes to support the seventy-
six-year-old Anna Hazare from Maharashtra. I would write about

the presence of RSS cadre in the movement[11] (when Yoga guru, Baba Ramdev also brought in large crowds). In hindsight, one can say that it was a good strategy for the RSS to be involved in the Anna movement as it helped hollow out the Congress.

Yes, the AAP as a party (not rooted in the RSS) would emerge two years later, and did strike roots in Delhi. But nationally, the beneficiary of the loss of face for Congress was the BJP, that soon came to be led by Narendra Modi. To use his vocabulary, the empire or the 'Delhi Sultanate' was shaking. It was time to push forward.

The Aam Aadmi Party's emergence had another significant ripple impact that also worked to shore up the candidacy of Narendra Modi. With its pitched campaigns against India's most powerful business groups, AAP was seen as disruptionist and anarchic by those who were at the top of the economic pyramid. The Congress was anyway sinking; it therefore made sound business sense to generously back the campaign of Narendra Modi, the business-friendly chief minister. Therefore, the arrival of AAP and the fall of the Congress proved to be catalysts for cementing the alliance of big business with Hindutva.

In my view, one of the amazing feats that Narendra Modi has achieved is not just winning elections, but in controlling the narrative around it. For instance, no one in the media has seriously asked his party to account for the source of funds for India's most expensive election campaign that would roll out in 2014—according to expenditure accounts submitted with the Election Commission, the BJP spent over 700 crores.

Meanwhile, the pace quickened by the end of 2013, after the results to the Assembly elections in Rajasthan, Madhya Pradesh and Chhattisgarh were announced. The BJP had won all three states, while the AAP got twenty-eight out of seventy seats in

Delhi, where its leader, Arvind Kejriwal, defeated the three-term Congress chief minister Shiela Dixit in her seat. By then it was clear that the Congress party was marching towards an imminent eclipse—it did not have state leaders of reckoning who could stem the tide, nor organized cadres to fight against the tide. The Manmohan Singh government wasn't just lame duck, it was swiftly becoming a 'dead duck'.

In retrospect, one can spilt hairs over whether the BJP's performance in three states was the result of Modi having been declared the prime ministerial candidate. But what was undeniable was that after the announcement, the Sangh Parivar cadre had united and were back to being a fighting-fit unit after a decade in the doldrums. As 2013 ended and 2014 began, it was certain that the BJP would be the single largest party in the next Parliament.

* * *

In the interim, the capitulation and surrender by L.K. Advani was abject. On 7 April 2014, at the release of the BJP's manifesto for the general elections, the octogenarian said that he didn't remember feeling such 'joy' during the sixteen elections that he had witnessed in his lifetime. He then went on to endorse precisely what he had bitterly fought over the past year: 'I don't remember ever such an advantageous reaction to the announcement of a PM candidate . . . the campaign that followed has been unprecedented.'[12]

The day Advani made his speech and the 2014 manifesto was released, the BJP headquarters in Delhi looked different. A sort of food court with various stalls was put up: pizzas, the famous Gujarati khakra and dhokla, dosa, Banaras ki chaat and so on. The traditional jalebi-samosa fare served by the BJP was passe, and I saw the imprint of Gujarat efficiency (and love for snacking!) in the manner in which the 2014 manifesto release was mounted.

The campaign had no complexities; there was complete clarity. It was Modi Shining, Modi Smiling, Modi Descending, Modi Coming, Modi Waving, Modi Speaking and so on. Brand Modi was all around us, on TV, in billboards, on radio, in print ads. The phrase 'presidential style' would be somewhat inadequate to describe the contours of the campaign to those who did not see it for themselves.

Henceforth, in parts of India where the party's election symbol, the lotus, had no recall value, Modi, the name and the face would subsequently be recognized.

Equally, it must also be said that Narendra Modi had opened up great possibilities even for those who weren't formally part of his ideological fraternity but supported the idea of a strong Hindu leader. Besides the traditional BJP apparatus, independent groups of professionals took time off to work on the campaign. A month ahead of verdict day, there was slow acceptance in Delhi's corridors of power that the Modi blockbuster was clicking on the ground. I would do stories about how the Congress had stopped disbursing party funds in some parts of India anticipating defeat; something that was actually a breach of trust between the party and candidate.

While influential Congress leaders were privately conceding defeat, key players in the Modi campaign had moved to the next stage of planning: how Modi would perform *when* (and not *if*) he became prime minister.

Atal Bihari Vajpayee too was a leader around whom a personality-based campaign was built. But he did not canvass to the extent that Modi did. At the most, he would address two rallies at the peak of an election campaign; Modi addressed four to five a day, many in far-flung areas where the BJP had no expectations of winning a seat. In his entire campaign, Modi adopted a two-pronged approach: on the one hand, he used modern technology to reach voters; at the same time he gave great importance to mass rallies.

It is worthwhile to examine the process behind the huge production that would be the Modi campaign. At the heart of the planning was, obviously, Narendra Modi himself, while the Leader of the Opposition in the outgoing Rajya Sabha, Arun Jaitley, and national treasurer of the BJP and head of the party's 'Information Communication Campaign Committee', Piyush Goyal, played the role of facilitators and enablers of the campaign. Sushma Swaraj did at one point suggest making the campaign more about the party than a personality, but no other voice endorsed it.

The campaign then moved at various levels. Inside a building in Lodhi Estate in New Delhi, professionals brainstormed about getting the pitch right for each stage of the electoral battle. They looked into details about getting traction in social media platforms, jingles and slogans. Then came the formal release of advertisements that were created by a subsidiary of the advertising agency, O&M. But as mentioned before, at each stage, various loyalists were consulted.

Meanwhile, Narendra Modi chose to operate out of Gandhinagar in Gujarat, and did not set up camp in Delhi. He also began a process of toning down his 'Gujaratiness' and adopting a less distinctive regional persona. While working on this book, I established contact with some Gujarati NRIs now back in India, who are part of the prime minister's inner circle. These are individuals who prefer to keep their identities private, but throughout the 2014 process gave valuable inputs to Modi and have fascinating insights into the process. They told him that the Gujarati language, sweet as it is, does have a certain degree of bluntness that can come across as abrasive if not softened at the edges when the same thought is delivered in Hindi. There is also a great tradition of satire and humour in Gujarati that does not easily translate into Hindi, they told Modi. Since Narendra Modi was proficient in Hindi too, the idea was to just get him to approach the delivery of speeches with subtle changes in style. These were significant inputs that went into polishing up the image of the prime ministerial candidate.

Indeed, much has been written about Modi's early life in Vadnagar, his RSS background in several biographies, but what hasn't been recorded are his dealings with affluent and sophisticated Gujaratis both in India and abroad. According to a reliable source, who knows Modi well, 'All the biographers completely missed out on how he reached out to Westernized people also, and how they opened a window for him to things he wasn't aware of. People have mostly focused on his RSS background.' The same source also reiterated that contrary to the image of his having limited interests, Modi is curious about things that he didn't have access to as a young man. For instance, he was sent Pakistani plays, Western classical music, and representations of other cultures, and he showed interest in learning about all these things.

One of the Gujaratis who was willing to speak on record was the London-based Manoj Ladwa, a graduate from the London School of Economics, solicitor, and expert on FDI, who had parked himself in India for six months to alter several key facets of the 2014 campaign. Ladwa was then a member of the Labour Party in the UK, and chairman of its community engagement forum, and therefore had some exposure to political messaging. As founder of the MLS Chase Group plus India Inc, Manoj Ladwa headed a group called RAM (Research, Analysis, Messaging) which operated out of BJP's headquarters at Delhi's Ashoka Road, whose brief was to 'amplify the Modi message', and provide the required spin to spokespersons across the country.

The way the group operated during the 2014 campaign evokes media outreaches in Western democracies as depicted in TV shows and movies. Through the night, twelve to fifteen researchers followed the news, and by 8 a.m., there would be a summary of what could possibly be said; by 9.30 a.m., this would be gone over with spokespersons; in another hour, a briefing would be prepared, and by 1 p.m., an audio bridge to 250–300 spokespersons in different states would be linked up. Most critically, the content was carefully calibrated and it was all done under the supervision of an NRI Gujarati.

Although Manoj Ladwa's closeness to Modi slowly became apparent, certain details of what he contributed remain unknown. For instance, it was Ladwa who was instrumental in changing the colour of the lotus, BJP's election symbol, from saffron to black-and-white, a change effected without much ado in February 2014. The reason for this subtle, albeit significant change was executed to make the symbol appear 'exactly' the way voters would see it on the EVMs (Electronic Voting Machines). I remember asking Ladwa the obvious question about two famous Gujaratis, M.K. Gandhi and Narendra Modi, being so different, and pat came his reply, 'If we must look at things from such a perspective, then we can say that after Gandhi, Modi was the first Indian leader who had such a connect with the diaspora across the world, both Gujarati and non-Gujarati.'

Additionally, there were other operations functioning with military precision during this famous campaign. One such was led by a one-time public health expert who had worked in the UN, called Prashant Kishor, who has now become an expert in managing elections. Modi had actually read a paper written by Kishor on malnutrition and asked him to help reduce it in Gujarat, but Kishor got swept into brainstorming and was asked to strategize for the 2012 Assembly elections in Gujarat. For 2014, Kishor set up a non-profit group called Citizens for Accountable Governance (CAG), which began work on several aspects of the campaign, yet again reminiscent of US presidential elections. At the height of the campaign, CAG consisted of fifteen chapters in the states, over a thousand full-time members and a lakh volunteers. It was, however, smartly pitched as an independent advocacy group that was helping in operations. Some of the key innovations of the 2014 campaign, such as 'chai pe charcha' (a discussion over tea), and the brief mobilization of a force of student volunteers were executed by CAG. In 2015, Kishor parted ways with Prime Minister Modi and went on to establish a new outfit called the Indian Political Action Committee (I-Pac) and began working with the then chief minister of Bihar, Nitish Kumar, during the 2015 Assembly elections (in which the BJP was defeated). He would subsequently emerge as one of the most successful political consultants who has worked with the TMC, YSR Congress, AAP, DMK and TRS. Currently, he is working on the ground in his home state Bihar to create his own political movement and claims to have given up doing consultancy for others.

* * *

The 2014 campaign was mounted on an unprecedented scale in the history of Indian elections using modern technology, data and resource. One of the most useful tools was the realtime poll tracker, one of the firsts to be used by any political party in India on this scale. It would periodically throw up possible results to examine the status of a BJP win or defeat in specific constituencies, using a scientifically determined sample size. The results were shared with a select core group involved with the campaign strategy, and was later regularly studied by Modi (who is good with reading data) as it apparently helped him decide where and when he needed to make certain interventions to mobilize greater support for the BJP.

For instance, it was particularly useful in Uttar Pradesh, the state with the largest number of Lok Sabha seats at eighty, that was being handled by Narendra Modi's key aide, Amit Shah (later BJP president and currently Home Minister). The UP election unfolded in the backdrop of a vitiated atmosphere, post the Muzaffarnagar riots (August–September 2013). In the aftermath of the violence, which was the result of a clash between the dominant Jat peasant caste and Muslims, the region was simmering. In the election season, it helped certain BJP candidates who kept up an openly communal discourse on the ground.

On his part, Narendra Modi was promising *acche din* (good days), that became synonymous with a strong leader fixing the rot and corruption. But the electoral calculus in Uttar Pradesh would only fall into place if communities could be united over their traditional caste differences that had kept regional parties such as the SP and BSP in power in the state over the last two decades. Modi's task therefore was to break their voter blocs and transfer support to the BJP. He would eventually manage this spectacularly with the BJP winning seventy-one of the state's eighty seats and getting 42.5 per cent of the vote share.

The voting in Uttar Pradesh was staggered for over a month in six phases, beginning on 10 April 2014, when ten of the eighty constituencies went to polls, and culminating in the last phase on 12 May when Varanasi, Narendra Modi's constituency, also voted.

If Modi's rhetoric changed along the course of the campaign, it was also in response to the poll-tracker that suggested that a certain momentum could be gained by playing on the old, existing fault lines. By now, Narendra Modi needed no tutorials and was skilled enough to both fly high and strike low.[13]

Therefore, in this very presidential run for the prime ministership, there were enough references to issues that polarize on religious lines. It wasn't as if this was new to electioneering in India, but it was overtly vicious in 2014, carried out by sundry foot soldiers, cadre and candidates on the ground. Minorities were referred to in derogatory terms by candidates of the BJP, including incendiary remarks by senior leaders while referring to a rival as a 'Pakistani agent', or talking of the 'pink revolution' (the alleged promotion of slaughterhouses and meat export by the Congress-led UPA).[14] There was no doubt that the prime minister-in-waiting had the knack of pressing every subliminal button, yet it was also undeniable that Modi's packaging was seemingly about development and growth, and the 'diversions', as one strategist called them, took place in particular venues.

The basic plan was simple: one individual rising like a colossus should prevail over differences of caste that was usually the first reference point for voters' choice in the big Hindi heartland states of Uttar Pradesh and Bihar. The campaign was also intended to ride rough-shod over traditional arguments of secularism and communalism, even socialism and capitalism. It was intended to surmount the conventional wisdom that the BJP could never cross a certain threshold. The campaign, the most expensive, the most lavish, and the most ambitious in India's electoral history, would succeed beyond the wildest expectations of its early promoters.

* * *

Narendra Modi carefully chose Varanasi, the holy town on the river Ganges, to make his all-India debut outside Gujarat and thereby, the site of his intervention into national politics. Once the announcement was made, Varanasi transformed into a BJP fortress with RSS cadres descending from across India. I made three trips to Varanasi in the course of the campaign: in late March, six weeks before polling day, I found the party's local office buzzing as late as at 8 p.m.

I met Prem Kapoor, the treasurer for fourteen districts of Uttar Pradesh, and we began a conversation. 'There has been an unprecedented pouring in of money into our coffers by almost everybody,' he said and was supported by Laxman Acharya, then the president of the Varanasi BJP, who said that contrary to reports of some 'hot-headed' cadre picking fights with AAP volunteers (as Arvind Kejriwal had decided to fight Modi in the city), the real truth was that the people of Varanasi felt privileged that they had been given the responsibility of electing a potential prime minister of India. He then reeled out the statistics. 'We are well prepared. There are five video vans across the town, 15–20 cadres for each booth in the city.'

The ancient city of Varanasi, which is believed to promise the dead release from the cycle of life-and-death, was swamped during the election. Every street corner in the city, where space has to be negotiated between devotees, cows and food vendors, had Narendra Modi's face plastered on walls and hoardings. Laxman Acharya broke my reverie to interject and informed me that most of the hoardings across the city were put up by 'well-wishers', who believed that they had a duty towards the incumbent prime minister. (Modi himself would come in early April, and eventually didn't have to make too many visits to claim Varanasi.)

In another room, the IT cell was active. It was headed by Sailesh, who had left the Indian Navy eight months ago to work for Modi's campaign. He said that their main job was to facilitate the net registration of BJP voters and fine-tune booth management. He also pointed out that the Congress was hardly visible in Varanasi, and only the AAP was beginning to show bursts of energy for the battle on social media.

The core of the campaign in Modi's chosen constituency was about asserting a strong Hindu identity even though Modi was speaking about *ache din* (good days). I was repeatedly told that Lord Shiva, the primary diety of Varanasi, had Himself descended in Kashi. Ashok Pandey, one of the state BJP spokespersons said, 'We will chant Har Har Modi! He is an avatar of Shankar bhagwan (Shiva). He is therefore standing from every seat in India.'

Towards the end of the campaign, the national BJP team booked an entire floor in Varanasi's Surya hotel in the cantonment area where the roads are broader than the narrow alleys of the old city. The hotel became the venue for press conferences which were held each day by BJP spokespersons. Next to the Surya Hotel is the Radisson Hotel, where the big guns of the party moved in. Amit Shah stationed himself there, as did journalists Swapan Dasgupta and Ashok Malik who were expected to explain the Modi phenomenon to foreign journalists. After his election campaign in Punjab, Arun Jaitley also came over for a few days.

On one of my several trips to Varanasi that year, I sought time with BJP leaders and ended up being there when the top leaders sat down for lunch. As always, Arun Jaitley was playing host, even as Amit Shah joined in. I didn't know the latter well, but took the opportunity to ask him about his assessment of his party's prospects. Amit Shah sounded supremely confident and said that after decades, both arithmetic and chemistry were working in tandem for the BJP in Uttar Pradesh. 'We shall sweep this election,' he said. Meanwhile, I stuck my neck out and told him that I had predicted around fifty-five seats for the BJP in UP and was being critiqued for 'over estimating' the party.

The results came on 14 May 2014. India had shifted on its axis and elected an individual who projected himself as a Supreme Leader. Narendra Modi became prime minister following an emphatic mandate that marked the end of coalition politics. Even within his own party and the Sangh Parivar, he had prevailed, leaving little room for those quiet manoeuvres and petty skirmishes that had been part of the BJP growth trajectory. The pitch turned into reality. Modi created the wave, with media and advertising acting as force multipliers, and then he deftly rode to a stupendous victory.

* * *

Atal Bihari Vajpayee was sworn in on a morning at a modest ceremony at Rashtrapati Bhawan. It was evening by the time Prime Minister Narendra Modi took the oath of office at a blockbuster ceremony at the same venue on 26 May 2014. Journalists like me with the necessary passes had to arrive hours in advance on a hot day where temperatures were hovering around forty degrees. More than 4000 guests watched Modi take oath a little after 6 p.m., including heads of state from the SAARC region; the then prime minister of Pakistan, Nawaz Sharif; captains of industry; heads of religious orders; editors; MPs; and some Bollywood stars. As the sun began set against the backdrop that defines the Republic, Narendra Modi claimed the evening as his own. History was being made and I was standing there watching it.

34

BJP INC.

On 18 February 2018, Prime Minister Narendra Modi inaugurated the new national headquarters of the BJP on Deendayal Upadhyay Marg, between New Delhi Railway Station and the crowded ITO crossing.

The BJP was the first party to have complied with the Supreme Court order that political parties shift their offices from Delhi's Lutyen's Zone: the construction on the 1.7 lakh square feet plot was completed in a record one-and-a-half years. The BJP president Amit Shah swiftly declared that the new office is bigger than the office of any political party in the world.

It's like a swank, shiny headquarters of a mega corporation and very different from the old headquarters in a rambling bungalow.

The media briefing room matches the best auditorium in Delhi and on my first trip, I was delighted to note that the many women's restrooms were as good as any in upmarket hotels. (This marked a real change from most political party offices in the Lutyen's Zone.)

The building itself is an imposing structure on top of which several flags of the party flutter. It has Wi-Fi, an underground parking, conference halls, a studio, a reading room and naturally, the best communication facilities that make it possible for apparatchiks to keep in touch with all the state units.

It is a monument to the BJP's successful enterprise in the country since the 2014 win built on unlimited funds and by perpetuating a leadership cult, spreading the social base and the Hindutva ideology. There is a large map of India in the compound. On the map, the party's geographical spread is coloured saffron and the only strip left white is the stretch along the coast from Kerala to Bengal in the east. I see that map as the statement of intent of the Modi–Shah-led BJP: there are just a few territories left to conquer, though the job has mostly been done.

At this point, the BJP seems poised to be as central to the nation's future as the Congress was to the past. As mentioned in the beginning of the book, its coffers are full, and there is no parity left in political finance.[1]

Consider this data. When the UPA came to power in 2004, the Congress got 58 per cent of receipts given to national parties. But by 2013–14, the last year of UPA II, the Congress's share was down to 39 per cent, while the BJP's jumped to 44 per cent. The point this reinforces is that money moves in the direction of political power, and by 2013, big corporates where shifting donations from Congress to the BJP.

After a decade out of power at the Centre, in 2014, according to figures filed with the Election Commission, the BJP spent 712 crores on the campaign. As mentioned earlier, it was by far the most expensive campaign in the country's history.

In 2019, according to figures given to the Election Commission, the BJP spent Rs 763 crore (ADR data). The 2019 campaign in India was according to estimates put out by the New Delhi based Centre for Media Studies, the most expensive in the world. Their report released to the media said all parties together spent aroung Rs 500 billion that came to $7 billion while the 2016 US Presidential and Congressional race in which Donald Trump was elected cost $6.5 billion.

It's shocking data in a country where millions remain malnourished and earn salaries that add up to a few dollars a month.

If election costs are spiralling up it's because the BJP, now the pre-eminent party in the country, is the bull pushing up costs in social media, advertising, cadre support and transportation.

In 2014, the irony was that after a decade in power, the Congress, mid-campaign, stopped sending funds to candidates in some parts of India who were expected to lose.

Senior leaders told me so with explicit details.[2]

Having ruled over India for most of its history, and presided over the opening up of the Indian economy, the only explanation for the Congress being broke was that fund collection was carried out in such a haphazard and ad hoc manner that there was no real accountability.

The BJP today, with a more centralized fund collection than during the Vajpayee era, puts the money where its mouth is. Under Modi's dispensation, the funds are available for every expansion plan, every audacious move that involves getting members of other parties to join in or of bringing small regional players around, if required, for government formation. In the age of Narendra Modi, the BJP gets its money from the same corporate conglomerates, but it is used for political work. As costs of elections in India have only spiralled, when there is money on the table, it creates incentives for individuals to join and/or support a particular party. And unlike what happened during the Congress era and even the Vajpayee era (refer to chapter on Pramod Mahajan), in the age of

Modi and Shah, large amounts are unlikely to be pilfered down the line, as it apparently happens with other parties, regional and national, that operate with funding from business (hence the phrase, 'crony capitalism').

According to the updated Annual Audit Report filed with the Election Commission of India, dated 8 February 2018, the BJP's income in 2016–17 soared to 1,034 crores (from 570 crores in 2015–16). And according to an analysis by ADR, the BJP has shown the highest income of ₹1,917.12 crore during the financial year 2021–22.

History has indeed been made and is underwritten with a lot of money.

EPILOGUE

ENGINEERING SOCIETY AND COUNTRY: THE FUTURE

The first time I saw a press conference held by Amit Shah during the 2014 campaign, there was a digital monitor behind him that kept ticking and showing changing numbers even as he spoke. He was showcasing the number of new members joining the party during its growth trajectory in 2014. They appeared to be joining by the seconds. That presser will always be etched in my memory as a statement on the Amit Shah maximalist approach to politics.

In 2023, Shah, right hand man to Modi, is just fifty-nine years old. The home minister of India is without doubt the individual who oversees party expansions and electoral management and is at the core of the project that has already changed India. In Gujarat, where his journey with Modi began, he excelled in breaking established power centres. For instance, he is credited with being behind the end of the Congress stranglehold on the cooperative sector that is powerful in the state. Since his move to Delhi, he has gone from strength to strength and must be credited with putting the apparatus in place to claim UP for Modi in 2014. After this, there has been no looking back for the party in the state.

Here again, it is necessary to emphasize and is mentioned earlier in the book, that as organization general secretary of the BJP in the late 1990s, it was Modi who always stressed the importance of booth management and constant training of cadres for this. Now that he has been in mass politics for over two decades, it is Shah who does the work and has created the party apparatus in vital states conquered in the Modi era. Shah worked on UP for a year, starting 2013, putting structures into place, so that the momentum Modi was getting could be translated into victories on a ground where the BJP had not been in power since 2002.

Earlier in 2010, when the UPA was in power at the Centre, Shah was charged with ordering fake encounters in Gujarat and imprisoned for a short period.[1] When out on bail, he was not allowed to enter the state of Gujarat and that is the time I first met him as he would frequently be present in the room Arun Jaitley was allotted as Leader of the Opposition in Parliament. Since that room was a regular haunt of journalists, Shah could hold forth with clarity on political assessments down to every detail.

The cases against him were dismissed by a CBI special court in December 2014, months after Modi became PM. In 2021, his son Jay Shah became the secretary of the Board of Control for Cricket in India (BCCI), a powerful post in a cricket-crazy country. If anyone knows about the ruthless application of power in this age, it is Amit Shah.

Modi is in 2023 seventy-three years old. Were he to win and serve a third term, he would be seventy-eight by the time of the 2029 general election. Anything is possible, but if we were to look for successors, theoretically, there is the much younger right-hand man, Amit Shah, and there is too now the CM of UP, Yogi

Adityanath, just fifty-one in 2023. Of course, the RSS would have a say in the anointment of any successor but after the PM, the UP CM is the campaigner who is the most in demand in the BJP.

The head of a religious order in Gorakhpur, UP, Yogi Adityanath has also created narratives that have resonated outside the state such as the template of 'bulldozer rule'. Briefly, this means that properties of individuals considered 'troublemakers' would be bulldozed without the due process of law. The so-called troublemakers could be protestors (mostly from the minority community) so there is an ethical problem with what has unfolded in the state.[2]

It is also interesting to note that in recent months, as the world sees visuals of the war in Gaza, authorities in Israel also use bulldozers in the occupied West Bank and Gaza to demolish homes of individuals believed to be protesting, resisting or supporting Hamas. UP is also known for what are called 'fake police encounters' in which criminals or political opponents can be killed without the due process of law. 'Bulldozer rule' and police encounters are the template in the nation's most populous state.[3]

In India, we now do live in an age when shocking levels of polarization against the large Muslim minority has become acceptable. In such a psychological atmosphere, the bureaucracy goes along with the political will, the police take intimidatory action and the lower judiciary can become pliant. The bulldozer template has actually been a hit with BJP members and supporters and has only been challenged at the level of opinion but not on the ground; Madhya Pradesh, which shares a long border with UP, sought to replicate the model in the state during the reign of Shivraj Singh Chouhan and there have been demands made in other BJP-ruled states to also apply 'bulldozer justice', whatever that oxymoron means.

On the face of it, the BJP's leadership triangle appears to be now settled on the personas of Narendra Modi, Amit Shah and Yogi Adityanath, but politics is full of unexpected twists and turns. The three at the top currently are all ideological hardliners, impatient with due process and thereby un-democratic in their instincts even as they have prevailed through an electoral democracy. India has actually turned out to be a remarkably fertile terrain for authoritarian figures who emerge through the ballot box. This is mapped quite thoroughly by some of the best international scholars on India besides many who continue to work inside the country.[4, 5] There is an excellent book on the process of authoritarianism coming through by ballot box across the world by Harvard professors Steven Levitsky and Daniel Ziblatt titled *How Democracies Die*.[6] In the book they write, 'Democracies may die at the hands of elected leaders who subvert the very processes that brought them to power'.

Yet, we must note that the BJP is winning elections because more people across sections of society are voting for it. As noted, the social outreach of the Sangh Parivar is phenomenal and there have, in recent times, been books and studies that have elaborated on the large presence of OBCs and Dalits in the party structure.[7, 8] The promotion of small caste groups, their gods and sacred spaces, an outreach that seeks to include them into the expanding fold, is all done very methodically by the RSS.

Yet, it would still be a generalization to say that the BJP has become a party of the subaltern communities and the stereotype of high-caste Brahmins from the RSS headquarters in Nagpur running the BJP project is now entirely false. For if we look at the data, even after the 2022 UP election, where the BJP was praised for its social outreach, 43 per cent of the BJP MLAs come from the upper castes—who represent only one-fifth of the state society, whereas its OBC MLAs form one-third of its MLAs when OBCs are about 50 per cent of the state population.[9]

Among the upper-caste MLAs of the BJP, 17 per cent are Brahmins and 16 per cent are Rajputs, whereas these two groups are estimated to represent about 10 and 7 per cent of the society of UP, respectively. There is, of course, no Muslim representation although they constitute 20 per cent of the state population.

Likewise, if we see the national council of ministers of the Modi regime in Delhi, all the important portfolios are held by individuals from the upper castes though there are OBCs and Dalits holding the not-so-important portfolios. I would not include Modi himself in this analysis since he must be seen as holding an exceptional position that transcends caste. From the very beginning of his innings in mass politics, he positioned himself as a Hindu icon as opposed to a Backward Caste leader. In fact, he has often spoken of politics around caste in a way that is in sync with the RSS world view.

Indeed, it must also be noted that since acquiring a simple majority in Parliament 2014, the party has actually jettisoned the trend of anointing CMs from the backward castes and/or giving the leadership to castes that are numerically and traditionally dominant in politics of the state. The old BJP had consciously tried to do what it called social engineering, to project and build up mass politicians from OBC communities, such as the former UP CM (at the time of the demolition of the Babri mosque), Kalyan Singh and later, Modi himself.

But attaining simple majority rule in 2014 made those at the top of the BJP/RSS decision-making pyramid jettison that approach in the matter of choosing state leaders. To elaborate, in October 2014, just some months after the national mandate that made Modi the PM, the BJP came to power through state

elections in Maharashtra (then in alliance with the undivided
Shiv Sena) and Haryana, replacing regimes led by the Congress.
In both states, they would go on to choose leaders who came
from social groups that are not politically powerful or numerically
strong but from the upper castes. Both candidates came from the
RSS stable (it is an established fact that the Sangh leadership is
overwhelmingly in the hands of Brahmins).

Devendra Fadnavis, then unknown, was chosen for
Maharashtra. He is the second Brahmin to be CM of Maharashtra
(the other, Shiv Sena's Manohar Joshi, had to make way for
the Maratha leader, Narayan Rane, in 1999), a state where the
Maratha community is a dominant social group, besides Dalits
and OBCs. Currently, after upheavals and breaks with the old
Shiv Sena, Fadnavis is deputy CM of Maharashtra and remains
the main BJP figure in the large and financially significant state.

Simultaneously, in Haryana, a Punjabi Khatri (or Kshatriya,
and second in the rung of the traditional varna or caste system),
Manohar Lal Khattar, a former RSS pracharak, was chosen and
remains in power for a second term with the support of a local
Haryana party. He would be the first non-Jat CM of the state;
his reign has been marked by large caste-based protests by the Jat
community, but he remains in power with the support of non-
Jats and a small regional party led by one of the state's traditional
ruling Jat dynasts.

But the point to note is that in both Maharashtra and Haryana,
the BJP went against what I would define as the 'dominant caste
syndrome', which means choosing candidates outside of the
social group that has a large and influential voter base. The third
such choice was made in Jharkhand that the BJP would win in
December 2014, although it would lose the state in the 2019
election. It is a state that was carved out of Bihar and initially

projected as a homeland for adivasis or tribals who make up 27 per cent of its population.

Since the formation of Jharkhand in November 2000, only tribals had been CMs. That is, till 27 December 2014, when Raghubar Das from a backward caste was appointed CM by the BJP. But in the 2019 state election, the BJP would be defeated and JMM's Hemant Soren, an adivasi, is CM again in alliance with the Congress.

All three choices were unusual in all the three states and did have the consequence of making the dominant caste groups restive. Modi himself managed this in Gujarat where he replaced a Patel leadership (Modi is from a small caste group referred to as Ghanchi-Teli, which is categorized as an OBC in Gujarat). But the larger point is that once it had won a simple majority in Parliament, the BJP has been ready to make choices in keeping with the RSS's thinking about not giving a caste group veto power (if you don't have to).

Earlier, the BJP had responded to the emergence of Mandal era politics, by projecting a figure such as Kalyan Singh as CM in UP and Uma Bharti in Madhya Pradesh, both belonging to the OBC Lodh community. But we must remember that with the exception of Modi, OBC figures such as Kalyan Singh and Uma Bharati did not have smooth journeys in the BJP just as Bangaru Laxman, the sole Dalit party president, was swiftly discarded after a cash on camera scam emerged involving a not very large sum.[10]

The most significant abandonment of the policy of giving 'real' power to OBCs has been seen in UP, where Yogi Adityanath is from the forward Thakur community and he has prevailed, winning a second term in 2022. With a Brahmin leading the party in Maharashtra and a Thakur in UP, we could argue that 'real' power is still vested in the higher castes, although the BJP's support among Dalits and OBCs has increased.

The RSS ideology is committed to a post-caste era when all Hindus have united. Simultaneously, as the BJP has become a hegemonic force in the Modi era, it no longer feels the need to make such notional gestures at the leadership levels. The engineering of society that Govindacharya spoke of decades ago, now requires just symbolic representation of Dalits, tribals and OBCs while the *savarnas* or upper castes are still on top of the political pyramid in many decision-making roles.

At the same time, we must note that the BJP/RSS is very good with symbolic gestures such as appointing a Dalit president in Ram Nath Kovind and following this up in 2022 with an adivasi woman president in Droupadi Murmu. All of this counts particularly as the PM is indeed from an OBC community. We can argue about real and symbolic power sharing with backward castes and Dalits. Yet, we must note that in the history of the contemporary world, few parties have struck such deep roots in such a cross-section of society in such a short span of time as the BJP has done.

* * *

Between Vajpayee to Modi, it is not just the institutional subculture of the party that has changed, but India itself is being transformed into what many would call a majoritarian nation. The capture and consolidation of power at the hands of the BJP, with Modi at the pivot, however, remains a work in progress. If the Opposition is unable to come together and fight back and the BJP maintains its hold on power in New Delhi, in the near future I also see the transformation of the federal nature of the

Republic. This can theoretically happen through delimitation, the act of redrawing boundaries and increasing the number of seats in state assemblies and the Lok Sabha to reflect the changes in population. Currently, there is a freeze on this exercise till 2026, but logistical preparations have been undertaken to accommodate many more MPs.

A new Parliament building was inaugurated by Modi on 29 May 2023. It was a telling ceremony that appeared to be a coronation amid a boycott by the Opposition parties. *The Hindu* would write in an editorial:

> A multi-religious prayer was a part of the ceremony, but there was no mistaking that Hindu ritualism overshadowed all else. By weaving an artful tale around a Sengol, a sceptre gifted to the first Prime Minister of India by a Shaivite sect of Tamil Nadu, the current dispensation has sought to reimagine the founding principles of India's republican sovereignty. A Sengol symbolised divine right and is now installed in the Assembly of people's representatives.[11]

The date of the inauguration also fell on the birthday of Vinayak Damodar Savarkar, the ideological founder of Hindutva. But beyond the symbolism, the new building also brings us to the question of delimitation of constituencies that could reduce the power of the southern states and linguistic minorities vis-à-vis the nation's Hindi speakers. The BJP currently has 38 per cent of the popular vote, but 55 per cent of Lok Sabha seats because the strike rate and percentage of support in its Hindi heartland bases has been impressive. The new Parliament has been constructed as part of the Central Vista in New Delhi which is very much a Modi project through which the PM seeks to leave his imprint in the nation's capital. It has a Lok Sabha chamber that can seat many more MPs up from the 543 in the current House.[12]

In 2026, whosoever is in power at the Centre can unroll the delimitation exercise where new constituencies will be created on the basis of population growth. It would certainly be in the BJP's interest to see that the number of seats in the Hindi belt states, where the party has its bases, should increase while those in the South could potentially decrease. Going by demographic trends, in the future, therefore, we can certainly project that the Lok Sabha seats of UP, currently eighty, could go into triple digits. Indeed, all states that have not been able to control population growth, which is typical of poorer and less developed regions, would get more seats in Parliament, and eventually a greater proportional share in the Rajya Sabha. The details of what precisely could and would happen are not clear, but it would happen in the not-so-distant future. It's a very tricky issue. There has been a freeze on the number of parliamentary constituencies since 1971 and the concept of equal number of voters in all seats is likely to open a Pandora's box.

That is because there is a clear and present danger confronting the better-performing states such as Tamil Nadu, Kerala, Telangana and Karnataka that would lose out in such an exercise as they have done well on population control and the overall development indices. The political leadership in the southern states says that delimitation would create a big north–south rupture because such an exercise penalizes them for successful family planning and population control while those states that fail to perform would get even greater national clout.

As it is, for some years now, many South Indian states have been flagging the issue of distribution of the central pool of tax revenue in the Finance Commission. The grounds for concern have been that the southern states collect more taxes and have brought down their populations, but the larger shares of revenue go to the poorer states with bigger and expanding populations. In other words, the South Indian states have been arguing that they are already 'penalized' for controlling the pace of population growth.[13]

Meanwhile, all Opposition-ruled states complain that in the Modi era, their fiscal autonomy is being systematically curtailed through cess and taxes and by attempting to turn states into implementation agencies of central schemes that are pitched and structured around the persona of Modi.[14]

The potential recasting of the federation of India as we know it is therefore a ticking time bomb. All the evidence points to this being factored into the long game that the BJP/RSS plays. In an affidavit filed in the Supreme Court, the Central Public Works Department (CPWD) has said that the new Lok Sabha chamber could accommodate 876 members and 1224 during joint sessions as it would be three times the size of the current chamber in Parliament. In the same affidavit filed in the context of suits against the Central Vista project, the CPWD stated that the current strength of the Lok Sabha has remained at 545 as per the delimitation carried out after the 1971 census but 'it is likely to increase substantially as the freeze on the total number of seats is only till 2026'.[15]

Meanwhile, although there is a swanky new Parliament building, the institution per se has been functioning in a very ad hoc manner since the Covid-19 pandemic struck. As multiple catastrophes began in 2020, from the pandemic to the reverse migration and consequent economic mayhem caused by the lockdown, the institution that should have been debating it all became virtually defunct.[16] In 2020, the budget session of Parliament was ended abruptly on 24 March after panic over an MP being in contact with a Covid-19 patient. The year of the greatest crises confronted by independent India would, therefore, also be the year of the suspension of Indian Parliament—following which even the state assemblies stopped meeting.

The Executive, principally the PM, would implement decisions through the bureaucracy without any parliamentary oversight, bad for the health of any democracy. The argument that this was the outcome of the pandemic does not hold true as countries around the world with healthy democratic traditions had responded with virtual sessions or with limited meetings by groups of elected representatives or a hybrid of both. India adopted the Westminster model of the United Kingdom. The British Parliament functioned through hybrid debates, although then PM Boris Johnson had landed in hospital with Covid-19.

In India, meanwhile, some Opposition MPs did raise the issue of convening Parliament and some suggested that at the very least, meetings of parliamentary standing committees should be allowed to take place virtually. The response was that proceedings need to be confidential and, therefore, cannot be online for fear of a security breach.

The law mandates that the break between sessions of Parliament should not exceed six months. When Parliament did reconvene in September 2020, it would be to witness epic scenes in the Rajya Sabha when the Upper House passed the controversial farm laws through a voice vote without agreeing to a division of votes, which the government was not in a position to win.[17] Eventually, these laws would have to be taken back by the government in November 2021 following a year-long agitation, and that too was done without any parliamentary debate.

It is also worth noting that seven sessions of Parliament till August 2022 were cut short on one pretext or the other.

Broadly, the government also used the post-Covid era to block the numbers and access of media-persons inside Parliament. Debates demanded by the Opposition have not been allowed on any subject the government does not wish to discuss, while important laws and amendments are passed without discussion or as money bills to avoid scrutiny in the Rajya Sabha where the BJP does not have a majority as it does in the Lok Sabha. This is precisely how the 2019 amendment to the PMLA was brought in and is now being challenged in the Supreme Court.[18] The data is quite shocking: during the life of the 17th Lok Sabha elected in 2019, 115 bills were introduced, of which eighty-five saw no consultation prior to introduction. Almost nine out of ten bills introduced in Parliament were done so with zero or incomplete consultation.[19]

In 2023, the budget session of Parliament was another disaster as the government refused to allow a debate or create a Joint Parliamentary Committee (JPC) to discuss the scandal engulfing the Adani Group after a US-based short-seller produced a damning report. The PM refused to answer any questions about his alleged proximity to Gautam Adani. Instead, in a speech in Parliament, he said that he had the love of 140 crore Indians.[20]

He basically implied that he was so wildly popular that he did not have to answer direct questions. Meanwhile, large chunks of critical speeches made by Opposition figures such as Rahul Gandhi were expunged from parliamentary records. By the time the session ended, Rahul had been disqualified as an MP because of a sudden decision by a court in Gujarat that held him guilty and gave him the maximum sentence of two years for a defamatory remark he had made in 2019 about the name Modi, with the reference extending to businessmen Lalit Modi and Nirav Modi, who fled India after being mired in cases of mega corruption.[21]

Rahul Gandhi's parliamentary membership was restored only after the Supreme Court put on hold his conviction in the 2019 defamation case.

The camaraderie and civility between ruling party and Opposition members is now missing in an institution that relies on actions based on good faith and tradition. It has instead become an arena for gladiatorial contest and the institution does not function in the manner in which it was intended to. The bricks and mortar are there, but the soul of parliamentary democracy—that demands the cut and thrust of debate—has left the building.

* * *

Between the eras of Vajpayee and Modi, the BJP has lost most of its significant allies even as it has orchestrated splits in many parties. The Modi-era BJP has a political strategy that plans mergers and acquisitions of other political parties with the ruthlessness of a booming business that intends to become a monopoly. In the Modi era, partnerships with regional parties have been used to give the national party a toehold and a chance to eventually dominate, through psychological and financial means.[22]

To elaborate, examine the 2020 Bihar election where the BJP encircled its own ally Nitish Kumar, leader of the JD(U) and CM of the state, in order to ensure that the national party gets a larger number of seats. In that election, the BJP actually outdid its well-honed technique of financing independents and splinter parties to wean away small sections of various voter blocs to max the first-past-the-post game with the minimum numbers of actual votes.[23]

In the 2020 Assembly election, the BJP/RSS cadre occupied the structures of another party, in that instance, the Chirag Paswan-led LJP, in order to bring down the votes of its partner, the Nitish Kumar-led JD(U). So not only does the BJP now run itself, but it's also in the business of running other parties, like empty shell companies or ghost corporations.[24]

The breakaway faction of the Shiv Sena led by Eknath Shinde could be another empty shell corporation, at the mercy of the BJP. There was an attempt to do so with the AIADMK in Tamil Nadu in the post-Jayalalithaa scenario (the former CM passed away in 2016), but it's yet to yield electoral dividends and currently the AIADMK has split from the BJP. Still, the AIADMK does have assets that can be used to make it a vehicle for the national party's own ambitions in the future. When the BJP cannot make it on its own, the strategy is to win over individual influencers inside various political parties and slowly steer the course in a direction that is useful to them.

The strategy frequently works but can also boomerang as it has with Nitish who would again dump the BJP in August 2022 to join hands with the RJD and remain CM.[25] To recap briefly, Nitish Kumar would become CM of Bihar in 2005 in alliance with the BJP, but in 2014, he would part ways with the national party on the issue of the projection of Modi as PM. He would contest the 2015 Bihar election in alliance with Lalu Prasad Yadav's RJD that would win comfortably, but in 2017, Nitish would abandon that alliance on the issue of 'corruption' and take his MLAs to form a government with the BJP. Obviously, it was an uneasy relationship as in the next election, the 2020 state poll, the national party would encircle its own CM face. Less than two years later, Nitish would return to the arrangement with the RJD, that is believed to be formidable in terms of its caste/community reach.

It is the Bihar coalition government that has released the data from a caste census that puts the state's backward castes at 63.14

per cent. The national Opposition has picked up the issue of caste for 2024 and would be hoping it would threaten the BJP's carefully nurtured 'Hindutva unity' exercise. Yet, there are contradictions in the Opposition front even on the caste issue.

Still, the departure of Nitish from the NDA after the old Shiv Sena and the Akali Dal in Punjab (they left over the farm laws) all reveal that although the BJP of the Vajpayee era was India's most successful coalition, the current BJP runs a solitary path seeking a hegemony that threatens its own allies. Any partner that remains with the BJP can become cash-rich but would eventually become politically redundant. The business plan—of taking over smaller parties—is now built into every political and ideological strategy. The BJP is after all propped up by a motivated cadre, and all that money, besides the psychological momentum given by helpful media narratives. It works on incremental gains and long-term strategy. Even in a state such as Odisha where it has not come to power, it has emerged as the main Opposition replacing the Congress.

The inner dynamics of the BJP have also shifted and other personalities that are seen as not kowtowing to the Modi–Shah combine have been cut to size. State satraps and former CMs of the party are barely tolerated and all the decisions, even pertaining to the states, are now made in New Delhi.[26]

Also revealing has been the saga of Nitin Gadkari, an old-world gentleman politician in the Modi council of ministers. He has been a good performer in the various ministries he has been given charge of, particularly Roads and Transport. He was also seen to be a favourite of the RSS that is headquartered in his home town, Nagpur. Both Gadkari and Fadnavis are from Nagpur and are Deshashtha Brahmins, as is the RSS chief Mohan Bhagwat.

Gadkari is likeable and has friends across the political spectrum, but it is precisely these traits that could make the current national leadership of the BJP suspicious of him. There has always been the theory in political circles that in the event of the BJP not getting a simple majority and needing to create a Vajpayee-style coalition again, Gadkari, and not Modi, would be the candidate of the RSS. Therefore, he has been diminished and was in 2022 dropped from the Parliamentary Board, the highest decision-making body in the BJP. From being a party of multiple power centres, today's BJP clicks its heels and salutes the leader.

Certainly, the BJP has a saleable leader in PM Modi. But the PM as a brand has been built up on mega campaigns and media narratives that discredit all other leadership, regional or national. But worship of one individual can be the means to a certain end of attaining a more uniform India. The Sangh Parivar is ideologically motivated to spread its reach across the length and breadth of the country and to do so is acquiring as many assets as it can. The stated goal is One Nation One Poll all centralized under One Leader.[27] Given the fact that India is a multilingual and multi-cultural nation, the BJP has already done remarkably well, but there are parts of India that still shun the party.

It is a party that ultimately seeks to transform India and towards that end, the cadre is actively engaged in creating multiple saffron storms. This has been seen explicitly and clearly during the recent Ram Navami and Hanuman Jayanti seasons that come each year in April. A very thorough study has been released titled 'Routes of Wrath: Weaponizing Religious Processions' that examines communal violence during Ram Navami and Hanuman Jayanti in April 2022. The foreword to the study is written by retired Supreme Court judge Rohinton Nariman (whom Arun

Jaitley would call the finest legal mind in the Supreme Court), and it has been edited by senior advocate Chander Uday Singh.

The report gives detailed insights into events that unfolded in eleven states where the processions sought to create an intense polarization. As each chapter ends with a media narrative that followed the tension and/or clashes, the report notes that ironically, the loyal broadcast media often spins a story slant of 'Hindus in danger' after aggressive processions deliberately chose to pass through areas where Muslims live in large numbers. The modus operandi of processions deliberately triggering clashes is as old as Partition and the 1947 Independence of India. What is noteworthy is that we as a nation are willfully allowing that to happen in contemporary times.

In 2022, in the city where I live, Delhi, there were clashes in the Jahangirpuri locality in the western part of the city when a Hanuman Jayanti procession organized by the VHP and Bajrang Dal went off the permitted route and attempted to hoist flags with Jai Shri Ram written on them on a mosque in block C. There are several recordings of members of the procession carrying weapons such as knives, swords, bats and a few country-made pistols even as they raise provocative and insulting slogans.

There was intense media coverage of the Jahangirpuri clashes in the national capital that were taking place just two years after full-blown riots had devastated the north-east part of the city. Yet, the data shows that between 2022 and 2023, the numbers of procession on Ram Navami in Delhi has only increased from twenty-two to fifty-two, that is more than double. Likewise, the numbers of processions of Hanuman Jayanti rose from seventeen in 2022 to fifty-one in 2023.[28] For the first time in my life, I saw a Hanuman Jayanti procession. This too is part of the saffron storm created by the BJP and its foot-soldiers.

As we have seen in the earlier chapters of this book, the BJP calibrated its ideology carefully through positions on the Ram temple at Ayodhya, the movement for which had actually catapulted the party on the national stage. Now, the journey has come full circle as the brand-new temple at Ayodhya—on the site where a medieval mosque was demolished—will be inaugurated on 22 January 2024. It is a date that shall now also define India, and the Ram temple is the greatest symbol of this new nationhood.

In conclusion, we can say that between the reigns of Vajpayee and Modi, the BJP as a party and the country it now rules from New Delhi, has changed. The change fundamentally lies in a greater acceptance of the ideas of Hindutva as opposed to the values enshrined in the Indian Constitution and a move towards centralizing power in the hands of Prime Minister Narendra Modi, be it in his own party or in the country. Some aspects of the change seem irreversible, but politics in India can always throw up new trends and a few surprises.

NOTES

Introduction

1 Sandipan Baksi and Aravindhan Nagarajan, 'Mob Lynchings in India: A Look at Data and the Story behind the Numbers', NewsLaundry, 4 July 2017. https://www.newslaundry.com/2017/07/04/mob-lynchings-in-india-a-look-at-data-and-the-story-behind-the-numbers (accessed 16 November 2023).

2 Walter K. Anderson and Shridhar D. Damle, *The RSS: View to the Inside* (Penguin Viking, 2018).

3 Anuj Kumar, 'Bhupendra Singh Appointed Uttar Pradesh BJP Chief', *The Hindu*, 25 August 2025, https://www.thehindu.com/news/national/other-states/bhupendra-chaudhary-appointed-uttar-pradesh-bjp-chief/article65809517.ece (accessed 16 November 2023).

4 Saba Naqvi, 'UP Polls: The Vanished Minority Voter', *Deccan Herald*, 14 February 2022, https://www.deccanherald.com/opinion/up-polls-the-vanished-minority-voter-1081295.html (accessed 16 November 2023).

5 Divya Trivedi, 'Missing Voters', *The Hindu Frontline*, 10 April 2019, https://frontline.thehindu.com/cover-story/article26781550.ece (accessed 16 November 2023).

6 'Missing Voters App Trending as Polls Approach', *The Hindu*, 19 March 2019, https://www.thehindu.com/elections/lok-sabha-2019/

missing-voters-app-trending-as-polls-approach/article26583861.ece (accessed 16 November 2023).

7 'Akhilesh Yadav Hits Back at Election Commission after Being Asked to Submit Proof of Deletion of Voter Names', *Hindustan Times*, 28 October 2022, https://www.hindustantimes.com/cities/lucknow-news/akhilesh-yadav-hits-back-at-election-commission-after-being-asked-to-submit-proof-of-deletion-of-voter-names-101666981385362.html (accessed 16 November 2023).

8 Sheryl Sebastian, 'Voters' Names Won't Be Deleted from Electoral Rolls Without Giving Them Prior Notice: Election Commission Tells Supreme Court', LiveLaw, 9 August 2023, https://www.livelaw.in/top-stories/voters-names-wont-be-deleted-from-electoral-rolls-without-giving-them-prior-notice-election-commission-tells-supreme-court-234828 (accessed 16 November 2023).

9 Udit Misra, 'Explained: How Electoral Bonds Work, and Why They Face Criticism', *Indian Express*, 7 April 2022, https://indianexpress.com/article/explained/explained-how-electoral-bonds-work-why-criticism-78 (accessed 16 November 2023).

10 'In 2019–20, BJP got 75% of poll bonds sold, Congress just 9%', *Indian Express*, 10 August 2021, https://indianexpress.com/article/india/in-2019-20-bjp-got-75-per-cent-of-poll-bonds-sold-congress-just-9-per-cent-7446293/ (accessed 16 November 2023).

11 Udit Misra, 'Explained: How Electoral Bonds Work, and Why They Face Criticism', *Indian Express*, 7 April 2022, https://indianexpress.com/article/explained/explained-how-electoral-bonds-work-why-criticism-78 (accessed 16 November 2023).

12 'Analysis of Donations Received by National Political Parties, FY 2020–21', 15 July 2022, ADR, https://adrindia.org/content/analysis-donations-received-national-political-parties-fy-2020-21-0 (accessed 16 November 2023).

13 P. Sainath, 'Forbes, India and Pandora's Pandemic Box', 16 April 2021, People's Archive of Rural India (PARI), https://ruralindiaonline.org/en/articles/forbes-india-and-pandoras-pandemic-box/ (accessed 16 November 2023).

14 https://www.ft.com/content/a01c8930-005d-48e1-8a52-cbd0850cbbff

15 'Adani Group: How the World's 3rd Richest Man Is Pulling the Largest Con in Corporate History', Hindenburg Research, https://hindenburgresearch.com/adani/ (accessed 16 November 2023).

16 Padmakshi Sharma, '95% Of Political Leaders Investigated by CBI & ED Are Opposition Leaders : Non-BJP Parties Tell Supreme Court', LiveLaw, 24 March 2023, https://www.livelaw.in/top-stories/95-of-political-leaders-investigated-by-cbi-ed-are-opposition-leaders-non-bjp-parties-tell-supreme-court-224653 (accessed 16 November 2023).

17 Bhanu Pratap Mehta, 'Pratap Bhanu Mehta Writes: By Upholding PMLA, SC Puts Its Stamp on Kafka's Law', *Indian Express*, 29 July 2022, https://indianexpress.com/article/opinion/columns/pratap-bhanu-mehta-by-upholding-pmla-sc-puts-its-stamp-on-kafkas-law-8057249/ (accessed 16 November 2023).

18 Vittal Shastri and DHNS, 'Money Looted from 40% Commissions Will Be Used by BJP to Buy Opposition MLAs in Karnataka: Rahul Gandhi', *Deccan Herald*, 17 April 2023, https://www.deccanherald.com/elections/karnataka/money-looted-from-40-commissions-will-be-used-by-bjp-to-buy-opposition-mlas-in-karnataka-rahul-gandhi-1210514.html (accessed 16 November 2023).

19 Harikishan Sharma, 'PM's Office Declares Assets of Ministers, Modi Donates Share in Only Property Owned', *Indian Express*, 9 August 2022, https://indianexpress.com/article/india/pms-office-declares-assets-of-ministers-modi-donates-share-in-only-property-owned-8079009/ (accessed 16 November 2023).

20 Bharat Bhushan, 'Why the Enforcement Directorate Is Being Seen as a Political Weapon', *Business Standard*, 1 August 2022, https://www.business-standard.com/article/opinion/why-the-enforcement-directorate-is-being-seen-as-a-political-weapon-122080100110_1.html (accessed 16 November 2023).

21 Dhananjay Mahapatra, '122 Sitting, Ex-Legislators Facing Laundering Cases, ED Tells SC', *Times of India*, 10 August 2021, https://timesofindia.indiatimes.com/india/122-sitting-ex-legislators-facing-laundering-cases-ed-tells-sc/articleshow/85196602.cms (accessed 16 November 2023).

22 Utkarsh Mishra, 'ED Raids Rajasthan Cong Chief; Summons Gehlot's Son', Rediff.com, https://www.rediff.com/news/report/ed-raids-

rajasthan-cong-chief-summons-gehlots-son/20231026.htm (accessed 16 November 2023).

23 'Narrow View: On the Supreme Court's PMLA Verdict', *The Hindu*, 29 July 2022, https://www.thehindu.com/opinion/editorial/narrow-view-the-hindu-editorial-on-the-supreme-courts-verdict-on-the-prevention-of-money-laundering-act/article65695526.ece (accessed 16 November 2023).

24 Supriya Sharma and Arunabh Saikia, 'How the Modi Government Has Weaponised the ED to Go after India's Opposition', Scroll.in, 5 July 2022, https://scroll.in/article/1027571/how-the-modi-government-has-weaponised-the-ed-to-go-after-indias-opposition (accessed 16 November 2023).

25 Harikishan Sharma, 'Govt Data: FEMA, PMLA Cases Triple in First 3 Yrs of NDA-II versus NDA-I', *Indian Express*, 26 July 2022, https://indianexpress.com/article/india/govt-data-fema-pmla-cases-triple-first-3-years-nda-govt-8051284/ (accessed 16 November 2023).

26 Deeptiman Tiwary, 'Since 2014, 4-Fold Jump in ED Cases against Politicians; 95% are from Opposition', *Indian Express*, 21 September 2022, https://indianexpress.com/article/express-exclusive/since-2014-4-fold-jump-in-ed-cases-against-politicians-95-per-cent-are-from-opposition-8163060/ (accessed 16 November 2023).

27 Saba Naqvi, 'Faith and Food in BJP's Big UP Win', *Deccan Herald*, 10 March 2022, https://www.deccanherald.com/election/uttar-pradesh/faith-and-food-in-bjps-big-up-win-1090004.html (accessed 16 November 2023).

28 Saba Naqvi, '2022 Assembly Polls Sound Death Knell for BSP', *Tribune India*, https://www.tribuneindia.com/news/comment/2022-assembly-polls-sound-death-knell-for-bsp-379541 (accessed 16 November 2023).

29 https://twitter.com/rautsanjay61/status/1491108614345728001?s=20&t=0oBMggIybKx487lFl1Q3-A (accessed 16 November 2023); Manoj Dattatreya More, '17-20 rebels are on ED radar, Eknath Shinde too, says Sanjay Raut', *Indian Express*, 23 June 2022, https://indianexpress.com/article/cities/pune/17-20-rebels-are-on-ed-radar-eknath-shinde-too-says-sanjay-raut-7986012/ (accessed 16 November 2023).

30 Shemin Joy, 'Only 23 Convicted in over 5,400 PMLA Cases Filed by ED in 17 Years, Government Tells Parliament', *Deccan Herald*, 25 July 2022, https://www.deccanherald.com/national/south/only-23-convicted-in-over-5400-pmla-cases-filed-by-ed-in-17-years-government-tells-parliament-1129964.html (accessed 16 November 2023).

31 Prem Shankar Jha, 'What Drives the Modi Government's Systematic Onslaught on AAP?' *The Wire*, 4 August 2016, https://thewire.in/politics/drives-modi-governments-systematic-onslaught-aap (accessed 16 November 2023).

32 Saba Naqvi, 'Sowing the Wind, Reaping the Whirlwind', *Tribune India*, https://www.tribuneindia.com/news/comment/sowing-the-wind-reaping-the-whirlwind-47748 (accessed 16 November 2023).

33 'ED Arrests Delhi Health Minister Satyendar Jain in Rs 4.8-cr Money Laundering Case', *Indian Express*, 31 May 2022, https://indianexpress.com/article/cities/delhi/satyendar-jain-arrested-enforcement-directorate-7944211/ (accessed 16 November 2023).

34 '34 West Bengal Legislators Went from TMC to BJP – only 13 of them got tickets to contest the election for the saffron party', *Business Insider*, 25 March 2021, https://www.businessinsider.in/politics/elections/news/bjp-has-given-tickets-to-only-13-out-of-34-west-bengal-legislators-went-from-tmc-to-bjp/articleshow/81689750.cms (accessed 16 November 2023).

35 'Narada Sting Case: Mukul Roy Questioned by CBI, Suvendu Adhikari by ED', *Indian Express*, 11 September 2017, https://indianexpress.com/article/india/narada-sting-case-mukul-roy-questioned-by-cbi-suvendu-adhikari-by-ed-4838781/ (accessed 16 November 2023).

36 'SSC Job "Scam": Rs 20 Crore Seized as ED Raids Houses of Bengal Ministers Partha Chatterjee, Paresh Adhikary, others', *Indian Express*, 23 July 2023, https://indianexpress.com/article/cities/kolkata/ssc-job-scam-rs-20-crore-seized-as-ed-raids-houses-of-2-bengal-ministers-others-8046500/ (accessed 16 November 2023).

37 'ED Raids Tejashwi Yadav's Delhi House in Land-for-Jobs Case', *Economic Times*, 10 March 2023, https://economictimes.indiatimes.com/news/politics-and-nation/ed-raids-tejashwi-yadavs-delhi-house-in-land-for-jobs-case/articleshow/98535255.cms (accessed 16 November 2023).

38 'Fearing Poaching by BJP, Jharkhand CM Hemant Soren Moves MLAs
    to Chhattisgarh', Firstpost, 30 August 2022, https://www.firstpost.
    com/politics/fearing-poaching-by-bjp-jharkhand-cm-hemant-soren-
    moves-mlas-to-chhattisgarh-11146231.html (accessed 16 November
    2023).
39 'Yediyurappa may Face ED Probe after IT Raids on His Close Aide',
    Statesman, 13 October 2021, https://www.thestatesman.com/india/
    yediyurappa-may-face-ed-probe-raids-close-aide-1503017454.html
    (accessed 16 November 2023).
40 K.V. Aditya Bharadwaj, 'Complaint to ED about BSY, family fuels
    rumour mills', The Hindu, 11 June 2021, https://www.thehindu.
    com/news/national/karnataka/complaint-to-ed-about-bsy-family-
    fuels-rumour-mills/article34784935.ece (accessed 16 November
    2023).
41 Devesh Kapur and Milan Vaishnav, Costs of Democracy: Political
    Finance in India (Oxford University Press, 2018).
42 Nagarjun Dwarakanath, 'Yediyurappa Resigns as Karnataka Chief
    Minister, Breaks Down, Says "People Lost Trust in Us"', India Today,
    26 July 2021, https://www.indiatoday.in/india/story/yediyurappa-
    resigns-as-karnataka-chief-minister-1832681-2021-07-26 (accessed 16
    November 2023).
43 Shelly Mahajan and Maj. Gen. Anil Verma (Retd), 'Transparency
    and Accountability in Political Funding', https://adrindia.org/sites/
    default/files/Transparency%20and%20Accountability%20in%20
    Political%20Funding_ResearchPaper_ADR%20V2.pdf (accessed 16
    November 2023).
44 Krishnadas Rajagopal, 'PMLA amendments | Money Bill Verdict
    Holds the Key', The Hindu, 28 July 2022, https://www.thehindu.
    com/news/national/scs-pmla-judgment-future-of-several-conclusions-
    depends-on-outcome-of-larger-bench/article65690860.ece (accessed
    16 November 2023).
45 Newly Purnell, 'Two Years Ago, India Lacked Fast, Cheap Internet—
    One Billionaire Changed All That', Wall Street Journal, 5 September
    2028, https://www.wsj.com/articles/two-years-ago-india-lacked-fast-
    cheap-internetone-billionaire-changed-all-that-1536159916 (accessed
    16 November 2023).

46 'India Is Now the Number One Country in the World in Mobile Data Consumption, Tweets NITI Aayog CEO, Amitabh Kant', Firstpost, 23 December 2017, https://www.firstpost.com/tech/news-analysis/india-is-now-the-number-one-country-in-the-world-in-mobile-data-consumption-tweets-niti-aayog-ceo-amitabh-kant-4271687.html (accessed 16 November 2023).

47 Ayushi Kar, 'Poor Show End of American Internet, India-China Contribute to 50% of World's Data Traffic', *The Hindu BusinessLine*, 4 December 2022, https://www.thehindubusinessline.com/info-tech/end-of-american-internet-india-china-contribute-to-50-of-worlds-data-traffic/article66222842.ece (accessed 16 November 2023).

48 'Delhi Riots: "Pro-Hindu" WhatsApp Group Promoted Enmity on Religion Ground, Says Charge Sheet', *New Indian Express*, 7 October 2022, https://www.newindianexpress.com/cities/delhi/2020/oct/07/delhi-riots-pro-hindu-whatsapp-group-promoted-enmity-on-religion-ground-says-charge-sheet-2207003.html (accessed 16 November 2023).

49 https://www.newslaundry.com/bloodlust-tv (accessed 16 November 2023).

Chapter 1: The Vajpayee Morning

1. Swapan Dasgupta, 'Perilously Yours', *India Today*, 30 March 1998.

Chapter 2: The Journey

1. L.K. Advani, *My Country My Life* (Rupa & Co., Delhi, 2008).
2. 'Hindu–Muslim Problem a Creation of Politicians', *India Today*, Nanaji Deshmukh in an interview to the author, 11 August 1997.
3. Saba Naqvi, 'BJP's Changing Colours: Is it for Real', *India Today*, 5 February 1998.

Chapter 3: The Mask

1. Nalin Mehta, *The New BJP: Modi and the Making of the The World's Largest Political Party* (Westland 2021).

Chapter 4: The Open House

1. In an interview with the author, *India Today*, 27 April 1998.

Chapter 5: The Householder

1. Saba Naqvi, 'Cats, Dogs and Disneyland', *India Today*, 20 April 1998.
2. ibid.
3. Saba Naqvi, 'The Enigma of Vajpayee: He Stands as the Archetypal Representative of What A Kinder and Gentler BJP Can Be', *Times of India*, 16 August 2018, https://timesofindia.indiatimes.com/blogs/et-commentary/the-enigma-of-vajpayee-he-stands-as-the-archetypal-representative-of-what-a-kinder-and-gentler-bjp-can-be/ (accessed 16 November 2023).

Chapter 6: The Atomic Fallout

1. L.K. Advani, *My Country My Life* (Rupa & Co., Delhi, 2008).
2. ibid.
3. 'Jai Shri Bomb!', *India Today*, 1 June 1998.
4. ibid.
5. ibid.
6. ibid.

Chapter 7: All the King's Men

1. 'Vajpayee's Health Becomes Matter of Speculation', *India Today*, 17 August 1998.
2. ibid.
3. ibid.
4. ibid.

Chapter 8: Satyamev Jayate

1. 'All Pomp, No Party', *India Today,* 29 March 1999.
2. ibid.

Chapter 9: The Collapse

1. 'Everybody Loses', *India Today*, 19 April 1999.
2. Jaswant Singh, *A Call to Honour: In Service of Emergent India* (Rupa & Co., Delhi, 2006).

Chapter 11: The Kargil War

1. Raj Chengappa, *India Today*, July 2004.
2. L.K. Advani, *My Country My Life* (Rupa & Co., Delhi, 2008), p. 562.
3. Jaswant Singh, *A Call to Honour* (Rupa & Co., Delhi, 2006), p. 229.

Chapter 12: The Sonia Factor

1. Sharad Pawar, *On My Terms: From the Grassroots to the Corridors of Power* (Speaking Tiger Publishing, Delhi, 2015).
2. 'Bizarre Cat and Mouse Game', *India Today*, 30 August 1999.
3. ibid.

Chapter 13: Campaign 1999

1. 'Old Hand Vs New face', *India Today*, 20 September 1999.
2. ibid.
3. 'Vajpayee a Habitual Liar', rediff.com, 24 August 1999.
4. 'Old Hand Vs New face', *India Today*, 20 September 1999.
5. Arun Gandhi, *Murarji Papers: Fall of the Janata Government* (Vision Books, 1984).
6. 'Slander Campaign', *Frontline*, 11–24 September 1999.

Chapter 14: From Kargil to Kandahar

1. Jaswant Singh, *A Call to Honour: In Service of Emergent India* (Rupa & Co., Delhi, 2006), p. 232.

Chapter 15: My Journey in the BJP

1. 'Needed a Love Jehad for the Soul', *Outlook*, 8 September 2014.

Chapter 16: The Advani–Vajpayee Push and Pull

1. 'Next Best Man', *Outlook*, 11 September 2000.
2. 'The Itinerary of Ideas', *Outlook*, 18 September 2000.
3. ibid.

Chapter 17: Guru Dakshina

1. 'One Man Band', *Outlook*, 9 October 2000.
2. ibid.

Chapter 18: The Tussle between the Big Two

1. 'Apostate Crown Prince', *Outlook,* 30 October 2000.
2. ibid.
3. 'I Never Intended to Attack Jaswant', L.K. Advani to the author, *Outlook,* 30 October 2000.

Chapter 19: Hey Ram!

1. 'The Second Coming of Lord Ram', *Outlook*, 18 December 2000.

Chapter 20: Enter: Narendra Modi

1. 'Shaky Ground', *Outlook*, 19 February 2001.
2. ibid.
3. 'Modish Twist', *Outlook*, 15 October 2001.

Chapter 21: Operation Corruption

1. 'Rigging the PMO', *Outlook,* 5 March 2001.

2. Vinod Mehta, *Lucknow Boy: A Memoir* (Penguin Viking, New Delhi, 2011), pp. 199–200.
3. 'The PM's Achilles Heel', *Outlook*, 26 March 2001.
4. 'With Daggers Sheathed', *Outlook*, 9 April 2001.
5. Vinod Mehta, *Lucknow Boy: A Memoir* (Penguin Viking, New Delhi, 2011), pp. 205–06.

Chapter 22: Dove vs Hawk: The False Binary

1. L.K. Advani, *My Country My Life* (Rupa & Co., Delhi, 2008), pp. 699–710.
2. ibid.
3. 'The Invisible Hand?', *Outlook*, 30 July 2001.
4. ibid.
5. ibid.

Chapter 23: When Terror Struck

1. Vinod Mehta, *Lucknow Boy: A Memoir* (Penguin Viking, New Delhi, 2011), p. 213.

Chapter 24: Atal and Jawaharlal

1. Atal Bihari Vajpayee's former press secretary, Ashok Tandon, in sifynews, 24 December 2014.
2. Saba Naqvi, 'Why India Must Continue with Ex-PM Vajpayee's Strategy of Not Getting Dragged Into a War', *Economic Times*, 17 November 2015.

Chapter 25: The Feel-Good Disaster

1. 'Fable of the Rooster', *Outlook*, 26 January 2004.
2. 'Old Man and the Holy Sea', *Outlook*, 17 February 2004.
3. 'Back to the Good Lord', *Outlook*, 24 May 2004.
4. ibid.

Chapter 26: The BJP Burlesque

1. 'Batter Familias', *Outlook,* 31 May 2004.
2. 'Iron Deficiency', *Outlook*, 8 November 2004.

Chapter 27: Jinnah's Ghost Spooks the BJP

1. 'Partition of a Party', *Outlook*, 20 June 2005.
2. 'Sudershan Asks Advani, Vajpayee to Make Way for Younger Leaders', *The Hindu,* 10 April 2005.
3. 'Advani Advises RSS to Leave Politics to the BJP', *Outlook*, 19 September 2005.

Chapter 28: The Baritone

1. 'Advani is not fit . . . to serve the interests of the country', Jaswant Singh to the author, *Outlook*, 7 September 2009.

Chapter 30: The Fiery Sannyasin

1. 'When the Last Dome Fell: A First-Person Account of the Babri Masjid Demolition', *The Hindu*, 6 December 2017.
2. 'This way to Freefall', *Outlook*, 20 December 2004.
3. ibid.

Chapter 31: BJP Burlesque: Part II

1. 'Iconoclast', *Outlook*, 12 February 2007.
2. ibid.
3. ibid.
4. 'Outlook interview contradicted', *DNA,* 31 July 2007.
5. 'Rajnath Singh's interview', *Outlook,* 6 August 2007.
6. 'Final Solution', *Outlook*, 31 August 2007.

Chapter 32: Arun Jaitley: The Ultimate Dilliwala

1. https://timesofindia.indiatimes.com/blogs/toi-edit-page/arun-jaitleys-relationshipsranged-far-and-wide-but-the-defining-equation-in-his-life-would-be-with-narendramodi/

Chapter 33: The Absolute Leader

1. Achyut Yagnik and Suchitra Sheth, *Shaping of Modern Gujarat: Plurality, Hindutva and Beyond* (Penguin Books India, New Delhi, 2005).
2. 'Gujarat's Guru', *Outlook*, 29 January 2007.
3. ibid.
4. 'Vendetta Vendor', *Outlook*, 17 December 2007.
5. ibid.
6. ibid.
7. 'The Masque of Augers', *Outlook*, 31 December 2012.
8. ibid.
9. 'Why Did BJP Oppose RSS Chief', *Economic Times*, 22 September 2015.
10. 'Adamant Advani opposes Modi as PM Candidate', *Times of India*, 12 September 2013.
11. 'The Jagran at Jantar Mantar', *Outlook*, 10 April 2011.
12. 'Modi Metrics', *Outlook*, 21 April 2014.
13. ibid.
14. 'Modi Targets Pink Revolution', *Telegraph*, 4 April 2014.

Chapter 34: BJP Inc.

1. 'BJP's Income Double that of 6 Other National Parties Together', *Times of India*, 11 April 2018.
2. 'Curtains on the Regnal', *Outlook*, 16 June 2014.

Epilogue

1 Dhananjay Mahapatra, 'Cases against Amit Shah & Chidambaram: It Is CBI That Is in the Dock', *Economic Times*, 2 September 2019, https://economictimes.indiatimes.com/news/politics-and-nation/cases-against-amit-shah-chidambaram-it-is-probe-agency-cbi-that-is-in-the-dock/articleshow/71043258.cms?utm_source=contentofinterest&utm_medium=text&utm_campaign=cppst (accessed 16 November 2023).

2 Venkitesh Ramakrishnan, 'Targeted Demolitions: Uttar Pradesh Back to Bulldozer Tactics Yet Again', *The Hindu Frontline*, 26 June 2022, https://frontline.thehindu.com/the-nation/communalism/targeted-demolitions-uttar-pradesh-back-to-bulldozer-tactics-yet-again/article65560390.ece (accessed 16 November 2023).

3 Omar Rashid, 'The Staged Spectacle of Encounters in Uttar Pradesh', *Outlook*, 29 April 2023, https://www.outlookindia.com/national/staged-spectacle-magazine-282187 (accessed 16 November 2023).

4 Christophe Jaffrelot, *Modi's India: Hindu Nationalism and the Rise of Ethnic Democracy* (Westland, 2021).

5 Aakar Patel, *Our Hindu Rashtra: What It Is. How We Got Here* (Westland, 2020).

6 Steven Levitsky and Daniel Ziblatt, *How Democracies Die: What History Reveals about Our Future* (Penguin 2018), pp. 3–10.

7 Badri Narayan, *Republic of Hindutva: How the Sangh Is Reshaping Indian Democracy* (Penguin, 2021).

8 Nalin Mehta, *The New BJP: Modi and the Making of the World's Largest Political Party* (Westland, 2022).

9 Prannv Dhawan and Christophe Jaffrelot, 'Is the BJP in UP Really More Representative of Society Than Other Parties? Not Really', *Indian Express*, 20 May 2022, https://indianexpress.com/article/opinion/columns/is-the-bjp-in-up-really-more-representative-of-society-than-other-parties-not-really-7926654/ (accessed 16 November 2023).

10 'Tehelka Sting Case: Former BJP Chief Bangaru Laxman Convicted', *India Today*, 28 April 2012, https://www.indiatoday.in/india/north/story/court-decision-in-bangaru-laxman-graft-case-100362-2012-04-26 (accessed 16 November 2023).

11   Sobhana K. Nair, 'An Opulent House: Art Lines ₹200-Crore Interiors', *The Hindu*, 28 May 2023, https://www.thehindu.com/news/national/new-parliament-building-is-dotted-with-installations-murals-and-artworks/article66904956.ece (accessed 16 November 2023).

12   Coomi Kapoor, 'Inside Track: Pandora's Box', *Indian Express*, 11 October 2021, https://indianexpress.com/article/opinion/columns/inside-track-103-7562822-amarinder-singh-sidhu-kamal-nath-rahul-gandhi-yogi-7562822/ (accessed 16 November 2023).

13   Saba Naqvi, 'Delimitation Double Standards: One Rule for J&K, Another for South India', *Deccan Herald*, 24 December 2021, https://www.deccanherald.com/opinion/delimitation-double-standards-one-rule-for-jk-another-for-south-india-1064017.html (accessed 16 November 2023).

14   Kalaiyarasan A., 'The Poor State of India's Fiscal Federalism', *The Hindu*, 28 July 2022, https://www.thehindu.com/opinion/lead/the-poor-state-of-indias-fiscal-federalism/article65690849.ece (accessed 16 November 2023).

15   Krishnadas Rajagopal, 'A New Parliament Building Is Prudent', *The Hindu*, 21 July 2022, https://www.thehindu.com/news/national/a-new-parliament-building-is-prudent/article32143173.ece (accessed 16 November 2023).

16   Saba Naqvi, 'Dysfunctional Parliament Impairing Democracy', *Tribune India*, https://www.tribuneindia.com/news/comment/dysfunctional-parliament-impairing-democracy-109989 (accessed 16 November 2023).

17   S.N. Sahu, 'The Way Farm Bills Passed in Rajya Sabha Shows Decline in Culture of Legislative Scrutiny', *The Wire*, 21 September 2020, https://thewire.in/politics/farm-bills-rajya-sabha-legislative-scrutiny (accessed 16 November 2023).

18   Aneesha Mathur, 'Supreme Court and Money Bill: Here's What's Next after PMLA Verdict', *India Today*, 31 July 2022, https://www.indiatoday.in/law/story/supreme-court-pmla-verdict-seven-judge-bench-money-bill-1981826-2022-07-30 (accessed 16 November 2023).

19   Arun PS, 'The need for a proper Pre-Legislative Consultation Policy', *The Hindu*, 25 November 2021, https://www.thehindu.com/news/

national/the-need-for-a-proper-pre-legislative-consultation-policy/
article37677558.ece (accessed 16 November 2023).

20 Saba Naqvi, *Times of India*, 14 February 2023, https://timesofindia.
indiatimes.com/india/if-a-pm-is-not-answerable-to-parliament-is-he-
answerable-to-people/articleshow/97838846.cms?from=mdr (accessed
16 November 2023).

21 Saba Naqvi, 'Why Rahul Gandhi's Disqualification Is Good News
for Opposition', *Times of India*, 28 March 2023, https://timesofindia.
indiatimes.com/india/why-rahul-gandhis-disqualification-is-good-
news-for-opposition/articleshow/99012783.cms?from=mdr (accessed
16 November 2023).

22 Saba Naqvi, 'BJP Ltd and Its Shell Companies: If Politics Was
Boardroom Strategy', Scroll.in, 25 November 2020, https://scroll.
in/article/979352/bjp-ltd-and-its-shell-companies-if-politics-was-
boardroom-strategy (accessed 16 November 2023).

23 Nalin Verma, 'BJP and LJP Are Hacking Away at Nitish Kumar's
Influence, Perhaps Irrevocably', The Wire, 7 October 2020, https://
thewire.in/politics/nitish-kumar-bjp-seat-sharing-jdu-bihar-election-
chirag-paswan (accessed 16 November 2023).

24 Saba Naqvi, 'BJP Ltd and Its Shell Companies: If Politics Was
Boardroom Strategy', Scroll.in, 25 November 2020, https://scroll.
in/article/979352/bjp-ltd-and-its-shell-companies-if-politics-was-
boardroom-strategy (accessed 16 November 2023).

25 Amarnath Tewary, *The Hindu*, 9 August 2022, https://www.thehindu.
com/news/national/other-states/bihar-political-crisis-nitish-kumar-
dumps-bjp-joins-hands-with-rjd/article65750757.ece (accessed 16
November 2023).

26 Liz Mathew, 'As Polls Near, the Centre Still Shines Bright in BJP. But
Are State Leaders Getting Blacked Out?', *Indian Express*, 24 October
2023, https://indianexpress.com/article/political-pulse/centre-shines-
bright-in-bjp-but-are-state-leaders-getting-blacked-out-8996470/
(accessed 16 November 2023).

27 'PM Modi Calls for Higher Polling, Discussion on "One Nation, One
Election"', *Economic Times*, 25 January 2022, https://economictimes.
indiatimes.com/news/india/pm-modi-calls-for-higher-polling-

discussion-on-one-nation-one-election/articleshow/89113270.
cms?from=mdr (accessed 16 November 2023).

28 'Delhi Saw 52 Ram Navami Processions This Year', *Indian Express*,
    13 April 2023, https://indianexpress.com/article/delhi/delhi-saw-52-
    ram-navami-processions-this-year-8553433/ (accessed 16 November
    2023).

INDEX

Scan QR code to access the
Penguin Random House India website